The Doha Round of Multilateral Trade Negotiations

The Doha Round of Multilateral Trade Negotiations

Arduous Issues and Strategic Responses

Dilip K. Das

First published in 2005 by
PALGRAVE MACMILLAN
Houndmills, Basingstoke, Hampshire RG21 6XS and
175 Fifth Avenue, New York, N.Y. 10010
Companies and representatives throughout the world.

PALGRAVE MACMILLAN is the global academic imprint of the Palgrave
Macmillan division of St. Martin's Press, LLC and of Palgrave Macmillan Ltd.
Macmillan® is a registered trademark in the United States, United Kingdom
and other countries. Palgrave is a registered trademark in the European
Union and other countries.

ISBN-13: 978–1–4039–4965–3
ISBN-10: 1–4039–4965–4

This book is printed on paper suitable for recycling and made from fully
managed and sustained forest sources.

A catalogue record for this book is available from the British Library.

A catalogue record for this book is available from the Library of Congress.

10 9 8 7 6 5 4 3 2 1
14 13 12 11 10 09 08 07 06 05

Printed and bound in Great Britain by
Antony Rowe Ltd, Chippenham and Eastbourne

To

Vasanti

*who is not only my dearest friend
but also my kindred soul*

'Impatience breeds apprehension and discouragement. Patience manifests itself in confidence, decisiveness, and a feeling of peaceful satisfaction. Adequate patience produces immediate results. One day at a time produces eternal results.'

Confucius

Contents

Preface	xi
About the Author	xvii

1 The Doha Round of Multilateral Trade Negotiations: Setting and Overture 1

The multilateral trade regime	1
The World Trade Organization	1
Multilateral trade negotiations	3
Launching a new round of MTNs	4
Trade and growth: the orthodox view	6
A global public good perspective	9
Reforming the global public good provision	11
From the vantage point of the Doha Round	12
The Uruguay Round	13
The Third Ministerial and the Millennium Round	16
Debacle at the Third Ministerial	18
Green Room consultations	18
A structural limitation of the WTO	21
Agenda in parentheses	22
Breakdown of the old GATT process	24
The single undertaking and deepening commitments	25
Backlash against globalization	25
The unbalanced harvest of the Uruguay Round	28
Conclusions and summary	30

2 Equilibrating the Global Trading System and the Doha Round 31

The changing emphases of successive MTNs	31
Rebalancing the country groups	34
Integrating goods markets	35
Striking a balance in modalities	36
Balancing the WTO architecture	38
Skewing the benefits of the Doha Round	41
Broad aspects of tariff-slashing modalities	44
Tariff-slashing modality in the Doha Round	46

Areas of specific focus for redressing the imbalances 48
The potential for welfare gains 50
Conclusions and summary 52

3 **Setback in Cancún: Salvaging the Doha Round** **54**
Launching the Fifth Ministerial Conference 54
The mechanics of failure 56
High stakes for the developing economies 59
Participation of developing economies in the
Doha Round 63
Market access for non-agricultural products 64
Progress since the launch of the Doha Round of MTNs 66
Causal factors behind the setback in Cancún 74
Negotiations on the Singapore issues 74
Negotiations on agriculture 75
The best thing about failure 77
Retreat from intransigence 79
Negotiations around the Derbez Text 81
Salvaging the Doha Round: the Framework Agreement 81
Conclusions and summary 84

4 **The Doha Round and the Developing Economies** **87**
The multilateral trade regime and the developing economies 87
A developmental round: abiding by the basic principles 90
Special and differential treatment 93
Beneficiaries of special and different treatment 95
Special and differential treatment in the Doha Round 96
The July package and the SDT 98
Hierarchies of beneficiaries and preferential market access 99
Small developing countries in the Doha Round 101
MFN-based liberalization: a possible Doha Round innovation 104
Intra-developing country trade and the Doha Round 106
Trade in textiles and apparel and the Doha Round 108
The Doha Round and global poverty alleviation 110
Conclusions and summary 112

5 **Trade in Services and the Doha Round** **115**
Trade in services 115
Some stylized facts about trade in services 119
Liberalization of trade in services 119
The impact of trade liberalization in services 123

Multilateral liberalization: detrimental or rewarding 124
Escalating services trade from the developing economies 126
Accord on trade in services 128
The Doha Round and services negotiations 129
  Stress-free negotiations 131
  Adopting modalities for the treatment of liberalization
  measures 132
Fourth mode: temporary labour mobility for supplying
services 133
  The Doha Round and the fourth mode of trade in services 137
  Programmes for labour movements under the fourth mode 138
Conclusions and summary 140

6 **Trade in Agriculture and the Doha Round** **143**
Dimensions of trade in agricultural products 143
The lingering tradition of excessive protectionism 144
A distorted and non-transparent trade regime 147
  Measuring OECD financial support 150
Long-standing irrational French antagonism 152
The Uruguay Round agreement on agriculture 153
  Dirty tariffication and the illusory decline in
  agricultural support 154
  The persistence of high tariff regimes after the
  Uruguay Round 156
  Implementation of the URAA and its impact 157
Agriculture negotiations in the Doha Round 159
  The complete lack of progress before the
  Cancún Ministerial 161
  An emerging 'framework' deal: post-Cancún developments 162
  An agreement for establishing modalities 165
The potential impact of multilateral liberalization
in the Doha Round 167
  Welfare gains from liberalization 168
  Welfare gains for the low-income developing economies 170
  The potential to ameliorate the plight of the rural poor 171
Conclusions and summary 172

7 **Intellectual Property Rights and the Doha Round** **174**
Intellectual property rights 174
Trade-related aspects of the intellectual property
rights agreement 176

The World Trade Organization and IPRs   178
Some stylized facts about the TRIPS regime   179
Development dimension of the IPR regimes   181
TRIPS in the Doha Round   182
Technology transfer and the Doha Round   183
    Technology transfer and protection of IPRs   184
    The TRIPS agreement and the lead-up to the Doha Round   186
    Proposed measures for the Doha Round   187
The Doha Round and public health concerns   188
    The Doha Round and patented essential medicines 189
    Agreement on an implementation procedure   190

Notes   194

References   210

Index   223

Preface

Multilateral trade has come to be a defining feature of national and global economic governance. Call it the global trading system, multilateral trade regime or the General Agreement on Tariffs and Trade/World Trade Organization (GATT/WTO) trade regime; it is a global public good of enormous significance. This public good is available to and affects the welfare of a large number of economies. The present membership of the WTO is 148, making it an almost global body. Cambodia, a least developed country (LDC), acceded to the WTO on the 13 October 2004, becoming the 148th member. To be sure, this regime is associated with non-excludable costs and benefits. To the extent that the joining of more countries does not detract from the existing members' benefits, the multilateral trade regime is also non-rivalrous. A global public good perspective of the multilateral trade regime reveals numerous possibilities of reforms which were not conceived or attempted in the past.

Individual case studies and cross-country analyses support the perception that open trade regimes lead to rapid growth and poverty alleviation. Tariffs and non-tariff barriers act as a tax on an economy, impeding its growth endeavours. Trade theory supports the view that elimination of trade barriers benefits both importing and exporting economies, and therefore is a win–win game for all the players. No doubt there have been disagreements among academic researchers, particularly regarding the causal links between trade and growth. Also, one cannot ignore the historic fact that the majority of today's industrial economies had high tariff walls during the initial stages of their economic growth, which they subsequently lowered. However, academics and public policy-makers concur on trade expansion underpinning the possibility of exploitation of comparative advantages, buttressing GDP growth rates and alleviating poverty by providing jobs and driving economic growth for developing countries. Casual empiricism reveals that economies that have entered export markets through trade with and that have integrated with the regional and global economies have tended to grow faster than those that have not. Neoclassical economics convincingly establishes that all the member economies have much more to gain than to lose by dismantling barriers to market access.

Liberalizing domestic markets expands global trade in goods and services. Notwithstanding a great deal of progress in multilateral reduction of tariff and non-tariff barriers (NTBs), barriers still beleaguer multilateral trade and create obstacles to market access. Liberalizing markets can be a potent instrument of stimulating trade and furthering economic growth. Whether trade expansion supports growth and alleviates poverty has been unremittingly debated by theorists and empirical researchers over the last four decades. The result is the existence of a large volume of literature, enough to fill a small library.

If trade is a driving force for economic expansion in developing and industrial economies alike, promoting its growth is essential for global economic prosperity. The Doha Round of multilateral trade negotiations (MTNs) can certainly help in achieving this goal. The Doha Round is the first round of MTNs under the aegis of the WTO. It is also considered a central pillar of the global strategy to achieve the Millennium Development Goals, which in turn is a strategy chalked out by the United Nations to reduce poverty by giving poor people the opportunity to help themselves. As indicated in Chapter 1, a group of developing economies has benefited from trade expansion and integrating with the global economy. The challenge ahead is to expand these opportunities and ensure that the small and low-income developing economies benefit from it as well. The Doha Round can make a tangible contribution in meeting this objective.

A noteworthy attribute of the multilateral trading system is that even after the implementation of the recommendations of the Uruguay Round of MTNs, trade barriers in the developing economies have remained high, although reasonable progress in binding tariffs was noted in the upper-middle and high-income developing countries as well as some lower-middle-income and low-income ones. This grouping of the developing economies is in accordance with the World Bank classification; see note 10 to Chapter 1. Trade barriers in the industrial economies against products of interest of the developing economies are still much higher than they are against the exports from other industrial economies. As noted in Chapter 1, these barriers have become more stringent in the post-Uruguay Round era. The same observation applies to trade in agricultural products where retrogression was observed and protection and subsidization increased after the Uruguay Round. In addition, it is now evident that welfare gains from the implementation of the recommendations of the Uruguay Round were overestimated by various quantitative exercises.

The Doha Round of MTNs has much to achieve for WTO members. It was launched in Doha, Qatar, following the Fourth Ministerial

Conference of the WTO during 9–13 November 2001. Trade ministers of 142 WTO member countries participated in the Doha Ministerial Conference. Although its agenda was not finalized until quite late, it was intended to be an extensive round of MTNs to cover a good number of critical areas of the multilateral trade regime. After a great deal of debating, disagreeing and foot-dragging, conflicting positions of members were brought into harmony, and the long-awaited and crucial framework agreement, the so-called July Package, was signed on 1 August 2004. If the participating WTO members look at the Doha Round through the lens of the global public good, their perspectives will certainly change and the usual intransigence among negotiating members or country groups – which led to failure of the Cancún Ministerial Conference in September 2003 – is sure to wane.

Multilateral organizations like the WTO, aided by the United Nations Conference on Trade and Development (UNCTAD), the World Bank and the International Monetary Fund (IMF) have been working to make the international trading system more supportive of developing countries' needs and policy priorities. The Doha Round of MTNs marked the first time that developing-country interests were placed at the centre of a multilateral round of trade negotiations. The Doha Development Agenda (DDA) is a major opportunity to attack poverty in developing countries. It favours lifting the protectionist measures that have locked small and low-income developing economies out of rich-country export markets.

According to estimates of the World Bank, a successful culmination of the Doha Round should result in substantial lowering of agricultural and manufacturing tariffs, as well as lowering or eliminating agricultural subsidies. It could certainly cut the number of people living in absolute poverty. A successful culmination of the Doha Round can be an instrument of meeting the first objective of the Millennium Developmental Goals (MDGs); that is, reducing absolute poverty by a half by 2015. In the short term, positive steps towards a new international trade agreement would boost confidence in the multilateral trade regime and global economic environment. For sure, to become participative partners – in the multilateral trade regime as opposed to passive onlookers – developing economies will need to lower their trade and non-trade barriers. There is a pressing need for action on this front.

An outstanding feature of this book is that unlike most books on multilateral trade, it is written in a comprehensive manner and covers large areas of the subject matter. The noteworthy areas of focus include the Doha Round and the multilateral trading system, the failure of the

Fifth Ministerial Conference in Cancún, developing economies' role in the contemporary multilateral trading system, and trade in agriculture. There are two chapters dedicated to trade in services and trade-related intellectual property rights (TRIPS) in the Doha Round. These two areas are referred to as two of the three 'pillars' of the WTO, the third one being merchandise trade. Thus viewed, in a succinct manner, this tightly written volume covers a great deal of ground and imparts substantive knowledge on multilateral trade-related themes to students, researchers and policy-makers alike. It is a worthwhile exercise because a knowledge gap has existed among various stakeholders on the Doha Round-related issues.

Another outstanding feature of this book is that in taking a contemporary view of multilateral trade, the book offers the most recent ideas, concepts and knowledge related to relevant themes. The book also deals with the principal normative and positive strands with which one needs to be properly familiar in this subject area. As it is essential for a book of this kind, parts of the chapters have been written in a 'just-the-facts-Jack' style. It inevitably draws on WTO sources, but does not stop at that because WTO reporting in most cases is static and misses the negotiation dynamics. The picture of both static and dynamic aspects of important economic themes related to multilateral trade has been painted with a broad brush. The selection and rejection of the thematic strands covered in the book have been done exceedingly carefully.

Although written in a reference book style, it can also be used as a textbook. As noted above, students and policy mandarins should find the latest knowledge and concepts on several important themes in the area of international trade in this book, presented in a manner which they can appreciate and absorb, as well as use as input in their decision-making. Students, particularly those from business schools, who may hold multilateral trade-related jobs after completing their studies, should find this knowledge extremely relevant, usable and helpful on the job.

The number of academic institutions offering courses related to multilateral trade and trading system is already significant and growing. The target readership of the book is master's-level students in economics, international political economy, international relations as well as MBA students. Ambitious senior-level undergraduates are also sure to find it valuable. Decision-makers in business as well as those with their hands on public policy levers can also benefit from the book. A background of initial micro- and macroeconomics, international trade and monetary economics should be sufficient to comprehend this book because it provides definitions and explanations of terminology and advanced concepts in its notes.

In addition, this book is neither overly technical nor highly model-oriented. I have avoided any excessive emphasis on technicalities, equations and econometric modelling, which would discourage many potential readers and narrow the book's appeal to a small expert readership. The book is easy to access for the target readership because of its descriptive analysis style, which stops short of mathematical formulations and econometric modelling. Many students and other readers who have good analytical minds and sound knowledge of economic principles feel lost in mathematical formulations. The writing style I have adopted should hopefully make the book accessible to a much larger number of readers.

As regards its structure, the book is divided into seven chapters. The first, introductory chapter offers a global public-good perspective of the Doha Round. Any discussion of the Doha Round has to start with the achievements – or lack thereof – of the Uruguay Round and the debacle at the Seattle Ministerial Conference. Therefore, the first chapter covers these two issues as a precursor of the primary analysis. The second chapter addresses how to equilibrate the global trading system and the role that the Doha Round can play in this important task. It also deals with the areas of specific focus as well as the potential welfare gains from the Doha Round. The setback during the Fifth Ministerial Conference in Cancún was one of the most important recent events for the multilateral trading system, which is thoroughly covered in Chapter 3. The chapter delves into the causal factors behind the Cancún failure, as well as the retreat from intransigence and the salvaging of the Doha Round. As the Doha Round is the first ever round of MTNs that was formally christened the 'Development Round', Chapter 4 has been devoted to the developing economies. A Development Round of trade liberalization should focus on improving the market access of developing economies to industrial-country markets and each other's markets. Issues of special concern to the developing economies, such as special and differential treatment, beneficiaries of special and different treatment and special and differential treatment in the Doha Round are discussed at length in this chapter. Chapter 5 focuses on the trade in services in the Doha Round. Liberalization and the bringing in of agricultural trade under the umbrella of multilateral trade discipline has a special place in the contemporary trading system. Chapter 6 follows the progress of liberalization trade in agriculture since the Uruguay Round Agreement on Agriculture (URAA), during the lead-up to the Doha Round, and after its launch. The final chapter delves into intellectual property rights and the Doha Round. The TRIPS agreement, in particular, technology transfer and the Doha Round and public health-related concerns are examined closely in this chapter.

Toronto   Dilip K. Das
November 2004

About the Author

Professor Dilip K. Das has been associated with several prestigious business schools around the globe, including the European Institute of Business Administration (INSEAD), Fontainebleau, France; the ESSEC, Paris; the Graduate School of Business, University of Sydney; the Australian National University, Canberra and the Webster University, Geneva. He was also Professor and Area Chairman at the Indian Institute of Management, Lucknow, India, and EXIM Bank Distinguished Chair Professor in the International Management Institute, New Delhi.

His areas of expertise include international finance and banking, international trade and WTO-related issues, international business and strategy, the emerging-market economies and Asian economies, including the Chinese and Japanese economies. His most recent interest is globalization and the global business environment. Professor Das has worked as a consultant for several international organizations, such as USAID, the World Bank, and the World Commission on Development and Environment in Geneva. He has organized 13 large international conferences during the last 10 years. He is presently a Toronto-based consultant to international organizations.

Dilip K. Das has an immense appetite for research and writing; he has written extensively and published widely. He is the author or editor of 23 books. He edited *The International Finance Reader*, published by Routledge, London and New York, in 2003. The last two books he authored were *Financial Globalization and the Emerging Market Economies*, Routledge, London and New York, 2004, and *Regionalism in Global Trade: Turning Kaleidoscope*, Edward Elgar Publishing, Inc., Boston, Mass., USA, 2004. He has contributed a significant number of articles to professional journals of international repute, and his papers have appeared in many prestigious research paper series. They have also been posted on the well-regarded websites of many business schools and universities.

He was educated at St John's College, Agra, India, where he took his BA and MA (Economics) degrees. He went on to study at the Institut Universitaire de Hautes Études Internationales, the University of Geneva, Switzerland, where he completed his MPhil and PhD in international economics. He is fluent in French.

1

The Doha Round of Multilateral Trade Negotiations: Setting and Overture

'Those who cannot remember the past are condemned to repeat it.'

Santayana, 1905

The multilateral trade regime

The contemporary multilateral trading system implies the system operated by the World Trade Organization (WTO). Most nations, including all the principal trading nations, are members of the multilateral trading system. Although it is treated as a *de facto* global body, some sovereign countries are not yet members. This includes countries like the Russian Federation, Saudi Arabia, Ukraine and several central-Asian republics which were part of the former Soviet Union. Therefore, the qualifier 'multilateral' is considered more apt to describe the contemporary trading system instead of 'global' or 'world'. In WTO affairs, 'multilateral' also contrasts with actions taken regionally or by other smaller groups of countries. While 'global trade' or 'world exports' are not incorrect expressions, they are not as precise as 'multilateral trade' or 'multilateral exports'.

The World Trade Organization

The WTO is one of the three supranational institutions that are charged with the task of global economic governance by the global community. The International Monetary Fund (IMF) and the World Bank are the other two institutions. The WTO is the multilateral institution that essentially deals with the rules of trade between nations. It has created the related regulatory structure and is based on numerous agreements and decisions which in turn create legally binding rights and obligations for all the member countries. Membership obligation of the WTO entails accepting the whole package of obligations, known as the 'Single Undertaking'. The multilateral trade regime, or the GATT/WTO system, forms the legal foundation of contemporary commerce. Its ultimate objective is to establish a rule-based multilateral trading system, which has no element of unpredictability.[1]

The General Agreement on Tariffs and Trade (GATT) – predecessor of the WTO – was born in October 1947 as an international treaty, with 23 signatories who signed the Protocol of Provisional Application of the General Agreement on Tariffs and Trade, at the Palais des Nations in Geneva.[2] The treaty came into force on 1 January 1948. Of these 23 original signatories of the GATT, 12 were industrial economies and 11 developing. The regulations and membership of the multilateral trade regime underwent a radical transformation and expansion since its naissance; so much so that the old GATT regime was subsumed into a new and much larger and comprehensive WTO, covering far greater swathes of world trade, with a substantially increased depth in the application of trade regulations. Since the naissance of the GATT in 1947, the volume of total merchandise trade has increased 18-fold in real terms (Ingco and Nash, 2004). Much of the credit for such rapid expansion in multilateral trade goes to trade liberalization under the GATT/WTO regime. The coverage of issues under the WTO expanded into new fields like trade in services, agriculture, protection of intellectual property rights, and trade-related investment issues. The WTO was built on the same base as the GATT, only its base was politically and legally broader. Unlike GATT, which was an agreement, the WTO is a multilateral organization whose larger institutional framework provides more substance in practice and moral suasion in effect. The WTO has an integral dispute-settlement process, having enforcement capabilities (Das, 2001).

The WTO is a forum for exchange of trade-liberalization commitments among its 148 sovereign member countries. With such a large membership, the multilateral trading regime represented by the WTO has become a *de facto* global trade regime.[3] The WTO oversees and governs multilateral trade and related issues, and to this end it has created the related regulatory structure which is based on approximately 60 agreements and decisions enshrined in the WTO *Legal Text*, which came into being at the time of culmination of the Uruguay Round (1996–94) of multilateral trade negotiations (MTNs).[4] A functional definition of the WTO could be as follows: The WTO in essence is a multilateral negotiating forum in which the member countries make trade policy commitments and exchange concessions for the purpose of improving access to each other's markets. Hoekman and Kostecki (2001) aptly referred to it as 'a market'. Bargaining and negotiations are the principal instruments used for reducing various types of market barriers to trade, as well as for mutually agreeing to abide by a rule-based system of multilateral trade.

As decided at the time of the Marrakesh Agreement of 1994, a Ministerial Conference is hosted biennially by the member states.[5] It is the highest decision-making body in the WTO system. Member states are represented by their respective trade ministers in the Ministerial Conferences, that, *inter alia*, decide on the need for a new round of MTNs as well as its agenda items.

Multilateral trade negotiations

The MTNs were the mechanism for reciprocally exchanging commitments for market access among the contracting parties (CPs) of the GATT, and now the members of the WTO. They have the advantage of offering a package approach to the participants; that is, MTNs augment the negotiating space in the system. A large number of issues can be more fruitful than negotiations on a single issue. By definition a package comprises numerous trade and trade-related issues and somewhere in it there is something for every participant. The package approach renders it feasible to make trade-offs in different issues, thereby making it easier to reach agreement. This has both political and economic implications. Concessions in one set of sectors can be balanced against gains in another set, which makes political defence of negotiations easier on the domestic front. This makes it feasible to reform the politically sensitive sectors of trade, and reform of agricultural trade during the Uruguay Round is an excellent illustration of such a trade-off.

Trade barriers have high welfare costs,[6] and MTNs are a multilateral endeavour to bring them down and liberalize trade. The MTNs have succeeded in bringing down tariffs on manufactured products; they have fallen continuously with each round of MTNs. At the time of the birth of the GATT, average tariff rates were 38 per cent; in 1962 when the Kennedy Round of MTNs began, they were 17 per cent; in 1972 during the post-Kennedy Round period they fell to 9 per cent; in 1987 after the Tokyo Round they declined to 6 per cent; while the post-Uruguay Round average in 1994 was 4 per cent. Tariff rates on agricultural products have continued to remain high. The MTNs provide a greater opportunity to developing economies, that wield little economic and political clout, to influence the multilateral trading system, more than they could ever do in bilateral negotiations with major trading nations. The flip-side of the coin is that having a wide range of issues in a round of MTNs may be not only a strength, it may also be a limitation. This has led to a debate on whether multi-sector rounds are more effective and purposeful than single-sector negotiations.

The rounds of MTNs often take many years to conclude; the Uruguay Round took seven-and-a-half years. Eight rounds of MTNs were sponsored by the GATT, of which the Uruguay Round was the last and is regarded as the most comprehensive of the GATT rounds. Its impact over multilateral trade has been thoroughly analysed by trade economists, spawning a good number of empirical studies. To be sure, it can be credited with more than a few notable achievements, although hindsight reveals that there were also numerous shortcomings that affected trade during the post-Uruguay Round period.

Launching a new round of MTNs

During the Third Ministerial Conference of the WTO in 1999, in Seattle, the members failed to agree on whether a new round of MTNs should be launched. This Ministerial Conference is universally considered to have been a comprehensive systemic failure. There were a host of reasons behind the discord and dissention, which are analysed later in this chapter.[7] The Conference caused apprehension among WTO members regarding its institutional soundness and ability to reach consensus on trade and economic policy issues, and its failure created a concern about the general stability of the world trading system and economic framework. However, two years later, 142 members of the WTO reached a consensus regarding launching a new round of MTNs. The Doha Round of MTNs was launched in Doha, Qatar, following the Fourth Ministerial Conference of the WTO during 9–13 November 2001.

The launch of the Doha Round, driven by the Doha Development Agenda (DDA), was something of a breakthrough and bolstered confidence in the WTO as a negotiating forum for multilateral traders and the multilateral trading system. In Doha, the WTO members agreed to take the 'the development dimension seriously across the board', although some thought of it as a mere post-Seattle spin (Lamy, 2003).[8] The Doha Ministerial Declaration acknowledged that the benefits of trade needed to be more widely distributed among the members of the WTO (WTO, 2001). The DDA made growth and development the principal focus of this round, and governments of the industrial countries have repeatedly pointed to the Doha Round as evidence of their commitment to create a more equitable pattern of globalization (Watkins, 2003).

The ongoing Doha Round is the first under the aegis of the WTO. The trade liberalization process has deepened and widened with each round of MTNs, through first binding participating nations to a particular tariff rate for a particular line of products, then increasing the number of products covered, and then further lowering the tariff rates to which participating nations were bound. The national tariff schedules of the participants of a round of MTNs list tariff rates on a product-by-product basis. Trade in goods and tariff reduction or elimination, however, is only one dimension of the multilateral trading system. The first five rounds of MTNs under the aegis of the GATT focused only on tariff reduction and elimination, but their scope from then on has expanded and evolved (see Chapter 2).

After prolonged deliberations, members agreed to include the following 20 issues in the Doha Development Agenda (DDA): implementation-related issues; agriculture; services; market access; trade-related intellectual property rights (TRIPS); trade and competition policy; trade and investment; government procurement; trade facilitation; WTO rules; dispute settlement understanding; trade and environment; electronic commerce; small economies; trade, debt and finance; transfer of technology; technical cooperation; least-developed countries; special and differential treatment; and organization of the work programme (WTO, 2001). Such a wide spread of agenda makes the Doha Round one of the most comprehensive rounds of MTNs, comparable to the Uruguay Round. The Doha Ministerial Conference was decisively influenced by lessons learned from the debacle in Seattle in many ways. In addition, in 2001 the global economy perceived a coming recession, which intensified the interest of the world business community and member governments in launching a fresh round of MTNs. Failure in Seattle had left a pall of frustration and disillusionment regarding the multilateral trading system, and the WTO members were raring to come out of it.

It is agreed in the community of trade analysts and economists that liberalizing markets for trade in manufactured products, services and agriculture can buttress global economic growth and development and can have a salutary influence over the absolute poor of the world. Furthermore, during the planning of the DDA, it was considered essential that the negotiations should deliver more to developing economies than the previous eight GATT rounds of MTNs. It was expected that liberalization of multilateral trade in agriculture would receive a great deal of attention from the Organization for Economic Cooperation and Development (OECD) countries, which in turn would benefit the poorest in several developing economies. Although not a part of the 'Single

Undertaking', a reform of Dispute Settlement Understanding (DSU) and addressing the vulnerability of least-developed countries (LDCs)[9] was also agreed to be taken up during the MTNs by the participating trade ministers during the Doha Ministerial Conference.

The objective of this chapter is to introduce the reader to the lay of the land by bringing into light the salient characteristics of multilateral trade. This section provides the definition of important concepts like the WTO, multilateral trading system, and MTNs. The focus of the next section is the contribution of trade to economic growth, as well as recent quantitative dimensions of multilateral trade. After familiarizing the reader to the role of the MTNs in the multilateral trading system, it explains the significance of taking a global public good (GPG) perspective in this regard. Given the background of polemics, disputations, controversies, sharp differences in stances and intransigence in negotiations leading to frequent obstructions, delays and breakdowns in MTNs, we then consider the vital importance that participating members of the WTO take a global public good perspective of the MTNs, and reform the global public policy provisions accordingly. Two developments are then discussed that were precursors to the Doha Round, namely the completion of a comprehensive round of MTNs, the Uruguay Round, and the debacle of the Third Ministerial Conference of the WTO in Seattle, that affected and inspired the launching of the Doha Round of MTNs. As both of these events were meaningful and imperative precursors of the Doha Round, it is essential to analyse them before launching into the core examination of the Doha Round and related issues, that would otherwise be incomplete. As the Doha Round is expected to rectify earlier problems, it is necessary to focus on the skewed inventory of accomplishments of the Uruguay Round.

Trade and growth: the orthodox view

As an area of intellectual curiosity as well as its tangible economic benefits and welfare gains, international trade has attracted the attention of noted scholars for centuries. The nineteenth century witnessed an avid intellectual debate on the benefits and limitations of free trade. While Adam Smith and David Ricardo preached the doctrine of free trade and adherence to the principle of comparative advantage, Alexander Hamilton and Friedrich List argued that trade barriers were required to protect infant industries. The contemporary mainstream view is that international trade helps in raising and sustaining growth in an economy. Any textbook would inform the reader that trade promotion provides domestic firms access to world markets of goods, services and knowledge. Trade expansion lowers prices and enhances the quality of consumer goods. It propels an economy in the direction in which it becomes feasible for it to exploit its comparative advantage, enhance specialization and thereby promote optimal resource allocation in the domestic economy. In addition, trade also has a strong and positive correlation with investment (Florax *et al.*, 2002). It not only creates investment opportunities, but also positive externalities that are associated with learning through absorption of technology (Irwin, 2001). Investment, in turn, is positively and robustly correlated to economic growth. Trade provides two channels of raising the investment level, namely exploitation of scale economies and the transfer of technology. Research and development (R&D) and capital investment have a symbiotic relationship and are known to reinforce each other, since new innovations are often embodied in advanced capital goods. Trade is also known to provide market opportunities to invest in R&D, as well as opportunities of introducing the results of innovation in the marketplace. Thus, an open economy tends to be far more R&D-oriented than one that is not open (WTO, 2003).

Trade policy liberalization since the mid-1980s and expanding trade contributed to new opportunities for growth and global integration in a group of rapidly globalizing developing economies. This observation applies particularly to several middle-income and a small number of low-income developing economies.[10] Many developing economies chose to be more open economies, and many related policy moves were made unilaterally by them, albeit that the multilateral organizations had made their contribution. Between the 1970s and 1990s, 24 developing countries remarkably increased their ratio of trade to GDP. This dynamic group did not include the newly industrialized economies (NIEs), of Chile, Hong Kong SAR, Korea, Singapore and Taiwan (WB, 2003).[11]

Both the trade and incomes of developing countries grew during the 1990s at twice the rate of the 1980s, and the developing economies that improved their integration with the global economy – through trade, investment and other channels – saw their income rise at more than three times the pace of those that did not integrate (Collier and Dollar, 2003). Liberalizing domestic markets by lowering or eliminating tariff and NTBs unilaterally, and under the aegis of the GATT and the WTO, facilitated trade expansion and underpinned economic growth in a number of developing economies. A spate of empirical cross-country studies has suggested that the impact of liberalization of trade in goods on the long-term rate of economic growth is positive.[12] The link between trade policy liberalization and economic growth, albeit not completely unambiguous and universal, is strong. Trade does seem to create, even sustain, growth, and there is little evidence to the contrary.[13] China is the latest as well as an outstanding illustration of an economy benefiting from liberalizing its trade policy regime and globalizing.[14]

However, the orthodox perspective did not go unchallenged. Rodriguez and Rodrik (1999) questioned the robustness of the results of these empirical cross-country studies. Rodrik (2001a and 2001b) disagreed and propounded an alternative viewpoint which attracted a good deal of scholarly attention. In a vigorous tirade against the orthodox viewpoint, he stated that those who believe in trade-promoting growth and development are labouring under delusion. He said that

> the WTO and the multilateral lending agencies have come to view these two goals – promoting development and maximizing trade – as synonymous, to the point where the latter easily substitutes for the former. Trade has become the lens through which development is perceived, rather than the other way round.

He goes on to say, 'In this conception, the WTO focus on market access and deepening integration through the harmonization of a wide-range of trade-related practices is precisely what development requires.' However, a debate over which is the cart and which is the horse, who is the leader and who is led, is not a momentous issue. Strategies aimed at trade expansion have had a growth payoff, discernible even to the untrained eye.

The WTO statistics indicate that multilateral trade expanded at a rapid rate over the decades of the 1980s and 1990s, and as stated above the average rate for the 1990s was much higher than that in the 1980s. After recording a negative growth rate in 2001, and a weak recovery the next year, multilateral trade recovered in 2003. Trade expanded by 4.5 per cent in real terms in 2003, which was below the average rate of 6.5 per cent recorded in the decade of 1990s. Nominal dollar trade values were far more buoyant than real trade due to the impact of higher commodity prices, particularly fuels, as well as exchange rate developments. World merchandise exports rose by 16 per cent (to $7.3 trillion) and commercial services exports by 12 per cent (to $1.8 trillion) in 2003. World trade could expand further in 2004 should the global economy continue to improve. In nominal terms, these were the strongest increases for both merchandise and services trade since 1990. Merchandise exports expanded by 17 per cent in the developing economies in 2003, slightly faster than imports expansion as well as the world average. The overall trade surplus therefore widened for these countries. However, according to estimates based on available data, developing countries' commercial services exports and imports expanded at only half the rate of world services trade in 2003 (WTO, 2004a and 2004b).

At country level, noteworthy trade developments in 2003 included the extraordinary expansion of China's merchandise trade. Many oil-exporting economies (particularly the Russian Federation and Saudi Arabia) recorded nominal export growth in excess of 20 per cent, as did countries with strongly appreciating currencies, in particular in Western Europe. Gains in the ranking of the leading commercial services traders in 2003 were principally recorded by Western European countries at the expense of the United States (US) and Asian economies. This observation is valid for both export and import rankings. It was estimated that in 2003 China became the largest exporter of commercial services among the developing countries (WTO, 2004a and 2004b).

A global public good perspective

In the process of rapid expansion, since the birth of the General Agreement on Tariffs and Trade (GATT) in 1947, international trade became a contentious issue for the global economy as well as for global economic governance. It has also become a defining feature of national and global economic governance. The multilateral trade regime governing international trade is a global public good (GPG); that is, using the concept in a positive sense, not in its normative meaning. A GPG by definition has a universal intertemporal impact over a large number of countries, a large number of people and on several generations. In terms of its benefits and costs the multilateral trade regime is a GPG. As alluded to in the preceding section, this regime is a set of rules, codes, agreements and institutions which are fundamentally intended to facilitate and expand international trade. As a GPG, the multilateral trade regime is essentially public in consumption, but the distribution of its net benefits is clearly skewed in favour of the industrial economies, giving rise to a great deal of understandable tensions in the global trade fora and the periodic MTNs.

Trade expansion touches a sensitive chord in the developing and industrialized economies, and all their sub-sets of country groups. Several acrimoniously controversial and debatable issues have arisen in the multilateral trading system as well as out of it. An example of the latter is the civil society organizations (CSOs), non-governmental organizations (NGOs) and anti-globalization lobby, which feel absolutely convinced that trade is harmful for the developing economies because it vitiates their economies and immiserates them. The dissonance and dissent among WTO members has exacerbated in the recent past, and the Ministerial Conferences at Seattle and Cancún are two recent illustrations. In this *mise-en-scene* one wonders whether the multilateral trading system has paid adequate attention to coherence and consistency of its professed objectives, and the objectives of the member economies it is intended to benefit.[15]

As set out earlier in this chapter, the multilateral trade regime, or the agreed code of conduct, has utility, benefits and costs for the 148 sovereign countries or customs territories. Its agreements and regulations are applicable and acceptable to the inhabitants of an overwhelmingly large part of the trading world. Services provided by the multilateral trade regime are a public good in that they facilitate multilateral trade between the member sovereign countries, making it more predictable than before. Mutually binding codes restrict destructive patterns of behaviour such as trade wars, for which the Great Depression period is known. Destructive behaviour is not limited to trade wars, retaliatory tariffs and NTBs however, and competitive devaluations have been infrequently witnessed even in the contemporary era. Trading economies can also have seriously pernicious influences over each other and over the multilateral trade regime by pursuing inefficient protectionist policies. Conversely, the multilateral trade regime, which comprises a shared rule-based framework among its constituent members, nurtures deep integration through trade. Its myriad benefits include cultivating cost-trimming scale economies in production and distribution of goods and services.[16]

The multilateral trade regime demonstrates the original public good properties of non-rivalry and non-excludability. The former is by nature, while the latter is by policy choice. As the application of the rules under the regime increases, their relevance and value to users is enhanced. By facilitating and thereby expanding mutually beneficial trade, the multilateral trading regime markets a non-rival public good more enticing to any country that wishes to enter into the global trading arena and expand its trade. Non-rival goods can be made available to additional users at no extra cost (Stiglitz, 2000). The multilateral trade regime is also non-excludable, or alternatively exclusion is not optimal, because benefits from the regime increase with the increasing number of participants. A rising number of consumers of GPGs enhance the functioning and improve the efficiency of the global marketplace. A positive network of externalities expands *pari passu* with the increasing number of trading economies as members. Mendoza and Bahadur (2002) noted that the wide-ranging and far-reaching impact of the multilateral trade regime over the global trade pattern is non-rivalrous and non-excludable for all the countries, members and non-members alike.

It is therefore fitting to consider the multilateral trade regime as a GPG, and analyse its benefits from that perspective. Expanding free trade under an enlarging multilateral trade regime is optimal for the participating economies because, first, it would increase global production of goods and services, and second, it would enable more economies to exploit their comparative advantage, improve resource allocation, and have opportunities to specialize in production structures.[17] Furthermore, there are more welfare gains from these than generally realized. Since the early 1960s developing countries have been gradually trying to integrate into the multilateral trading system, and as alluded to in the previous section, in the mid-1980s this process gained a sizeable momentum. These developing economies can certainly question the utility of this GPG, as its consumers.[18]

It is obvious that at this stage of development in the multilateral trade regime, the benefits are skewed and are heavily concentrated in the industrial economies, which had an absolute dominance of the multilateral trading system in the past. These economies are highly competitive, both at micro- and macro- levels. They are large traders and dominate the WTO league tables of large exporters and importers. They not only comply with the prescribed norms of the multilateral trade discipline almost effortlessly, but also implement related reforms without too much problem. Ideally, all WTO members should be able to consume the GPG and benefit from it evenly. This is *a fortiori* so because at this stage in the global economic development it is the developing economies, and their various sub-groups, that need to emphasize trade as an instrument of economic growth. To reach the objectives of evenness of benefits from the GPG, all participants need to determine that the multilateral trade regime is *ex ante* a balanced system. Only then can one expect a balanced outcome for all participants; that is, industrial and developing economies.[19]

Reforming the global public good provision

That a GPG can be under-provided and mal-provided leading to sub-optimal, even undesirable outcomes, is obvious from the current state of contentiousness in the multilateral trade system. 'What these imbalances have demonstrated is that the multilateral trade regime is fast advancing as a GPG in form, but lagging in its development as a GPG in substance' (Mendoza and Bahadur, 2002). It is apparent that there was overemphasis on the so-called 'level playing field', at the expense of the accommodation of the growth objectives of the developing country members. Reforms undertaken from a GPG perspective would necessarily have to concentrate on actual imbalances as well as on the decision-making process in the multilateral trade regime that was responsible for them.

In what she referred to as a 'grand bargain', Ostry (2001 and 2002) pointed out that during the Uruguay Round exchanges of trade concessions, developing economies agreed to exchange increased market access in two areas, namely agriculture and textiles and apparel, in the industrial economies in return for acquiescing agreements in intellectual property rights, services and investment. This grand bargain turned out to work only in the interests of the industrial economies through increased rent in market access. The original idea was that the cost for the developing economies of agreeing to the three agreements would be offset by the benefits from the increased market access in the two areas, which never happened. This is an illustration of an unequal exchange between the two country groups, and it led to adjustment costs that were asymmetrically distributed. Such exchanges put a question mark on net benefits to developing economies from the multilateral trade regime.

An intensive scrutiny of past multilateral negotiations reveals numerous instances of such uneven exchanges between the industrial and developing economies. Such imbalances in negotiations developed due to a flawed decision-making process in the GATT/WTO system. Improvement in the bargaining platform of the developing economies can potentially diminish the 'grand bargain'-like imbalances, which in turn would enhance their benefits from international trade and consumption of GPG. To this end, fundamentally recasting the multilateral trade negotiation in such a manner that the development objective remains an integral part of it, is another desirable goal. As indicated in the preceding section, the Doha Ministerial Declaration does so in its first paragraph (WTO, 2001).

From the vantage point of the Doha Round

Any analytical account of the Doha Round of the MTNs must logically take into consideration the achievements, or a lack thereof, during the post-Uruguay Round period. It should also benefit from the lessons from the ignominious Seattle debacle. It is crucial to take a look at the events surrounding these two events, because they are a sort of Rorschach test of how different constituencies view the multilateral trading system.[20] Different groups have looked at it from different perspectives and reached different conclusions.

The Uruguay Round

The Uruguay Round is widely regarded as the most comprehensive of the GATT rounds, with 123 contracting parties (CPs) participating in it. The decision to create two novel institutions, namely the WTO and the General Agreement on Trade in Services (GATS) was taken during the Uruguay Round. It was a veritable milestone and is justly celebrated for the innovations it represented. When it was launched in September 1986, at the initiative of the USA, with limited support from the other industrial economies, the developing economies – a fairly diverse group – were somewhat apprehensive about its launch. By the time the Round culminated, the majority of them had begun to expect substantial gains from it and grew impatient with the failure of the industrial economies to settle their outstanding trade differences.

Completion of the Uruguay Round ushered in a revitalized multilateral trading system in a globalizing world of greater integration. It also marked the beginning of the critical process of integrating the developing economies – or at least some sub-groups of them – into the global trading system. For the first time it was decided that no exceptions to the rules would be allowed for specific sectors or products. Therefore, the multi-fibre agreement (MFA) was scheduled to be phased out by the end of 2005, and more importantly it was agreed that trade in agriculture would be brought under the same multilateral trading system as that in other commodities. Correction of these two major flaws in the multilateral trade regime was attempted for the first time. Trade rules were also extended to services, trade-related aspects of intellectual property rights (TRIPs), trade-related investment measures (TRIMS) and government procurement.

Initially a lot was expected from the implementation of the recommendations of the Uruguay Round. According to one estimate, tariff reductions made in the area of merchandise trade were estimated to increase real income in developing economies by between $55 billion and $90 billion at 1992 prices and exchange rate, or between 1.2 per cent and 2.0 per cent of real income. On the heels of the Marrakesh Agreement, many supra-national institutions made quantitative projections of welfare gains from the implementation of the Uruguay Round recommendations. The World Bank and the OECD Secretariat estimated them of the order of $200 billion annually, while the WTO came to a higher figure of $500 billion.[21] However, not only did these estimates prove grossly optimistic, it has since been found that 70 per cent of welfare gains from the Uruguay Round went to the industrial economies. The rest went to a small number of large export-oriented developing economies (UNDP, 1997).

There were several reasons why these projections turned out to be erroneous. First, post-Uruguay Round events did not reflect the scenarios that were projected by the Uruguay Round. The reforms that were recommended, and that were going to be the sources of welfare gains, did not proceed as expected. The Agreement on Textiles and Clothing (ATC) is a typical case in point. Dismantling the quotas in textiles and clothing did not follow the predetermined structured pattern; instead, the reforms were postponed for the final stage of the 10-year period. The tariffication of agriculture, which was intended to liberalize this important sector and improve the market access of developing countries, was not implemented as visualized (see later in Chapter 6). Finally, the cost of implementing the Marrakesh Agreement – which was significant – was completely ignored by those who projected welfare gains for the developing economies from the Uruguay Round.

What was worse was that many of the developing economies were discontented with both the non-transparent manner in which the negotiations were conducted and their outcome. Evidence is available to show that the Sub-Saharan African economies were worse off as a result of the terms-of-trade effect resulting from the Uruguay Round agreement (WB, 2002b). The United Nations Development Programme (UNDP, 1997) estimated that under the post-Uruguay Round WTO regime, 48 LDCs would be worse off over the 1995–2004 period by $600 million a year, with the Sub-Saharan African economies worse off by $1.2 billion a year.[22] The developing countries expressed their concern about the trade restrictions that were 'allowed' to continue. The elimination of quotas under the Multifibre Arrangement (MFA) had an adjustment period of 10 years, with dismantling of the MFA taking place on 1 January 2005. However, in the first eight years of the adjustment period, only 20 per cent of the quotas on textiles and apparel were dismantled. The developing economies were concerned that at the end of 2005, either quotas would be supplanted by high tariffs, or other measures (like safeguards and NTBs) would be used to continue protection of the domestic textiles and apparel sector.

Stiglitz and Charlton (2004) asserted that the Uruguay Round agenda reflected the priorities of the industrial countries in large measure.

Market access concessions were negotiated but they were concentrated in the areas of interest of the industrial economies (see also the final section of this chapter). The priority areas of the developing economies – like agriculture and textiles and apparels – only benefited marginally in this respect. Consequently the asymmetry that had existed in multilateral trade before the pre-Uruguay Round period worsened. This was reflected in the post-Uruguay Round tariff structure of the Organization for Economic Cooperation and Development (OECD) economies; the average OECD tariffs for imports from the developing economies was four times higher than imports from the other OECD economies, and post-Uruguay Round protection to agriculture was found to be much higher in the OECD economies. On the eve of the launch of the Doha Round, for manufactured goods, averaged tariff rates in the industrial economies were 1.5 per cent if the goods originated from other industrial economies, but 11.5 per cent if these exports originated from the developing economies. Similarly, for agricultural exports average tariff rates in the industrial economies were 15.6 per cent if they originated in the other industrial economies and 21.1 per cent if they originated in the developing economies (Hertel *et al.*, 2000).

A recent World Bank study (Finger and Nogues, 2001) contended that the outcome of the Uruguay Round was unbalanced, and skewed against the developing economies. Developing economies gave more in terms of tariff-slashing than the industrial economies. They also accepted a large range of obligations and responsibilities, that imposed significant burdens on them. The study enumerated eight areas in which the developing economies granted more concessions to the industrial economies than they received from them. In many of these areas the concessions granted by the developing economies to the industrial economies were not necessary and 'remained entirely unrequited'. This happened due to essentially three reasons. First, developing economies had only limited experience in trade negotiations, which is a complex and slippery process requiring a good deal of acumen and knowledge of trade (Krugman, 1997). Second, the USA, which was the largest trading economy, took an intense mercantilist attitude in negotiations during the Uruguay Round.[23] Finger and Nogues (2001) posited that while the Uruguay Round negotiations and outcomes were justifiable by mercantilist logic (imports for imports, apples for apples), they could not be rationalized in a real economic sense (apples for oranges). Economies that follow mercantilist economic logic treat dismantling of protection as a favour or a concession to their trade partners, while in neo-classical economics any reduction or elimination in trade barriers is considered to have a positive effect on both trade partners.[24]

In return for accepting new obligations and responsibilities, the low-income developing countries – which included the LDCs – were promised financial assistance to defray the cost of implementation as well as extension of market access commitments by the industrial economies. However, this commitment was non-binding, and was subsequently more or less ignored by the industrial economies. Implementation costs of obligations in areas of TRIPs, customs valuation, technical barriers to trade, and food safety are high.

For a large number of developing countries, particularly the small, low-income ones, participating in the Uruguay Round in an active manner was a confounding experience for domestic reasons. For many of them, it was their first exposure to an MTN and they felt out of their depth. After the Round ended, many of them felt they had committed to obligations that they could not fulfil, and they inevitably approached the Doha Round with the intellectual legacy of the Uruguay Round. Razeen Sally (2003) observed that during the Doha Round, many of the small- and medium-sized developing economies

> did not wish to fall into the Uruguay Round trap of being rushed into agreements they cannot fathom and (subsequently) find very hard to implement. This accounts in some measure for their present defensive attitude.

The Third Ministerial and the Millennium Round

It was noted earlier in this chapter that the one requirement of the Marrakesh Agreement is to convene a Ministerial Conference biennially. Thus far five Ministerial Conferences of the WTO have taken place: Singapore (9–13 December 1996), Geneva (18–20 May 1998), Seattle (30 November to 3 December 1999), Doha (9–13 November 2001) and Cancún (10–14 September 2003). President Clinton invited the WTO members to hold the Third Ministerial in Seattle, Washington, and the trade ministers of 135 member countries accepted the invitation to define the trade agenda and negotiations on trade regimes and issues for the next millennium. The Seattle meeting of the WTO was dedicated by Mike Moore, the erstwhile Director General, to 'developing the framework for the global trading system in the twenty-first century' (Moore, 1999).

The global trading system of the initial years of the twenty-first century was profoundly influenced by what came to pass in the third Ministerial Conference in Seattle, that is regarded as a defining moment in the annals of multilateral trade. The failure in Seattle brought about a discernible shift in the multilateral trading system. Trade ministers of the member countries were going to review the implementation of the WTO agreements during the four days of plenary sessions, and during the closing session, were expected to launch the next round of MTNs, and, based on its timing, they were possibly going to name it the Millennium Round.[25] Mike Moore, the Director General of the WTO, had started referring to it as the 'Development Round' in his speeches. If launched, this Round would have been the ninth round of MTNs and the first under the aegis of the WTO.

The *modus operandi* for the Seattle Ministerial Conference was devised as follows. Five working or negotiation groups were planned, each to be chaired by a trade minister and that could be divided into sub-groups. Singapore was to chair the negotiating group on agriculture, Lesotho that on market access, and Hong Kong SAR on the four Singapore issues.[26] Brazil's name was proposed for presiding over the negotiation group on implementation of the recommendations of the Uruguay Round, and the one on systemic issues (transparency and relations with the civil society) was going to be chaired by Chile. Although the negotiating procedure was not decided, each group would have comprised 15–20 WTO members. The country participation was to be determined on the basis of a participating country's economic weight as well as the special interest a country might have in a given theme. A new 'Green Room' was planned for the Seattle Ministerial; if the working group reached a consensus, the text was to be introduced in the Green Room. The Green Room was to comprise 15–20 country delegations representing different regions of the global economy, and at different levels of economic development. Eventually the Green Room consensus was to be presented to the full WTO membership, which ultimately needed to approve it. *Prima facie* it was a logical, functional and even imaginative procedure (ICTSD, 1999).

The pre-Seattle global economic and trading environment was widely considered supportive, creating hope for a successful Third Ministerial. Despite the Asian crisis of 1997–98, good sense had prevailed among policy-makers and the WTO framework had helped keep markets open, providing the necessary base for recovery. The five crisis-affected Asian economies were busy making their V-shaped recovery. Additionally, global GDP grew by 3.3 per cent in 1999, substantially higher than that in the preceding year (2.5 per cent). A strengthening of global economic output in 1999 reversed the slowdown of world trade in the first half of 1999 and led to a dynamic expansion of trade in the second half. Global merchandise exports grew by 3.5 per cent in 1999 and those of commercial services grew by 1.5 per cent (Das, 2001).

Debacle at the Third Ministerial

Despite the good presage, the Third Ministerial Conference turned out to be a complete, if somewhat ignominious, failure and the Millennium Round could never be launched. The silver lining behind this cloud was that it provided a much-needed opportunity to stakeholders to deliberate and debate the significance of trade for achieving the Millennium Development Goals (MDG). The discord on the multilateral trading system was not about the system *per se*, but about how it could underpin economic growth and human welfare and how various consumers of this GPG can evenly consume it. The Seattle failure gave rise to an impression among stakeholders that the global trading system was in a state of dissonance and disarray. The principal reasons behind the debacle in Seattle were the Green Room consultations as described below.

Green Room consultations

Four out of the five mandated working groups, mentioned in the preceding section, came into being on 1 December 1999, while the fifth was scheduled to meet on 2 December. Aside from the release of some heavily bracketed text in the areas of agriculture, implementation and market excess, there were few advances made in reaching substantive agreement on most issues. Bracketed text implies disagreement over the bracketed part of the text; it has been a common practice during negotiations to have large parts of a text in parentheses. No text could be issued on the Singapore issues because the positions of the participants were so far apart that no reconciliation was feasible. Many delegations did not see any point in starting negotiations.

A preliminary Committee of the Whole comprised of representatives from all 135 WTO members and chaired by the US Trade Representative Charlene Barshefsky met on the morning of 1 December. Barshefsky had urged delegations to send senior officials with decision-making authority to mandated working groups, and she notified delegations that she reserved the right to hold Green Room meetings. She preferred an inclusive approach such as that afforded by the working-group structure. However, delegations continued to meet in a number of informal bilateral and multilateral sessions. An impromptu mini-Green Room process evolved, continued and picked up momentum. The pre-Seattle discord continued unabated, and if anything it worsened. All-night negotiating sessions between trade ministers turned into petulant feuding.

Although theoretically the WTO operates by consensus, in practice it is not so. The members of the Quadrilateral Group, the so-called Quad (Canada, the European Union, EU, Japan and the USA) traditionally functioned as an informal steering committee for the GATT/WTO system. They functioned in a non-transparent manner and held informal meetings on important issues in small groups. It must be stated that some large trading developing countries' ambassadors did participate in the deliberations. These meetings took place in a room next to the office of the Director General of the WTO at the Centre William Reppard in Geneva, which is painted parrot-green. This is how the so-called Green Room process began.

During the life and time of the GATT, the Green Room process worked well and facilitated consultations among the CPs. The GATT period is known for its businesslike diplomacy and negotiating effectiveness. The flip-side of this coin was that a lot of relatively smaller traders had to play the role of second fiddle. Since the birth of the WTO,[27] this legacy of the GATT came in for a lot of criticism and has been painted in villainous colours. An increasing number of WTO members were eager to contribute to the decision-making process, but accession of many sovereign countries in quick succession slowed down the decision-making process and promoted stasis and drift. Some analysts went so far as calling decision-making in the WTO a 'medieval' and irrelevant process. This was considered one of the *causae causantes* of failure in Seattle.

Participation in the Green Room process was decided on the basis of the issue, and only the most active delegations were invited to participate. As for the question which CPs were typically included for consultations other than the Quad, the answer is Australia, New Zealand, Norway, Switzerland, sometimes one or two transition economies and some developing economies. The last category included countries like Argentina, Brazil, Chile, Colombia, Egypt, Hong Kong, India, Mexico, Pakistan, South Africa and at least one large member of the Association of Southeast Asian Nations (ASEAN).[28] Most of the other developing economies were kept out for lack of resources or capabilities (Schott and Watal, 2000). The number of economies participating in the GATT/WTO system went on increasing steadily, and *pari passu* the number of participants in the Green Room process also increased with the passage of time.[29] For instance, during the Tokyo Round (1973–79) period Green Room consultations typically involved eight delegations. By the time the Seattle Ministerial started, this number had reached 25, occasionally 30. With the growth in membership of the WTO, the Green Room process had to exclude too many new members and it subsequently became impossible to build any consensus on any important issue.

During the third Ministerial the Green Room process turned out to be totally dysfunctional. Besides, the conference dynamics adopted by the US Trade Representative was seemingly undemocratic. On the second day she announced her 'right' as chairperson to use procedures of her own choosing to reach a declaration in the name of the Ministerial Conference. She, with the Director General of the WTO, set up several Green Room meetings on issues where disagreements existed. Putatively, the plan was to get the major trading economies to agree among themselves, apply pressure on the major developing economies to participate in a Green Room meeting, and then pull together a third Ministerial declaration to launch a new round of MTNs, which all the 135 members would be asked to accept in a general meeting on the last day.

Textiles and apparel-exporting developing economies were upset by the US press briefing during the Seattle Ministerial declaring that acceleration of its textile liberalization commitments and discussion of its anti-dumping mechanism were off the table. The developing-country delegations were also unpleasantly surprised when Pascal Lamy, the EU Trade Commissioner, opposed negotiations on implementation, although he acknowledged that implementation was problematic in 'certain areas' that could be addressed in the context of a comprehensive new round (Das, 2000). Thus viewed, the lack of a streamlined decision-making process was creating frequent problems.

For the first time, the number of participating members was as large as 135. As the majority of them had not participated in the Green Room process, they felt marginalized. They were not even onlookers because they were not informed about what was going on in the Green Room meetings. Their discomfiture knew no bounds on the third day of the Ministerial Conference when trade ministers from several African countries, the Caribbean Community, and some Latin American economies complained about a lack of transparency in the negotiation process. The WTO was resoundingly criticized for its lack of transparency.[30] They felt that they were excluded from the deliberations on issues vital for their growth, and therefore did not feel obliged to support a draft Ministerial Declaration text produced without their knowledge or consent. On the final day the draft declaration stood without support from a large number of members, and the Seattle Ministerial had to be suspended without a declaration.

A structural limitation of the WTO

Most stakeholders regarded transparency as the mainstay of the global trading system and, therefore, the WTO agreements. Members assign the highest priority to transparency in the conduct of trade, and therefore its absence was resoundingly excoriated in Seattle. On the one hand, the GATT, the WTO and the General Agreement on Trade in Services (GATS) call on members to publicize all measures that affect the operation of agreements. On the other hand, ironically, the negotiations, rules and requirements of the WTO have frequently been perceived as opaque. The famous Leutwilder Group of eminent persons' report[31] of 1985 noted that a

> major reason why things have gone wrong with the trading system is that trade policy actions have often escaped scrutiny and discussion at the national level. Clear analysis and greater openness in the making of trade policy are badly needed, along with greater public knowledge of how the multilateral system works. (GATT, 1985)

The global trading system ignored this advice. A decade and a half went by and the WTO was faced with the same charge in Seattle. That the WTO should be more transparent in its operations was the express wish of the Group-of-Eight (G-8) leaders in the Kyushu–Okinawa summit (2000). There have also been problems in obtaining information on the activities of the WTO; critics have felt that the organization was being secretive because it was trying to hide something that was not in the interests of stakeholders.

Opacity apart, the decision-making process that was developed half a century ago was found to be completely unsuitable for the contemporary period. Over the latter half of the last century, the global trade scenario underwent a sea-change. A good number of developing economies became successful exporters, and China emerged as a manufacturing–exporting juggernaut. These emerging traders expected to have deeper involvement in the WTO operations and decision-making. It cannot be ignored that 65 developing economies had participated in the negotiations that led to the formation of the WTO, and current membership entails more than 100 developing economies. Their number represents strength, and has changed the power structure in the WTO. The influence of the Quad over the WTO system declined after the Seattle debacle. Rapid growth and expanding trade in a group of developing economies has made them more important than they were in the global trading system of the past. The majority of these economies fall in the category of emerging-market economies (EMEs) (Das, 2004). The decision-making process in the WTO has not evolved to accommodate the agenda items of this group of economies.

Agenda in parentheses

In preparing for the third Ministerial, a draft agenda document was prepared by the WTO secretariat in October 1999, which had 79 para-graphs. They were all bracketed, implying that nothing was agreed upon. This document was a catalogue of contradictory positions rather than a basis for launching serious multilateral negotiations. The EU and Japan did not countenance demands from the USA and the Cairns Group for far-reaching negotiations on agriculture. Partly to deflect this pressure on its highly protectionist Common Agricultural Policy (CAP), the EU was emphasizing a broader negotiating agenda that included some of the Singapore issues, in particular investment and competition policy. To the US delegation, the EU stance looked like 'negotiate on anything but agriculture'.

A group of 15 substantial traders among developing economies (G-15) was formed, which held meetings in Bangalore, India, during 17 and 18 August 1999. The G-15 prepared a fairly pragmatic and plausible draft agenda, which could be taken as a starting point, but the decision-making machinery in Geneva could not accommodate such a diversity of views. The Ministers of the Group-of-Seventy-Seven (G-77) developing economies had issued a declaration in Marrakesh in September formulat-ing wide-ranging proposals on the future negotiations in Seattle, intended to be a Message to the Ministerial Conference. The Declaration stressed the problems faced by developing countries, arising from the implemen-tation of the WTO agreements, and put forward several proposals includ-ing ways of getting greater market access to the industrial economies' markets, operationalizing special and differential treatment (SDT), and ways of achieving greater equity in the trading system. The declaration also contained warnings about the inclusion of labour standards and the misuse of the environment issue. However, the declaration was silent on the G-77 position on the Singapore issues and reductions in industrial tar-iffs. In their message the G-77 ministers also said that they were strongly committed to liberal and open trade policies which integrated the development dimension. The challenge for the Third WTO Ministerial Conference was to make resolute progress along the path towards an open international trading system whose benefits are equitably distributed.

The disagreements in Seattle were compounded by US insistence on putting labour standards in all trade agreements, and endorsement of the use of trade sanctions to enforce them. The EU echoed the US demand for a firm link between trade and labour rights. However, the first Ministerial Conference, or the Singapore communiqué of 1996, was clear on this issue and had stated what a majority of the members believed, that is, 'the International Labour Organization is the competent body to set and deal with these standards'. Secondly, developing economies saw a pretext for protectionism in the trade–labour link. Thirdly, piling non-trade issues on to an institution specifically designed to address trade issues was a travesty of logic. The US insistence was a bad-faith violation of the understanding reached at the WTO's first Ministerial, and in making this demand it appeared that US President Bill Clinton had caved in to pressure from labour interest groups (Irwin, 2000). Developing economies correctly apprehended that labour standards could become just a new pretext for restricting their exports. Several Asian economies (in particular India, Pakistan and Thailand) were vociferously opposed to it, and developing economies presented a consensual front opposing the US demand on core labour standards. Some analysts regard this as the largest stumbling block at the Seattle Ministerial.

The USA tried to rationalize and push for a narrow agenda for the third Ministerial; the logic given was that it would help in speeding up the negotiation process. Many developing economies were still discussing the Uruguay Round recommendations, which they thought gave them a raw deal (see earlier), and some of them (India, Pakistan, the Philippines) were not interested in discussing any further trade liberalization until they were granted leeway in implementing previous commitments in areas like TRIPS and customs practices, which was bitterly opposed by the USA and was considered tantamount to 'reopening done deals'. These are only a few illustrations of disagreements. With such wide disparities of views, no consensus could possibly emerge. Delegations were looking for a canary in a coal mine.

An agenda document littered with parentheses was not an uncommon incident, and the scenario at the Punta del Este meeting in 1986, where the Uruguay Round was launched, had been precisely the same. Yet the prospects for launching a new round of MTNs were clearly there because the outline of a possible balanced deal that needed to be clinched existed for the participating delegations. As opposed to this, the ambiance in Seattle was comparable to that in 1982, when efforts to launch a new Round were squashed by French refusal to participate in any negotiation on agriculture.

After weeks of often acrimonious negotiations, the WTO ambassadors abandoned efforts on preparing a draft agenda a week before the Third

Ministerial; they were aware that going into a four-day Ministerial Conference without a script was a recipe for a catastrophe. Informal consultations continued until hours before the commencement address, but a last-minute attempt by the White House to generate political will by getting some 30 world leaders to join President Clinton fell flat.

Breakdown of the old GATT process

The Green Room process had evolved soon after the birth of the GATT, and as alluded to above, the eight rounds of MTNs under the aegis of the GATT successfully utilized this process in arriving at consensus among the CPs. The process *per se* entailed only a small number of CPs, others remained relatively passive and accepted what came out of the Green Room. Delegations worked together more or less harmoniously to produce concrete benefits for all the CPs as well as the global trading system. Delegations came to the GATT to 'do business' in a pragmatic manner; impasses did occur during GATT period, but ways were found to circumscribe them, and delegations left political rhetoric for the other international fora (Schott and Watal, 2000). While recounting this positive feature of the GATT, it must be borne in mind that the GATT system was limited in its coverage and had a much smaller number of CPs than the membership of the WTO. Several major areas of international trade were not covered, and it did not have a Single Undertaking.[32]

Although the old GATT system operated by consensus, voting or majority rule were not excluded.[33] If none of the CPs present disagreed with a decision, it was assumed that a consensus has been arrived at. Country groups had operational understanding about each other's stands, and the consensus rule was not abused. Large traders like the EU and the USA took the initiative in planning the draft agenda for meetings and they did not insist on full participation by the developing economies. Full participation was taken to mean 'full and/or immediate' compliance. On their part, the developing economies did not stall progress in negotiations for two principal reasons. First, trade accords made few demands on them; there was no compulsion to be part of the agreements. Second, they made large gains from the commitments of the industrial economies that were extended to them on a most-favoured-nation (MFN) basis.[34] As a group, the developing economies were not large traders; they were aware of the fact that, as weaker partners in the GATT system, they benefited significantly from a well-functioning, multilateral, rule-based trading system.

The unobtrusive, discreet and judicious consensus-building process profiled above broke down in the WTO era for two reasons. First, as noted earlier, the membership of the WTO is much larger. Many developing economies had found it necessary to join the new system as members, because by the time of the founding of the WTO several of them, particularly those in Asia, had evolved as significant traders in their own right. This issue is discussed at length in Chapter 2.

The single undertaking and deepening commitments

Unlike the CPs of the GATT, the WTO members cannot be 'free-riders' on negotiated agreements. The Single Undertaking clause of the Uruguay Round demanded commitment to all the 60 agreements and decisions covered by the WTO. The Uruguay Round was the first time that the concept of a Single Undertaking was formally incorporated in the global trading system, and became a part of the GATT lexicon. Subsequently it also became a part of the WTO jargon. It is not surprising that it has been given a variety of interpretations. The WTO, for example, lists it as one of the principles – together with others such as participation, transparency, SDT and sustainable development – that guide the Doha Work Programme.

The WTO further goes on to describe the Single Undertaking as 'virtually every item of the negotiation is part of a whole and indivisible package and cannot be agreed separately' (WTO, 2001).[35] The Single Undertaking created substantial commitment to greater reforms of trade barriers and domestic regulation for the member developing economies. The reform commitments were far more than those during the GATT regime, making it mandatory for members to be better informed about the issues under negotiations and the negotiation process. Several of them (like the Philippines) were disenchanted with the obligation they had accepted under the Uruguay Round without participating in the negotiations; they were facing difficulties in the implementation of regulations that were required to fulfil their WTO obligations. This added to the difficulties of crafting an agenda for a new round of MTNs.

Backlash against globalization

Another full-size challenge to the third Ministerial Conference came from the international backlash against globalization, which was more than merely economic and particularly reviled the global trading system. A strong perception that globalization had spawned winners and losers had taken hold. The very same enriching, competitive, liberalization process that neoclassical economists lauded does indeed exact its costs. The doctrine of competitive advantage, à la Michael Porter, has a salutary economic influence in a globalizing economy if you have the wherewithal with which to be competitive. If an economy has a history of poorly trained human resources, weak institutional structures and an inefficient government system, globalization can do little good. Globalization has patently worsened the economic lives of some people. It must, however, be understood that it does not imply that some have to lose for others to win. Instead of merely denying the failures of globalization, one needs to set them in some sort of context. One needs to try to work out what governments and people on the comfortable side of the 'red-lacquered gate' can do to solve them (Micklethwait and Wooldridge, 2000). One of the principal reasons why this issue tends to be so frustrating is that supporters and opponents of globalization rarely listen to each other. There is so much evidence available for the contenders on both sides of this argument that they can go on *ad infinitum* without ever bothering to acknowledge the other.

Some observers of the globalization process opine that it is ruled by the laws of the market applied to suit the powerful. Concerns regarding the negative influence of globalization have been expressed by a diverse range of noteworthy people, from Pope John Paul II to George Soros.[36] That a backlash against globalization could derail efforts to commence new international liberalization initiatives and promote protectionist pressures around the world was well-known before the Seattle Ministerial. Although some backlash could be found in the developing countries, there was little reaction against trade liberalization in the crisis-affected Asian economies. Paradoxically, despite the continuing strong economic performance, some worrisome tendencies were emerging in the USA. This trend was disconcerting because the USA was not only the largest exporting country in the world in 1999, but also played a vitally important role in the development of the global trading system.

'The WTO became to the leftist mythology what the United Nations had become to the militia movement, the center of a global conspiracy against all that was good and decent in human society' (Krugman, 1999). Several thousand disparate anti-WTO demonstrators from about 1,200 non-governmental organizations (NGOs) protested in the streets of Seattle against free trade.[37] They made the WTO the scapegoat for all that was wrong in an unequal world. These citizens' groups have become increasingly powerful at the corporate, national and international levels, ranging from environment groups and labour unions to human-rights activists and development lobbies, with differing agendas. They are well-organized and media-savvy, using media in a masterly fashion. They also have some successes to their credit. In the past they had succeeded in arousing enough public interest and pressure, and were successful during the Earth Summit in Rio de Janeiro in 1992 in pushing through an agreement on controlling greenhouse gases. During the World Bank anniversary meeting in 1994 they forced a rethink of the Bank's goals, and they sank the Multilateral Agreement on Investment in 1998, which was a draft treaty to harmonize the rules of foreign investment under the aegis of the OECD. These groups thought that the Seattle Ministerial was going to be their next noteworthy achievement.

In Seattle these citizens' groups expressed their displeasure over everything from genetically modified (GM) crops to fishing subsidies. They decried a panoply of global ills: deforestation, child-labour, over-fishing and pollution. It made for colourful television; red-jacketed steel-workers marched alongside environmentalists dressed as endangered green sea turtles and monarch butterflies. They were determined to stop or delay the launch of the new round of the MTNs. Although the demonstrators got a good deal of media coverage, they could not take the credit for the failure of the Seattle Ministerial which was foredoomed due to numerous and serious deadlocks at the negotiating table.

The game-plan of the anti-globalization movement was to attack the global economy by attacking the institutions of global economic governance. To this movement the international bureaucracies formed an unlovable symbol of the global economy. The Bretton Woods twins and the WTO had much to answer for when it came to their influence on economic development, or lack of it, particularly in the low-income countries. By placing these multilateral organizations at the centre of the debate, critics of free international markets in goods and services put their opponents on the defensive. To be sure, the economists' case in favour of national governments adopting policies of openness and competition to spur growth and opportunity is overwhelming. However, the issue for the anti-globalization movement is that unelected and unaccountable international bureaucracies should not impose their policy prescriptions over sovereign national governments (Lindsey, 2000). The targets of the anti-globalization movement were incorrectly, if naively, chosen. The institutions they attacked, reviled and scorned were not responsible for the policy outcomes they deplored. The real object of their hostility is the trend towards freer trade and free markets, unrestricted mergers, and the perceived power of the transnational corporations (TNCs) which have swept over the global economy during the past two decades. While multilateral institutions have promoted freer markets, whose beneficial impact is visible in the NIEs and EMEs, they were not responsible for the other trends. Besides, such trends would certainly persist even if the IMF, the World Bank and the WTO suddenly melted into thin air.

We need to answer the valid question as to whether unelected and unaccountable officials of international bureaucracies, like the WTO, should impose their policy prescriptions over sovereign national governments or not. To make international agreements work, international bodies have to have some quasi-judicial process and/or authority to ensure that domestic measures do not become trade barriers. When they do, they violate the international treaty – that is the WTO. Before the birth of the WTO this process of monitoring domestic policy and providing policy prescriptions was slow and cumbersome, but after the WTO came into being the process became swift and decisive. It needs to be emphasized that the much feared and maligned power of the WTO to overrule national laws is limited to enforcement of the spirit of the existing trade agreements. For sure, it cannot force countries that are skeptical regarding the benefits of globalization to open their markets to trade and their economies to foreign direct investment (FDI). Furthermore, if a large number of sovereign countries are eager, or willing, to participate in the WTO discipline and be part of the global economic dynamism, it is because they are convinced about the benefits of the WTO regime and globalization (Krugman, 1999). Therefore, should the target of the citizens' group wrath not be the national governments that are fervently interested in WTO membership?

The unbalanced harvest of the Uruguay Round

As set out earlier, the developing economies accepted a lot of commitments in the so-called new areas like services, TRIPS and investment. In turn, the industrial economies reciprocated by providing market expansion opportunities to the developing economies in areas of interest to them, namely in agriculture and textiles and apparel. When market access commitments for the developing economies are added up, they are no more than those of the industrial economies. NTBs in the agriculture sector had to be converted into tariffs by all participants, while those in other sectors had to be significantly brought down or eliminated (Finger and Schuknecht, 1999). The proportion of imports affected by tariff cuts in both developing and industrial economies was close to 32 per cent, but the depth of tariff cuts was 2.3 times more for the developing economies when all merchandise are taken into account, and 2.7 times more when industrial goods are considered.

Finger and Nogues (2001) argued that tariff reduction of 'x per cent on y proportion of imports' is imprecise wording and leads to 'smoke and mirrors'. Negotiations in textiles and apparel and agriculture used this concept, leading to a dubious outcome. The Uruguay Round Agreement in Textiles and Clothing (ATC) was so worded that it allowed industrial countries to postpone an overwhelming part of the liberalization to the end of the transition period. Similarly, the Uruguay Round Agreement on Agriculture (URAA) 'has proven to be much less than it appears to be'. To be sure, quotas were tariffied, but the tariff rates were so chosen that they reduced protection only minimally. In some cases tariffication even increased protection (see Chapter 6).

A meaningful diminution in agricultural protection, domestic support and export subsidies has not been negotiated up to the Fifth Ministerial Conference in Cancún, and even the first half of 2004. As regards how this came about it is easy to comprehend. That all NTBs would be eliminated and replaced with tariffs was made a legal obligation in the negotiations, but it was not written into the agreement as a legal obligation that industrial economies would reduce them by an average of 36 per cent in six years and developing economies by 24 per cent in 10 years, and that there would be a simultaneous reduction of export subsidies and domestic support to the farm sector. The *modus operandi* by which tariffs, export subsidies and domestic support would be reduced was published in another document, called the 'modalities' document, which did not have the status of legal obligations. The Uruguay Round strove for a reduction in protection for trade in agriculture in the industrial economies, but in reality it produced the opposite results. Support for agriculture increased from 31 per cent of gross farm receipts in 1997 to 40 per cent in 1999. In all major industrial economies, the aggregate support of agriculture was higher in the early years of the twenty-first century than before the Uruguay Round was launched (OECD, 2000; Stoeckel, 2004).

For the purpose of evaluation, the concessions given versus received logic cannot be applied to the new areas like services, customs valuation, TRIPS, TRIMS, and sanitary and phytosanitary measures. Implementation of measures negotiated in these areas during the MTNs was found to be expensive by the developing economies. In first three areas (customs valuation, TRIPs and sanitary and phytosanitary measures), implementation of the agreed measures was going to cost $150 million, more than a year's development budget in an LDC. To the industrial economies the implementation cost is nothing because the new WTO standards imposed were usually those that already existed in them. The new

norms ignored the development problems and the costs of implementation. Many developing economies, particularly the LDCs, therefore
faced difficulties in implementation of the negotiated measures, and
they vociferously complained in the international fora, including
during the Doha Ministerial Conference.

Conclusions and summary

The MTNs were the mechanism for reciprocally exchanging commitments for market access among the contracting parties (CPs) of the
GATT, and now among the members of the WTO. The on-going Doha
Round is the first round of MTNs under the auspices of the WTO. The
trade liberalization process tended to deepen and widen with each
round of MTNs. This chapter, *inter alia*, covers two of the most important events that took place before the launch of the Doha Round. These
two events were vitally significant *per se* and they inspired and influenced the launching and proceedings of the Doha Round. They were the
completion of a comprehensive round of MTNs, the Uruguay Round,
and the comprehensive systemic failure that the Seattle Ministerial
Conference stood for.

It is widely believed that trade expansion leads to economic growth
and welfare gains, though this issue is not without its thought-provoking
controversies. That said, there is little evidence to the contrary. Many
developing economies unilaterally adopted trade policy liberalization
from the mid-1980s, though the contribution made by multilateral
institutions in this regard cannot be discounted.

In the process of rapid expansion, international trade and the MTNs
became a contentious issue for the global economy as well as for global
economic governance. Controversies are rife, with sharp differences in
stances and intransigence in negotiations leading to frequent obstructions, delays and breakdowns in MTNs. The multilateral trade regime
governing international trade is a global public good (GPG). A GPG can
be underprovided and malprovided leading to suboptimal, undesirable,
outcomes. This is obvious from the current state of the contentiousness
in the multilateral trade system. Failures in Seattle and Cancún are two
of the most recent reminders. It is vitally important that the participating members of the WTO take a global public good perspective of the
MTNs, and reform the global public policy provisions accordingly.

2
Equilibrating the Global Trading System and the Doha Round

The changing emphases of successive MTNs

Although the United States took a great deal of initiative in championing the cause of free multilateral trade for decades, the global system was not created for or by the industrial economies. However, at the time of the inception of the General Agreement on Tariffs and Trade (GATT) they were the principal trading economies and, therefore, overwhelmingly dominated it until the commencement of the Uruguay Round of multilateral trade negotiations (MTNs) in 1996. Historically, the participation of the developing economies in the global trading system was limited, and therefore the evolution of many of the GATT rules reflects the perceived interests of the industrial economies. The international treaty creating the GATT in 1947 was signed by 23 nations – 12 industrial and 11 developing economies.[1] These 23 contracting parties (CPs) accounted for 60 per cent of the world trade at that point in time. The GATT contained tariff concessions agreed to during the first Geneva Tariff Conference (1947) and a set of rules designed to prevent these concessions from being frustrated by restrictive trade measures.

The following seven rounds of MTNs under the sponsorship of the GATT were dominated by industrial economies: the Geneva Tariff Conference (1947), the Annecy Tariff Conference (1949), the Torquay Tariff Conference (1951), the Geneva Tariff Conference (1956), the Dillon Round (1960–61), the Kennedy Round (1964–67), and the Tokyo Round (1973–79). The coverage of trade issues in these MTNs varied substantially. Tariffs were the only issue covered during the first five rounds (see Chapter 1), and as the tariff rates declined with progress in the rounds, policy-makers became increasingly creative in imposing non-tariff barriers (NTBs). The scope of the subsequent rounds was

31

progressively enlarged and extended to include NTBs of different genre. Each subsequent round covered more issues and entered new territories than the preceding one, and was correctly described as the most comprehensive round of MTNs so far. The Doha Round can also be qualified for such a description. For instance, the Kennedy Round covered tariffs, anti-dumping, agriculture and subsidies and countervailing duties. The Tokyo Round covered all that was covered in the Kennedy Round and also included technical barriers to trade (TBT), public procurement, safeguards, and the GATT articles. Being even more comprehensive, the Uruguay Round (1986–94) covered all the issue areas of the preceding two rounds, plus the rules of origin (ROO), pre-shipment inspection and textiles and apparel, GATT functions, WTO organizational issues, trade-related investment measures (TRIMS), trade-related intellectual property rights (TRIPS), and, most importantly, services. Following the same mode, the Doha Round covered all the issues of the preceding three rounds, plus industrial tariffs, regional integration agreements (RIAs), trade and environment, capacity-building and implementation issues. About the Singapore issues there remained some mystification. One group of participants thought that they were on the agenda, while another group thought not. This confusion continued until the Fifth Ministerial Conference in Cancún, Mexico.

If the GATT system was skewed towards the industrial economies, it certainly was not the intention of the founding fathers. That said, in the first seven rounds of MTNs the negotiations were focused on the areas of trade interest of the industrial economies because they dominated the world trade scenario as well as the multilateral trading system, and were the only meaningful participants in the MTNs and other GATT activities. Principal areas in which developing economies had comparative advantage, like agriculture and low-technology products like textiles and apparel, were not even included in the GATT discipline, and the developing economies remained complacent about this because trade had not become a significant part of their economic structures. Although the developing country CPs attended the MTNs and other GATT meetings, they were more or less passive participants. Their comprehension and preparation for the MTNs was highly limited, and therefore they were reduced to non-participants, looking on from the sidelines. Little wonder that the areas of interest of the developing economies were not addressed by the multilateral trading system. However, due to the most-favoured-nation (MFN) principle of the multilateral trading system the developing country CPs were able to avail themselves of the benefits of the industrial country liberalization,[2] but this is where their contribution to and benefit from the GATT system terminated.

The industrial country CPs accepted non-participation from the developing country CPs readily because it allowed them to ignore liberalization in what they considered 'sensitive' sectors for their domestic economies, particularly agriculture and textiles and apparel. What was more important was the fact that the developing country markets during this period were so small, in both relative and absolute senses, that they held little attraction for the exporting firms from the industrial economies. Also, the benefits of asking the developing country CPs to liberalize their small import markets were decisively much smaller than the cost of liberalizing their own markets in labour-intensive import sectors.

The growth endeavours and globalization during the 1980s and 1990s changed this scenario. First, many developing countries were no longer insignificant import markets and exporters; both their market size and export volume began to matter. The emerging-market economies (EMEs) and the newly industrializing economies (NIEs)[3] deserve a particular mention in this regard. Close to 25 of the developing economies earned the status of EMEs and integrated well with the global economy (Das, 2004a). This changed situation was evident during the Uruguay Round (1986–94), and for the first time at least the EMEs, many of whom had turned into successful traders, were brought into the fold of the GATT. They were expected to adhere to the reciprocity principle[4] of the WTO because the industrial economies felt that at their level of development they could. This was the time to establish a new equilibrium among the CPs of the GATT.

Hindsight reveals that since the Uruguay Round, the developing economies – small and large – no longer played the role of sideliners; their influence on the global trading system was undeniably on the rise. More than 90 developing economies participated for the first time in the Uruguay Round, and although they were a highly disparate group and disagreed with each other on a wide range of issues, they made their presence felt in the negotiations. Deardorff and Stern (2003) disagree with the developing country participation in the Uruguay Round being a wilful unilateral decision. They believe that the developing economies were 'brought on board by promises that were misleading or not likely to be kept'. Notwithstanding the disagreements among them, developing economies made several forays to influence the outcome in their favour, although their success in this endeavour was rather limited.

As the earlier rounds of MTNs focused on issues of interest to the industrial economies, a good deal of institutional and academic dialogue took place between 1995–2001 on the need for a round concerned with issues of interest to the developing economies. The intervening period covering the completion of the Uruguay Round and the launch of the Doha Round was focused on an elongated intellectual dialogue and policy debates on the need to redress the imbalance in this regard. That there was a need to integrate various sub-groups of developing economies fully into the global trading system was emphasized by many trade analysts. Various such sub-groups have differing expectations from the global trading system, and extensive suggestions for a future development round with a development-oriented agenda centred on issues of concern for those developing economies were made. Each proponent of a development round posited an appropriate agenda that would meet the needs and demands of different groups and sub-groups of developing economies and match the ever-altering multilateral trade scenario. Organizational changes in the WTO and those in its operations and emphases were also suggested by academic scholars and practising trade economists.[5]

Rebalancing the country groups

As the industrial economies overwhelmingly dominated multilateral trade, they also dominated the MTNs and the agenda-making procedures and exercises during the pre-Uruguay Round period. Members of the Quad, namely the EU, Canada, Japan and the USA, have dominated global trade in terms of value and volume, with a clear supremacy over the system even during the Uruguay Round. The global economy has undergone a considerable transformation since then, and several other country groups have emerged that are making their presence felt globally. Important in this regard are the emerging-market economies (EMEs) and the newly-industrialized economies (NIEs). Not only have these new country groups emerged, they have also integrated well with the global economy, including goods market integration as will be discussed.

Failure is a great teacher. One lesson from the skewed outcome of the Uruguay Round and from the Seattle debacle is that WTO members would naturally deliberate more on the agenda of any future MTNs. The broad framework of the Doha Round was being given more attention by members than in the past, in an attempt to strike a balance between the interests, priorities and tangible outcome of an MTN for both industrial and developing economies alike. The latter group is pragmatically subdivided into the EMEs and the NIEs on the one hand, and the low-income developing economies on the other, and their trading and economic priorities are markedly different. The last named group of developing economies was given the formal name of the Group-of-Ninety (G-90) during the Fifth Ministerial Conference in Cancún for the first time, albeit it had always existed. Any future round of MTNs must not limit its focus to issues and sectors that are of interest to one group of economies alone, such as financial services, information technology and some of the Singapore issues, but also include sectors of interest and benefit to the developing economies, like agriculture, construction, textiles and apparel, and maritime services.

While the Quad and the industrial economies have controlled the multilateral trading system in the past, presently the developing economies dominate at least the membership of the WTO in terms of sheer numbers. To be sure, they continue to be a highly diverse group, although they see strength in numbers. Besides, the WTO league tables of the 30 largest exporters and importers published annually comprise the NIEs and several EMEs in important places. Also, the People's Republic of China (hereinafter China), which acceded to the WTO during the Doha Round, was the fourth largest exporter in the world in 2003, after Germany, the USA and Japan, in that order. It was also the third largest importer in the world after the USA and Germany, in that order, making it a large and globally significant trading economy (WTO, 2004a).[6] China was invited to the Group-of-Seven (G-7) meeting held in Boca Raton, Florida, in February 2004. Additionally, a group of developing economies has done a laudable task of integrating with the global economy during the last two decades (Das, 2004a). Given the increasing economic interdependence between the industrial countries and the NIEs and the EMEs, a larger more representative group of finance ministers would be a more useful and representative group for deliberations on global economic, financial and trade issues. The old G-7 concept (founded in 1978) is progressively becoming outdated and irrelevant. It needs to be upgraded to a new Group-of-Twenty (G-20), founded by Paul Martin, the erstwhile Finance Minister of Canada in 1999.[7] Therefore, the global trading system cannot possibly treat the interests and priorities of the NIEs, the EMEs and the G-90 economies as merely marginal. Stubbornly adhering to the longstanding principle of G-7 and not moving nimbly and adapting to the changing global economic realities is sure to lead to global economic disarray.

Integrating goods markets

As stated in the preceding section, not only have a number of developing economies emerged as important global economies, but many of them have also done a good task of integrating with the global economy. Goods market integration has increased significantly over the decade of the 1990s, taking place through trade flows, with larger trade flows implying greater goods market integration. It is often estimated using data for bilateral trade flows, which are easily available. Price dispersion is another method of estimation, with smaller price differentials between trading economies implying greater goods market integration.

Several recent empirical studies have used price dispersion to quantify goods market integration across a large number of economies.[8] Prices of a large number (90+) of goods across a large (say, 100) number of cities are used, the goods chosen being generally highly disaggregated. The studies have concluded that the pattern of goods market integration has increased markedly during the last decade, and that regional integration arrangements (RIAs) have a positive effect over such integration.

Under these new circumstances, the notion of disregarding the priorities and trade interests of the developing economies in an MTN agenda would indeed be suboptimal. It would amount to creating a flawed system. Wisdom lies in addressing and integrating those priorities squarely into the MTN agenda because they are likely to produce systemic benefits. All consumers of the global public good stand to gain.

Striking a balance in modalities

Not only issues and sectors have to be paid careful, calculated and conscientious attention in any present and future MTN agenda, but attention should also be extended to the 'negotiation modalities'. In the contemporary trading world, balancing negotiation modalities has enormous significance; a lack of balance frequently jeopardized the MTNs and Ministerial Conferences in the past, and is certain to do so in the future as well. Determining what comprises a legal obligation needs to be done in such a manner that none of the trading country groups feel that they are being considered of secondary importance and, therefore, are being marginalized by the multilateral trading system. Intellectual property rights provide an interesting example. For sure, an MTN agenda must include the protection of intellectual property rights in which the industrial economies are interested, but at the same time it should not ignore issues of current and potential concern to developing economies, such as property rights to knowledge embedded in traditional medicines, and access of life-saving drugs and pharmaceuticals by the developing economies (Stiglitz, 1999a; Das, 2001).

The term negotiation modality in the context of tariff negotiations takes on a specific nuance and will be elaborated upon later in the chapter. Both in GATT-1947 and GATT-1994, the member governments were mandated to enter into negotiations to reduce tariffs and NTBs.[9] Negotiations were expected to be conducted 'on a reciprocal and mutually advantageous basis'.[10] Article XXVIII *bis* goes on to clarify that they 'may be carried out on a selective product-by-product basis or by application of such multilateral procedures as may be accepted' by the negotiating member countries. Conventionally, the CPs or the WTO members carried out negotiations on a product-by-product basis, and also devised mutually agreeable formulae for tariff reduction and trade liberalization. An assortment of instruments and techniques were deployed to this end. The term modality is used for the method used in tariff negotiations. Application of a particular method or modality also involves agreement on important related aspects, such as the base rate and staging. The base rate means the tariff level taken as a base for applying the agreed-upon tariff reductions, while staging means the period over which the tariff reduction would be phased (Hoda and Verma, 2004).

A balance on the above-mentioned lines cannot be struck until the member delegations take into account the institutional disadvantages that many developing economies have in participating meaningfully in negotiations. For instance, while 19 of the 42 African WTO members are not even represented at the WTO headquarters in Geneva, the average number of trade officials from each one of the Organization of Economic Cooperation and Development (OECD) countries is seven. In addition to the differences in the level of growth of the members, Stiglitz (1999b) correctly draws attention to the 'suspicions born of a legacy of past power imbalances'. The developing and industrial economies play on an uneven playing field, which is tilted against the former. Developing economies face greater volatility, and under certain circumstances trade liberalization can also create volatility. They find it relatively more difficult to deal with economic adjustments which are a consequence of trade liberalization. A closely related fact is that developing economies either do not have social safety nets or have very weak ones. Unemployment has been a persistent problem in a majority of them. Thus regulations and liberalization measures that *prima facie* look even and fair to both the country groups may have very different and unequal consequences for them.

After the foundering of the Seattle Ministerial, those members who consciously sought agreement and harmony between industrial and developing economies paid explicit attention to the agenda of the Doha Round. The Doha Declaration document showed that every aspect of developing country needs were paid attention to, in particular their implementation-related requirements. The Doha Ministerial communiqué document uses words like 'development' and 'developing' 63 times in 10 pages and 52 paragraphs (WTO, 2001). Could this be mere lip-service? Only the final outcome of the Doha Round would be able to provide an answer.

Balancing the WTO architecture

In five-and-a-half decades since the creation of the GATT/WTO system, the global economy has evolved out of recognition. Therefore, the current architecture of the WTO needs to be given serious reconsideration to accommodate the evolution and alterations in the global economy. The modalities and scope of negotiations need to be expanded in such a manner that mutually beneficial bargains can be struck between the participating country groups, resulting in enhancement of global welfare. Mattoo and Subramanian (2003) proposed a vigorous and coherent, albeit achievable, set of alterations and expansion in the WTO architecture, based on the following five principles:

1 The coverage of the improved global trade architecture must be comprehensive, including not only trade in goods and services but also factors of production.
2 The new WTO architecture must enforce national treatment[11] or non-discrimination, both *de facto* and *de jure*, between domestic and foreign products and suppliers of services, after they have entered the domestic market.
3 While there can be some flexibility in allowing restrictions on the entry of foreign goods and suppliers of services, they must be negotiated and bound at the current levels. In allowing the restrictions, only the most efficient instrument, namely tariffs, should be used. Inefficient instruments, like quotas, must be avoided.
4 Regulatory harmonization needs to be attempted only in a narrow range of situations where lack of harmonization is spawning negative externalities. For securing regulatory changes compensation is a superior instrument to sanctions.
5 Regional integration agreements (RIAs) need to be allowed as long as the interests of non-members of the RIA are protected.

These principles need to be explained. The first principle proposes expansion of the WTO and the General Agreement on Trade in Services (GATS) under multilateral discipline. To be sure, bringing services transactions within the ambit of the global trade discipline was a major step forward. The neoclassical argument supporting liberal trade in goods and services, including factors of production, is that it would lead to efficiency gains at the multilateral level and eventually enhance global welfare. The GATS *inter alia* covers trade in factors of production, that is capital and labour. The industrial economies had insisted on inclusion of the trans-border movement of capital, while the developing economies had insisted on the inclusion of the temporary movement of labour for delivering services. These are worthy suggestions for the consideration of the new WTO architecture.

Inclusion of the movement of factors of production in the WTO regime would augment the negotiating space in the WTO system and in rounds of MTNs. It should logically lead to the greater possibility of mutually beneficial negotiations between the developing and industrial economies. The opportunity of labour mobility is especially beneficial for the developing economies because it offers a distinct possibility of dwarfing the gains from improvement in market access in goods. Winters (2000a) and Winters *et al.* (2002) computed gains from labour mobility using a computable general equilibrium (CGE) model. According to their estimates, if industrial economies allow inward movement of unskilled temporary workers equivalent to 3 per cent of their workforce, it would generate global welfare gains worth $150 billion per annum. Two important features associated with these gains are: first, both developing and industrial economies share in these gains; and, second, gains are larger if labour mobility of both low-skilled and high-skilled workers is permitted. Mattoo and Subramanian (2003) point out that these gains 'dwarf the estimated gains from complete liberalization of trade in goods and any of the initiatives currently contemplated under the Doha Development Agenda'. While the Doha Development Agenda (DDA) covers investment in paragraphs 20 through 22 of the Doha Ministerial Declaration (WTO, 2001), it excludes the temporary movement of labour, which is a stark asymmetry in the DDA. To offset this imbalance the WTO needs to encompass the temporary movement of labour, so that this anomaly is offset in the WTO architecture. This issue has become a little more complex than it was after the tragic events of 11 September 2001. If it cannot be included in the Doha Round, it can be made an intermediate-term target for deliberation and negotiations.

The second improvement in the WTO architecture would come through adoption of unfettered national treatment. For maximizing efficiency, national treatment in trade in goods and services should be completely unrestricted. In the case of trade in services, the mode of delivery and the point of delivery must be immaterial. To be sure, this would be a trying requirement for both developing and industrial economies and many of them would find its countenance challenging. Nevertheless, this principle quintessentially provides support to sound multilateral trade policy, and therefore while adopting it a certain degree of flexibility is necessary. In the case of the GATT, national treatment is a general obligation (Article III), which applies to goods post-entry. That is, economies were not allowed the flexibility to impose restrictions. As opposed to this, in the GATS national treatment is applied both pre-entry and post-entry, but it is not a general obligation and countries have the flexibility to apply it to the selected sectors and modes of entry. The GATS needs to expand the application of national treatment. Application of the GATT principle to the GATS in this regard would indeed strengthen national treatment under the GATS. Enhanced transparency in domestic trade policy is one important merit of application of national treatment. Flexibility in the matter of domestic subsidies to producers may be tolerated for a while because they are the least inefficient instrument for remedying domestic distortions.

Thirdly, in allowing WTO members restrictions on the entry of foreign goods and suppliers (in case of services), some freedom can be allowed. Additionally, members can be allowed to choose in which sectors to allow foreign direct investment (FDI) and temporary movement of labour, albeit these freedoms need not be totally unrestricted. In this regard, application of the GATT principle of choosing only the less-inefficient instrument for restricting market access would indeed circumscribe this freedom on market restriction.

Fourthly, regulatory harmonization in the WTO system is desirable, but only if the final outcome is global welfare enhancement. Furthermore, if it is, it should be encouraged, attempted and achieved with the help of compensating instruments or rewards, not with sanctions or threats. There are situations in which both economic and non-economic externalities exist and members would be enticed towards regulatory harmonization of their own accord. In situations where there are no such externalities, there is little reason to harmonize the regulatory differences. In addition, the WTO system should be flexible enough to respect national trade-offs in this regard. For instance, the European Union's (EU) choice of higher safety standards for beef, or developing economies' option for lower environmental standards must be respected. In the latter case, one would expect that the developing economies would try and emulate the industrial economies as they move up the development ladder with the passage of time.

Finally, small regional or sub-regional groups that plan to form RIAs and seek shallow or deep integration must remain free to do so. Under Article XXIV of the GATT-1947 they have been free since the birth of the global trading system.[12] The integrating regional economies voluntarily choose to harmonize or mutually recognize each others' standards. What is important is how to accommodate those trading partners that did not participate in the RIA and are outsiders. In the absence of a mutual recognition agreement (MRA), an outsider may be discriminated against, which in turn would result in trade diversion from the non-members of the RIA. This is important because successful RIAs like the EU can form MRAs with little effort. They cannot do so with the developing economies like Egypt or the Philippines, making them potential victims of trade diversion. To minimize this problem, Mattoo and Subramanian (2003) suggested using the approach taken by GATS Article VII, which 'allows countries to harmonize or mutually recognize standards, provided such arrangements are not used as a means of discrimination and outsiders with substantially similar standards are afforded an opportunity to negotiate similar agreements'. This provision provides a pragmatic openness *vis-à-vis* non-member countries.

Skewing the benefits of the Doha Round

What policy actions need to be taken to equalize the previous tilt in the global trading system towards the industrial economies? Deardorff and Stern (2003) have made several noteworthy, effectual and spirited policy recommendations. The first relates to the decision-making process in the WTO. In Chapter 1, it was pointed out that the Green Room process is no longer an appropriate negotiating and decision-making tool in the WTO, and that it has outlived its utility. What is needed is the establishment of a formal decision-making process, which should be so devised that the developing economies realize that the trade issues of their interest are not being ignored and that they are 'represented in a manner that is commensurate with the importance' that these economies have in the global trade and multilateral trading system. One recent and functional improvement in this area is organizing 'mini-Ministerial meetings' of a subset of WTO members, say, approximately 25 of them. Such meetings have the advantage of facilitating rapid and fruitful decision-making, which is not feasible in the presence of the entire membership of the WTO. While organizing the 'mini-Ministerial meetings', care should be taken in selecting the representative developing economies in such a manner that the decision-making process not only becomes fully representative of developing country interests, but is also seen to be so by the stakeholders.[13] This is sure to inspire confidence in the developing economies regarding having a voice in the multilateral trading system.

Due to the presence of stringent protection, trade in agricultural products became a bone of contention. Deardorff and Stern (2003) made strong, if somewhat blunt and no-nonsense, policy recommendations on trade in agriculture, affecting the whole gamut of agricultural policies in the industrial economies. These recommendations are forthright and logical from the perspective of a trade theorist. These authors would prefer to see a clear commitment by industrial economies to not only eliminate agricultural export subsidies completely, but also reduce their agricultural output, which happens to be heavily subsidized. This must be done without delay, particularly in areas of export interest of developing economies. Tariffs on agricultural imports in the industrial economies and other policies that depress world market prices of agricultural products must also be eliminated. These prices are artificially depressed by subsidized farm production in the industrial economies as well as high import tariffs and other trade barriers. Many developing countries are adversely affected by these policies, and the burden is disproportionately borne by rural populations. The industrial economies also need to submit a clear and explicit schedule for adhering to these correctional moves in their policies. Although before the launch of the Doha Round this set of recommendations would have seemed like chasing an impossible target, it is no longer so. After the failure of the Ministerial Conference in Cancún, the industrial economies offered to eliminate an agricultural export subsidy, which is discussed in the next chapter. Negotiations on agriculture are of special interest to developing economies and should affect the whole range of agricultural policy structure in the industrial economies. The final objective of these negotiations should be to ensure that these policies do not distort global agricultural trade and undermine the ability of developing economies to exploit their comparative advantage in this vital sector (Brown *et al.*, 2003).

Market access is another crucial area of negotiations, which is sure to have far-reaching implications for global trade. During the Doha Round, all the WTO members need to commit to tariff reduction, particularly eliminating their most restrictive trade barriers, quotas and the so-called high tariffs or 'spikes'.[14] There is a pressing need to rationalize tariff escalation and rules of origin (ROO) because they are acknowledged to be biased against the developing economies. In the contemporary world trade scenario, the highest trade barriers exist predominantly against labour-intensive exports from the developing economies, particularly against textiles and apparel. These barriers stand in the way of the developing economies to pursue their comparative advantage, and run counter to what David Ricardo (1772–1823) recommended two centuries ago.[15] In the present-day world trade regime, labour-abundant economies feel handicapped in exporting labour-abundant products. What is worse is that the trade barriers in the developing economies are more restrictive and cover a larger range of products than the industrial economies, constraining trade between developing economies.

Market access is frequently constrained by administered protection, which includes measures like safeguards, countervailing duties, and anti-dumping duties. It is widely acknowledged that these measures are applied in an unjustifiable, if not totally illegitimate, manner. The rules regarding administered protection need to be rewritten in such a manner that they are not abused as protectionist devises to limit market access. Most often the anti-dumping laws are unjustly used for protection of specific industries; it has become customary to use these administered protection measures whenever a specific industry has to be protected. Although trade covered by administered protection is not large, they continually pose a threat to free trade.

The GATS came into effect in 1995, and since then definite progress has been made in negotiations in the services sectors of interest to the industrial economies. Negotiations on services must push ahead under the Doha Round and all-round progress should be made, without ignoring the services in which developing economies have comparative advantage, namely construction, maritime shipping, outsourcing, particularly business-process outsourcing (BPO), and movement of natural persons. On their part, developing economies need to pursue these negotiations in a thoughtful manner in the labour-intensive services areas where they have comparative advantage. How these negotiations are conducted and the modalities of negotiation will be important, and therefore developing economies need to prepare carefully and pragmatically, bearing in mind the tangible final outcome of what they are negotiating. For instance, liberalization of the movement of only high-skilled persons would result in limited gains for them. Conversely, as alluded to earlier, short-term movement of low-skilled persons is sure to spawn enormous benefits for the developing economies, making the GATS a vehicle of significant benefits for them.

Many developing economies need assistance in complying with their WTO obligations. In the Doha communiqué, paragraph 38 directly, and paragraphs 40, 42 and 43 indirectly, deal with the provision of technical assistance and capacity-building programmes (WTO, 2001). 'Technical cooperation and capacity building' mentioned in the Doha communiqué implies preparing developing economies, particularly low-income ones, for integrating into the multilateral trading system. The WTO needs to set up a formal mechanism of providing this assistance and finance it. However, the WTO is a small organization; its secretariat has limited professional strength and financial resources. Its 2004 budget was SFr 162 million and its total (professional and non-professional) staff strength is only 600. It would indeed be difficult for the WTO to meet the obligation of providing these public goods. Negotiators need to deliberate and decide on how to fulfil this institutional requirement and earmark resources for an institutional facility.

Bearing in mind the constraints faced by developing economies, the WTO members reaffirmed special and differential treatment (SDT) for the developing economies in paragraph 44 of the Doha communiqué (WTO, 2001). Although SDT implies exemption from market liberalization, it should be taken to imply 'acknowledgement of the adjustment cost of liberalization and a plan to provide assistance with bearing those costs' (Deardorff and Stern, 2003). It should include the technical and financial assistance noted in the preceding paragraph.[16] It would not be feasible in the short term but this issue must be debated during the Doha Round and the possibility of such assistance for the least developed countries (LDCs) explored.[17]

Broad aspects of tariff-slashing modalities

The first four GATT rounds followed Article XXVIII *bis* of the GATT-1947 closely, and adopted product-by-product modality of tariff-slashing without being imaginative or venturesome about it. Even in the fifth Dillon Round (1960–61), little progress was made towards bringing in innovative ideas in the modality. In the basic framework of tariff-slashing negotiations, reciprocity was an important consideration, although Article XXVIII *bis* did not specify how it was to be quantified. Therefore, strict reciprocity was followed in the first five rounds under the aegis of the GATT. All the CPs of the GATT, developing and industrial, exchanged tariff concessions on the basis of reciprocity. In the mid-1960s, however, the concept of reciprocity underwent a change. In view of the macroeconomic and financial problems faced by the developing economies, non-reciprocity was accepted as a norm for negotiations between developing and industrial economies. On later examination, some adjustments were also made. It was felt that while strict reciprocity may not be expected from the developing economies, they need to make concessions for the industrial economies, consistent with their individual development, financial and trade needs. As an afterthought, zero reciprocity was no longer considered acceptable by the industrial economies.

The product-by-product tariff cuts principle resulted in only small reductions in tariffs, and there was a general discontentment among the CPs. Besides, as the number of CPs participating in the negotiations was rising, product-by-product modality was growing increasingly cumbersome and unwieldy to operate. Therefore, the modality adopted during the Kennedy Round (1964–67) had to have some innovation, and for the first time the product-by-product modality was replaced by a linear tariff reduction. The working hypothesis of 50 per cent tariff cuts was accepted by the industrial economies, which quickened the pace of tariff reduction. The linear approach was applied to industrial products, while the modality of product-by-product tariff-slashing continued to be applied to agricultural products. The linear tariff reductions applied only to the negotiations between industrial economies, as the non-reciprocity principle was accepted for negotiations between developing and industrial economies. To be sure, exceptions to tariff reductions were granted, but they were kept to the very minimum.

The tariff slashing modality further changed in the Tokyo Round (1973–79), and the CPs from the industrial economies agreed to deploy a formula for general application based on the principle of the higher the tariff rate the greater the cut. Although a number of formulae were proposed, final agreement was on the Swiss proposition, which was as follows:

$$Z = AX/A + X$$

where coefficient A was equal to 14 or 16, X was the initial tariff rate and Z was the resulting rate of duty. The CPs had an option to choose the value of A; 16 resulted in slightly lower reduction than 14. As agreed in the Kennedy Round, the developing economies did not use the formula at all.

Several new negotiating modalities were proposed for the Uruguay Round (1986–94) by the EU, the USA, Japan, Canada and Switzerland, with each proponent certain about the superiority of its proposal. There was no agreement on which modality to adopt. Deliberations, discussions and foot-dragging continued until the mid-term review in Montreal, after which a general principal was accepted that a target overall reduction in tariffs should take place. The target was fixed at 33.3 per cent. Determining the modality to reach the target was left to the individual CPs. In principle, target reduction was applied to the developing economies but the expectation was that they should increase the coverage of their bound tariff schedules.[18] The public policy-makers in the developing economies were having a change of heart during – even before the launch of – the Uruguay Round and many of them began to take the initiative in unilaterally liberalizing their trade policy regimes. In the context of wide-ranging macroeconomic reforms, trade barriers began to come down or were eliminated. Despite no pressure to commit to the 33.3 per cent target, many of them made generous concessions in their tariff rates. Korea even overshot the targeted rate. The principle of non-reciprocity began to be treated by the developing economies as irrelevant. Four Latin American economies (Argentina, Brazil, Chile and Mexico) had 100 per cent of their tariffs bound soon after the Uruguay Round ended, while in Thailand the bound tariff rate had soared to 64 per cent at the end of the Uruguay Round; its pre-Uruguay Round bound rate was 1 per cent. However, negotiations on the reduction of international tariff peaks by 50 per cent were only partially successful.[19]

Tariff-slashing modality in the Doha Round

In paragraph 16 of the Ministerial Declaration at Doha, the WTO members agreed

> to negotiations which shall aim, by modalities to be agreed, to reduce or as appropriate eliminate tariff peaks, high tariffs and tariff escalation, as well as non-tariff barriers, in particular the products of particular interest to developing countries. Product coverage shall be comprehensive and without *a priori* exclusions. The negotiations shall take fully into account the special needs and interests of developing and least-developed country participants, including through less than full reciprocity in reduction commitments, in accordance with the relevant provisions of Article XXVIII *bis* of GATT-1994 ... To this end the modalities to be agreed will include appropriate studies and capacity-building measures to assist least developed countries to participate effectively in the negotiations. (WTO, 2001)

The mandate given by paragraph 16 of the DDA is fairly explicit.

The Negotiating Group on Market Access (NGMA) met several times after the Doha Ministerial, but no agreement on modalities was in sight. After several proposals and counter-proposals, the Chairman of the

NGMA submitted a draft of the 'Elements of Modalities for Negotiations on Non-Agricultural Products' in May 2003, but an agreement eluded this attempt as well. Several well-thought-out and result-oriented modality proposals were put forth by the USA, Hong Kong SAR, Japan, Korea, the EU, MERCOSUR countries,[20] the People's Republic of China and India, in that order (Hoda and Verma, 2004). Some of them were variations on the Swiss formula on the Tokyo Round, and disagreements regarding the base rates, implementation period and staging continued until early 2004. Not all the modality proposals can be taken up for discussion here through lack of space.[21]

This was a sensitive area of negotiations. The EU and the USA were in favour of adopting a 'blended formula' which was fiercely opposed by the G-21 for being against developing countries' interests. After pro-longed negotiations, the WTO members reached an agreement in this regard on 1 August 2004, in the so-called 'July Package', which contains frameworks and other agreements. The text of the General Council's decision on the Doha Agenda work programme noted that a single approach for developed and developing country members meets all the objectives of the Doha mandate, and noted that 'tariff reductions will be made through a tiered formula that takes into account their different tariff structures'. To ensure that such a formula will lead to substantial trade expansion, the following principles will guide its further negotiation:

- Tariff reductions will be made from bound rates. Substantial overall tariff reductions will be achieved as a final result from negotiations.
- Each member (other than LDCs) will make a contribution. Operationally effective special and differential provisions for developing country members will be an integral part of all elements.
- Progressivity in tariff reductions will be achieved through deeper cuts in higher tariffs with flexibilities for sensitive products. Substantial improvements in market access will be achieved for all products.

The number of bands, the thresholds for defining the bands and the type of tariff reduction in each band were not specified in the July Package, or the framework agreement. The role of a tariff cap in a tiered formula with distinct treatment for sensitive products was also left for future evaluation (WTO, 2004b). Thus, a lot in the 'tiered-formula' approach 'remain under negotiation' (paragraph 30), which implies that its development impact is almost impossible to appraise. This lack of detail hides major divisions between importing and exporting countries in developed and developing countries which will be very difficult to reconcile. The agreement includes references to 'sensitive products' designed to take into account the interests of the EU and Japan, and 'special products' designed to take into account the food security, development and poverty concerns of developing countries. Loopholes of this kind have been abused in the past, and this scenario warrants only cautious optimism.

Areas of specific focus for redressing the imbalances

Notwithstanding the notable achievements of the eight rounds of MTNs in multilateral trade liberalization, a lot remains to be done in several areas of multilateral trade, particularly for offsetting the imbalances in gains from the earlier rounds of MTNs. However, a successful culmination of the Doha Round can result in sizeable welfare gains to the participants, irrespective of the country group or sub-group they belong to. The past rounds of MTNs succeeded in achieving tariff cuts, reduction or elimination of NTBs, and liberalizing trade by other means. Tariff-slashing was most notable in manufactured goods. At the time of the genesis of the GATT, average tariffs on manufactured goods were around 40 per cent. By the time the Tokyo Round was completed (1979), this rate had fallen to 6 per cent, and when the recommendations of the Uruguay Round are implemented (end of 2005), they are expected to fall further to 4 per cent. The Uruguay Round agreement also succeeded in binding tariff rates in all the industrial economies as well as larger traders among the developing economies. When the Uruguay Round recommendations are completely implemented, tariff-free trade will be expanded to take hold in some products (like information technology-related goods). In the same vein, international trade can be reasonably expected to benefit from the Doha Round of MTNs.

Indubitably, tariffs still influence and distort multilateral trade patterns, and they *pari passu* distort the resource allocation patterns in the domestic economy. These distortions are substantially higher in many developing economies because tariffs are significantly higher in them than those in the industrial economies. Average MFN tariffs are the highest in South Asia, Latin America, North Africa and sub-Saharan Africa, in effect impeding trade, including intra-developing country trade. Early during the Doha Round, it was realized that tariff rates on manufactured goods traded between developing economies continue to be twice as high – or frequently more than twice as high – as for trade in similar goods between industrial economies.

The structure of tariffs is another problem that adversely affects market access, and tariff-related distortions persist. Tariff peaks and escalation continue to create serious hurdles. Economies that tend to upgrade their structures by moving up the technological ladder soon discover that tariffs were lower on the low-technology, labour-intensive products than they are on higher-technology, capital- or knowledge-intensive goods. This kind of tariff escalation between product categories is a disincentive to the developing economies and their technological advancement endeavours (IMF/WB, 2002).

Some of the principal areas of focus in the DDA have been taken up for discussion in this section. Negotiations on agriculture would certainly demand a good deal of time, endeavour and skills, because agriculture has continued to be the most illiberal area of multilateral trade, having exceedingly high tariffs no matter which country group one chooses; tariff rates vary widely among countries, ranging between 36 per cent and 63 per cent (IMF/WB, 2002). The situation in agriculture has been further complicated by having quotas and tariffs operating together; that is, having differential tariff rates inside and outside quotas. For instance, an importing country may set a tariff rate of 15 per cent for the first 150,000 units of a certain grain, but once this limit is reached the tariff rate is raised to 50 per cent. Tariff peaks are particularly high and frequent on several exports of developing country interest, such as textiles and apparel, leather, rubber and footwear, travel goods and transport equipment. Likewise, tariff escalation also affects developing country exports most in products like tobacco, leather, cocoa, wood and paper.

Two of the areas of special focus in the DDA are the so-called 'environmental goods'[22] and textiles and apparel. The former line of products were targeted by WTO members because they are instrumental in improving the environment, a global public good as well as a local public good, and therefore are badly needed in most countries. Thus far trade in environmental instruments follows the usual pattern of tariffs, that is, high when traded between the developing economies and relatively lower when traded between the industrial economies. Lowering of tariffs in this sector would encourage their use in more developing countries and spread environmental protection technology.

Phasing-out of the multi-fibre agreement (MFA) by 2005 is one of the much-celebrated recommendations of the Uruguay Round. As the phasing-out is completed, trade in textiles and apparel will be brought under WTO discipline, after which the importance of tariffs in this sector will increase. The reason is that once the MFA is dismantled, multilateral trade in this sector is likely to increase between 34 per cent and 60 per cent, and will certainly face tariffs in the industrial economies. In mid-2003 the average tariff rate in the textiles and apparel sector in the Organization of Economic Cooperation and Development (OECD) economies is 12 per cent, not far below the international peak level. As opposed to this in metals, a low-tariff sector, imports face a 1 per cent tariff rate. It is well-known and lamented that tariff peaks abound in textiles and apparel in the OECD economies; approximately 30 per cent of imports face tariff rates higher than 15 per cent.[23]

The potential for welfare gains

If negotiations around the DDA take place with an objective of offsetting past imbalances in the MTNs, there are possibilities of welfare gains for the participating developing economies which can be quantified using standard models. When economies liberalize their trade policy regimes in a non-discriminatory manner during MTNs, they tend to benefit. However, such liberalization should accompany appropriate domestic compensating policies, particularly macroeconomic, social and labour-market policies. The immediate impact of such liberalization works as follows. The MTN negotiations lead to changes in the production and consumption patterns, which in turn are the sources of these benefits and welfare gains. As to how this happens, let us begin with a traded product. Tariff reduction or elimination under an MTN exercise results in rising imports of the product in question, and therefore its prices fall in the previously protected importing country. Concurrently, production and prices of the goods in question rise in the exporting country that is an efficient producer of this product. Productive resources in the importing countries are reallocated to more efficient uses, in the process raising allocative efficiency. The final result is welfare gains in the importing country. The exporting country would be a mirror image of the importing country and would benefit from welfare gains because it would deploy more productive resources in the liberalized sector in which it has comparative advantage. In addition, for consumers in the importing country declining import prices would lead to an increase in consumer surplus.

The welfare gains process does not stop here, because there are a series of second-round effects. Changes in prices of traded goods result in changes in terms-of-trade in the trading economies. Decline or elimination of some tariffs cause rises in world prices of some traded goods, and falls in others. Depending upon the composition of their trade, some countries may gain by tariff liberalization while others may lose. However, the flip-side of the coin is that the economies that rely on custom revenue as a key source of public revenue stand to lose by tariff liberalization.

Like the previous rounds of MTN, the negotiations on the lines of the DDA and their implementation have a significant potential for welfare gains for WTO members. A time-tested method for quantifying welfare gains is by using a computable general equilibrium (CGE) model of the global economy, since such models can produce a wealth of projected economic indicators. Lippoldt and Kowalski (2004) used the Global Trade Analysis Project (GTAP) model for their modelling exercise. A static, multi-region, multi-sector modelling framework, the GTAP is designed to facilitate quantitative analysis of policy issues. It is a general equilibrium model that includes linkages between economies and between sectors within economies. It reflects an assumption of perfect competition; industries are characterized by constant returns to scale; imports are treated distinct from domestic goods; and imports from different sources are also treated differently. Developed from the Global Trade Analysis Project established in 1992, the model was extensively used to examine such issues as the impact of the Uruguay Round, trade liberalization in the Asia-Pacific Economic Cooperation forum, and future patterns of multilateral trade.[24] Lippoldt and Kowalski (2004) used data from the GTAP version 5 database, modified to reflect the information on MFN applied and bound tariffs contained in the updated *OECD Tariffs and Trade* database of 2003, with a base year of 1998.[25]

Academic researchers and international financial institutions (IFIs) had attempted similar exercises after the Uruguay Round and overestimated its potential welfare gains. One reason was their focus on applied tariffs, assuming that the negotiated reductions in bound tariffs were going to yield proportionate reductions in applied tariffs (Anderson *et al.*, 2000). In reality, the gap between the bound and applied tariffs was never proportionate. Cuts in bound tariffs did not always produce similar cuts in the applied tariff rates that exporters and importers faced. In order to assure more conservative and realistic estimates of tariffs, Lippoldt and Kowalski (2004) used a conditional applied tariff procedure comparable to the method adopted by Walkenhorst and Dihel (2002).

Principal conclusions arrived at by Lippoldt and Kowalski (2004) may be summarized here as follows:

1 The corrected (on the above-mentioned lines) and reestimated results of welfare gains from the Uruguay Round show an annual gain

of $18 billion, of which 70 per cent would be captured by the developing economies. South Asia, Latin America and sub-Saharan Africa were found to benefit most.

2   In the baseline scenario of the DDA, in which all the merchandise tariffs were removed and trade facilitation (reduced trading costs) was implemented, total welfare gains amounted to $173 billion, of which $97 billion were attributed to tariff cuts and $76 billion to the reduced cost of trading. The largest benefits went to Western Europe, and Southeast Asia and North Asia.

3   In the scenario where merchandise tariffs were reduced by half, and trade facilitation measures were introduced, the welfare gains amounted to $117 billion, of which $41 billion can be attributed to tariff reduction. Developing countries benefit substantially from market access in the industrial economies.

4   The deployment of the Swiss formula led to benefits ranging from $121 billion to $158 billion, depending upon the value of the coefficient used. The scenario with five tariffs spawned maximum benefits, second only to a complete liberalization scenario. In terms of welfare gains from tariff liberalization, the Swiss formula was found to have the advantage of producing gains for every region of the global economy.

5   Without exception, under all the different scenarios considered, the combination of reduced tariffs and trade facilitation produced welfare gains for all the regions.[26]

Conclusions and summary

The focus of different rounds of MTNs kept on shifting constantly. As the GATT system was essentially skewed in favour of the industrial economies, successive rounds of MTNs were largely conducted on the issues of interest to the industrial economies. These economies dominated multilateral trade as well as the multilateral trade regime. Developing economies were not active participants in the MTNs. However, this dominance of the industrial economies changed during the Uruguay Round.

Although developing economies are highly diverse, many sub-groups among them are neither insignificant import markets nor exporters. However, both, their market size and export volume has now begun to matter. Since the mid-1980s, not only have a number of developing economies emerged as important global trading economies, but many of them have also done a good task of integrating with the global economy. Two conspicuous sub-groups among the developing economies emerged as significant traders, namely the EMEs and the NIEs. Given the new circumstances, the WTO architecture needs to be rebalanced.

To be functional and efficient, the contemporary multilateral trading system must reflect these changing equations of the global economies. Not only issues and sectors of interest to the developing economies and various sub-groups among them have to be paid careful, calculated and conscientious attention in any present and future MTN agendas, but the 'negotiation modalities' of the MTNs should also be influenced by these considerations.

One way of striking the balance in the WTO regime would be skewing the benefits of the Doha Round. To this end, this chapter makes several noteworthy policy recommendations, beginning with a change in the decision-making process in the WTO. Tariff-slashing modalities have been debatable during most rounds of MTNs. The Negotiating Group on Market Access (NGMA) met several times after the Doha Ministerial, but no agreement on modalities was in sight until early 2004, although several proposals and counter-proposals were made. The WTO members reached an agreement in this regard on 1 August 2004, in the so-called framework agreement or the July Package.

A lot remains to be done in several areas of multilateral trade, particularly for offsetting the imbalances in gains from the earlier rounds of MTNs. To name a few, areas like agriculture, high tariffs in the products of interest to developing economies, tariff spikes and tariff escalation, environmental goods and textiles and apparel, have to be paid especial attention from the negotiators for redressing the long-time tilt against the developing economies. If the negotiations around the DDA take place with an objective to offset the past imbalances in the MTNs, there would be greater possibilities of welfare gains for the participating developing economies, which have been quantified using the oft-used modelling exercise.

3
Setback in Cancún: Salvaging the Doha Round

Launching the Fifth Ministerial Conference

The Fifth Ministerial Conference of the World Trade Organization (WTO) was held during 10–14 September 2003, in Cancún, Mexico. One of its objectives was to review the progress, or lack thereof, made in the Doha Round of multilateral trade negotiations (MTNs) so far. Its culmination without an agreement had little element of surprise for the cognoscenti in the area of international trade.[1] Its successful conclusion would, indeed, have been astounding. Other than being a tough grind, such negotiations are strongly failure-prone. Although this failure was indeed a setback to the trade liberalization efforts of the global community, such failures had occurred in the past. According to one observer, of the nine Ministerial Conferences under the aegis of the GATT and the WTO, four were considered complete failures.[2] The debacle in Seattle (1999) is fresh in our memories. The Uruguay Round (1986–94) of MTNs collapsed and had to be dextrously pulled back onto its feet by the erstwhile Director General[3] of the General Agreement on Tariffs and Trade (GATT). Originally it was to have been completed in three years, but its deadline had to be extended several times and it took seven-and-a-half years to be completed. The fate of the Doha Round of MTNs seems to be heading the same way. It was originally scheduled to complete in January 2005, but it was apparent early on during the negotiations that the probability of its concluding on schedule was remote, if not non-existent.

While the Doha Round running into the sand in Cancún is a setback to the global trading system, it would be wrong to conclude that this failure would undermine the legal and organizational foundations of the world trading system embodied in the WTO. The flip-side of this coin is that following Cancún, the penchant towards bilateral trade agreements among WTO members increased.[4] Such bilateral deals are based on narrow national interests of the partner economies and have been on the rise. Although the United States was endeavouring to restart the MTNs, it has announced that it is preparing to enter into a bilateral free trade agreement (FTA) or regional integration agreement (RIA) with Thailand. However, bilateral FTAs are not an easy way out of the MTNs, as was demonstrated by the recent failure of negotiations between Japan and Mexico to form an FTA. The two potential partners disagreed on several substantive issues and eventually abandoned the idea.

As set out in Chapter 2, the issues and emphases in the MTNs have varied, and the coverage of each successive round expanded. Not only the value and volume of multilateral trade has undergone a marked transformation, but also its structure has changed radically since 1980. This transformation was squarely based on the changing comparative advantage of the economies participating in the multilateral trading system. In 1980, the largest volume and value of world trade was in primary products and medium-technology manufactures. By 2000, primary products became the smallest component of multilateral trade, while high-technology products surpassed them by a wide margin, soaring from 10 per cent of world exports in 1980 to a quarter in 2000. During this time span, the growth in world exports had a high and positive correlation with the level of technology. While the highest growth rates were recorded in the high-technology product categories, resource-based manufactures were at the other end of the spectrum. The lowest overall growth was recorded in the primary exports category – a paltry 3.2 per cent per annum on average.[5]

The objective of this chapter is to delve into the launch of the Doha Round, examine what was needed to be achieved in the round, and whether or where progress has been made in the MTNs, if any. This chapter also examines the principal causes of failure in Cancún, as well as the gains to be expected from a successful conclusion of the Doha Round, against the backdrop of current levels of protectionist barriers in the developing and industrial economies. It also analyses how the Doha Round can possibly improve the plight of the developing economies as well as that of the multilateral trading system *per se*. Its focus also includes modalities and paradigms of participation by WTO members. It first focuses on the intransigence of the members, followed by taking an adaptable, accommodative and constructive attitude towards the MTNs. It culminates with the identification of the principal causes behind the disillusionment in Cancún, and the progress made by the four principal negotiating blocs in breaking the Cancún impasse.

Flexibility adopted on the salient issues led to the so-called 'July Package' or framework agreement of 1 August 2004 (WTO, 2004). This was a critical and long-awaited step in the Doha process. The *causae causantes* of the setback in Cancún were disagreements and conflicting positions among the 146 participating members of the WTO, which were divided into four main negotiating blocs: the US, the European Union (EU), the so-called Group-of-Twenty-One (G-21)[6] developing economies and the Group-of-Ninety (G-90) which included small and low-income developing economies and the least-developed countries (LDCs).[7] The disagreements were principally in two areas of international trade, agriculture, which is an age-old chestnut, and the so-called Singapore issues.[8] Preceding the Third Ministerial Conference in Seattle, disagreements among the WTO members were all around, across north–south, east–west, north–north and south–south axes (Das, 2001), but this time the disagreements among the members followed a clear north–south axis.

As for the structure of this chapter, we begin with the *mise-en-scene* of the Doha Round of the MTNs and its launch in the next section. As it was christened the 'development round' by the outgoing Director General of the WTO, Mike Moore,[9] we then explore whether it could benefit the developing economies, before focusing on residual protection in non-agricultural products. Notwithstanding the spectacular failure in Seattle, we then describe the slow but tangible progress that was indeed made in the 22 months between November 2001 and September 2003 by the MTNs. Later in the chapter, participation of the developing economies in the Doha Round and Cancún Ministerial Conference is profiled; the causes behind the failure and the learning process that followed are discussed; finally focusing on the retreat from intransigence.

The mechanics of failure

The publicized objective of the Fifth Ministerial Conference was to 'take stock of the progress in negotiations, provide any necessary political guidance, and take decisions as necessary'.[10] As ministers could not agree in Cancún on the negotiating framework and future agenda, the future of many relevant issues of negotiations seemed uncertain. A valid apprehension was that the Cancún setback was not only likely to make the round lose its momentum, but also bring it to a grinding halt. For these reasons, the outcome of the Fifth Ministerial Conference became a disappointment to the global trading community. In the end the participating trade ministers could not summon the necessary flexibility, adaptability, accommodation and political will to bridge the gaps that separated their respective positions. They could not agree in Cancún *inter alia* on whether to launch negotiations on the four Singapore issues, namely, (i) trade and foreign investment, (ii) trade and competition, (iii) transparency in government procurement and (iv) trade facilitation.[11] Developing economies felt that the Singapore issues were primarily going to further the interests of the industrial economies in the multilateral trading system, which was not entirely correct because the fourth Singapore issue was going to benefit all WTO members. Many developing countries believed that the Singapore issues not only did not benefit them but also amounted to an incursion into their domestic economic affairs and infringed their sovereignty. This was becoming a throwback to the Uruguay Round era, when developing economies believe that they accepted restricting policies to be a part of multilateral regulatory discipline, without any tangible gain to their domestic economies.

The developing economies' concern regarding an oppressive burden on their administrative capacity was valid. The creation of a new institutional regime and its enforcement has high costs, particularly in areas like competition policy, investment regulation, and trade and customs procedures. The developing economies are concerned about these costs because many of them failed to meet their Uruguay obligations for this very reason. An estimate of the cost of three Uruguay Round agreements (customs reforms, TRIPs, and sanitary and phytosanitary measures) that called for institutional creation and regulatory developments revealed that the average cost of restructuring domestic regulation in 12 developing economies could be as high as $150 million (Finger, 2000). It is indeed a large burden on the small budgetary resources of a developing economy.

The level of political sensitivity varied widely on the Singapore issues, which caused serious disagreements among members. The EU – the principal *demandeur* – and within it the United Kingdom (UK), insisted that the decision to launch negotiations on the Singapore issues was taken in Doha, but the G-21 and other developing economies were of the view that this was not the agreement. They asserted that these issues were to be addressed *after* the Cancún Ministerial Conference not *during* the conference. By June 2003, the developing economies had developed a significant opposition to the Singapore issues, and at that point 77 of them, that is more than half of the WTO membership, publicly expressed their aversion to the inclusion of the Singapore issues in the Doha Round. They made it clear that these issues were nowhere on their priority list. Objectively viewed, in a round of MTN basically intended for development, the first three Singapore issues were completely incongruous. This complete inability to agree and compromise in the global trade forum was likely to affect the poorest G-90 countries most. A more open and equitable trading system would provide them with an important tool in alleviating poverty and raising their levels of economic development (Panitchpakdi, 2003).

As discussed in Chapter 2, even after eight rounds of MTNs under the GATT, some of the most illiberal policies in agricultural trade, protection in the form of tariff peaks[12] and continuing protection of markets in services still persist in the industrial economies. Furthermore, developing economies have their own set of protectionist measures, limiting trade among them, which imposes a large cost on domestic consumers and developing economies in general. Elimination of trade-distorting policies in both industrial and developing economies can lift millions out of absolute poverty. Therefore, the Doha Ministerial Declaration promised to 'place needs and interest (of the developing economies) at the heart of the Work Program adopted in this Declaration'.[13] Successful conclusion of the Doha Round would go towards reaching the Millennium Development Goal (MDGs) of cutting down income poverty by a half by 2015 (Winters, 2002). Therefore, disagreement in Cancún on negotiating 'modalities' and a framework, and subsequent failure, was a pernicious development for the developing economies first and the global economy second. Apparently, the Doha Round was not living up to its name of being a development round.

The seeds of failure in Cancún were sown in Doha, where the launch of the round was marked by acrimonious disagreements between the developing and industrial economies. The impressive launch rhetoric promised reductions in trade-distorting farm support, to slash tariffs on farm goods, cut industrial tariffs in areas that developing countries cared about (such as agriculture and textiles and apparel), free up trade in services, and negotiate global trade rules in the four Singapore issues. Was so much achievable? After the launch of the Doha Round, country groups began disowning important parts of the DDA. For instance, the EU denied ever having promised elimination of export subsidies in agriculture. Similarly, the developing economies denied ever having agreed to talks on the Singapore issues. The majority of the low-income G-90 and some lower-middle-income countries[14] (like the Philippines) still complained about their grievances over the Uruguay Round and felt absolutely no need to launch a new round of MTNs. This kind of posturing meant that brisk progress in negotiations could not be realistically expected. Countries and country groups continued in their intransigence and grandstanding in

Cancún, instead of working towards compromises on which MTNs are squarely based (*The Economist*, 2003). In addition, the domestic and bilateral action of several industrial economies (discussed later in the chapter) soon after the Doha Ministerial led to questions about their commitment to the DDA (Stiglitz and Charlton, 2004).[15]

The possibility of acute discord and a north–south divide was apprehended well-before the Fifth Ministerial started in Cancún.[16] The divergence in positions of developing and industrial economies existed on several other substantive issues also. It included (i) the negotiating 'modalities' (discussed in the following section), (ii) modalities for strengthening the present WTO provisions on special and differential treatment (SDT) for developing economies and (iii) addressing the implementation problem of developing economies which were not able to implement the recommendations of the Uruguay Round. Progress in negotiations during the Doha Round was spasmodic. It missed important self-imposed deadlines – in some cases such as agriculture deadlines were missed repeatedly. Many of the difficult political decisions were being continuously put off, which overburdened the Cancún conference.

However, not all the developments in Cancún – and in negotiations that were undertaken before the beginning of the Fifth Ministerial Conference – were negative. Movements were made in reaching some partially agreed positions and a formula-based approach in trade support to the agricultural sector and market access in both agricultural and non-agricultural sectors, as well as in addressing some of the most trade-distorting policies in the areas of export subsidies and tariff peaks. In addition, two areas in which a bridge could be built – albeit uneasily – between the positions of developing and industrial economies were trade-related aspects of intellectual property rights (TRIPS) and public-health-related issues. Thus viewed, the negotiations scenario was not entirely bleak and bereft of progress (its details are discussed later in the chapter). Officially, the negotiations were not abandoned after failure to reach an agreement in Cancún on 14 September, but the members decided to continue them in Geneva. Negotiations to resuscitate the Doha Round began in October in Geneva, with an initial focus on two core issues, namely lowering agricultural subsidies and disciplining the tariff peaks and tariff escalation on non-agricultural goods.

High stakes for the developing economies

There are realistic possibilities of valuable and gainful results for the developing economies, who therefore had soaring expectations from this round of MTNs. It was well-recognized in Doha that developing economies required improved access to technologies and markets – which means expansion in their trade – for underpinning their growth endeavours. To be sure, world trade has grown and developing countries have not been excluded from it. Several developing countries that were classified as low-income economies in 1980 have successfully managed to raise their level of manufactured exports from 20 per cent of the total to 80 per cent. Many of them have entered the ranks of today's middle-income countries or the emerging-market economies (EMEs) (Das, 2004a). Between 1980 and 2001, the share of developing economies in world trade increased by 20 per cent, from 15 per cent to 35 per cent of the total. Expansion of exports in manufactures – not agriculture – accounted for the bulk of their trade growth (WB, 2003).

One far-reaching consequence of liberalization of tariff and non-tariff barriers (NTBs) by developing economies since the mid-1980s has been an increase in their competitiveness in the global marketplace, leading to a larger volume of their exports. Some 25 EMEs have made impressive strides in exporting low- and medium-technology goods.[17] Others have succeeded in exporting high-technology products, particularly electronics goods, computer components, semiconductors, IC chips and various information-technology (IT)-related products. Exports of automobile parts from the low- and middle-income developing countries have accelerated with a rapid pace, at more than 22 per cent per year (WB, 2003; Das, 2004a). Between 1981–2001, the growth rate of exports of these products from the developing economies was much higher than the global average export growth rate. Regional or global production networks, or production sharing, have also helped in raising export volumes of the EMEs. Integrated production networks, which are based on the principle of 'slicing the value chain',[18] tend to benefit the participating economies by allowing production to be broken into discrete stages; each stage is performed in the country best suited for it. For instance, labour-intensive stages of production are undertaken in labour-abundant countries, while capital- or knowledge-intensive stages take place in matured industrial economies. Production-sharing can greatly expand the range of industrial activities that can be undertaken in a developing economy.[19]

The growth rate in export expansion of traditional low-technology goods, such as textiles and apparel, from the low-income developing economies was 14 per cent per year over the 1981–2001 period. The export growth of other products accelerated even faster. For instance, exports of electronics products grew at 21 per cent per annum – fast enough to double in value every few years. This category of exports did not exist in 1980 in any developing economy. Not only market shares but also the range of markets of the developing economies increased considerably during this period, and all the developing regions further improved their competitiveness during the 1990s and gained in market share at the expense of the industrial economies. This was not true for the decade of the 1980s.[20]

The disturbing aspect of this trade expansion was its uneven distribution among the developing economies. The entire expansion occurred due to the trade expansion of the middle-income developing economies, while, conversely, the global share of 49 LDCs did not increase at all. In fact, in 43 countries in this sub-group exports contracted over the 1981–2001 period (WB, 2003). Even in the early 2000s the multilateral trading system discriminates against export products from the developing economies, and Stern (2003) has identified 'pockets' of stringent protection in products for which developing economies have comparative advantage. For instance, Canada and the USA still have tariff 'spikes' in textiles and apparel, while the EU and Japan have them in agriculture, food products and footwear. These pockets of tariffs have proved to be effective barriers to exports for a large number of low-income developing economies, particularly for those developing economies that are on the initial rungs of the technology ladder.

The global population of the absolute poor, who subsist on $1.08 a day, was 1,093 million in 2001, and those who subsisted on $2.25 a day was 2,736 million (Chen and Ravallion, 2004).[21] About three-quarters of the world's poorest people live in rural areas, where agriculture is the mainstay of their economy. They cannot export their agricultural products to OECD markets because the tariff barriers faced by them are 10-times or more than those on typical inter-OECD trade. In 2001, agricultural subsidies and other support in the OECD economies amounted to $311 billion, which was 1.3 per cent of the GDP of this country group. The level of support to the agriculture sector has not reduced much over the last decade-and-a-half. The bulk of farm support – which led to large agricultural output in the OECD economies – tended to depress the international prices of agricultural products that low-income G-90 economies have been attempting to export (Stern, 2003).

The whole array of agricultural subsidies in the EU and the USA is an imperative issue for the developing economies because agriculture is typically a big part of their economies, but they often have trouble competing with produce from rich countries because of those countries' export subsidies. Poor nations also find it hard to compete in the home markets of rich countries because of domestic subsidies. Together, the European Union and the United States support farmers to the tune of $300 billion a year. Watkins (2003) emphasized the pernicious effect of subsidies on farmers in the developing economies because they have to compete in global and domestic markets against the surpluses of the EU and the USA, which are exported at prices that bear no relation to the costs of production. In addition, the developing country farmers cannot enter the industrial country markets because of some of the highest trade barriers in the multilateral trading system, alluded to earlier in this chapter. Although governments in the industrial economies unmistakably support human development and poverty-alleviation goals, their policies on agricultural produce continue to be at the heart of a system that is perpetuating poverty and uneven globalization. While in the Cancún Ministerial Conference a number of industrial economies sought the use of WTO rules to promoting trade liberalization in financial services and foreign investment – areas in which they have comparative advantage – they systematically failed to apply the open-market principles to their agriculture sectors. Double standards and the difference between rhetoric and actions are self-evident.

In a majority of the important sectors in manufactured products, exports of developing economies face barriers in both industrial and developing economies' markets. The former impose five times higher tariffs on exports of manufactures from the developing economies than they do on exports of manufactures from other industrial economies. Tariffs and other NTBs imposed by other developing countries are even higher than those imposed by the industrial economies (WB, 2003). Protectionist measures in the developing economies generally take the form of non-ad valorem tariffs. Quantitative restrictions (QRs), specific tariffs and anti-dumping measures are presently endemic in the developing countries against exports from other developing economies. On average, anti-dumping duties are 10 times higher than tariffs in industrial economies, while they are five times higher than tariffs in the developing economies.

There is a pressing need to rectify such anomalies – absurdities, if you please – in multilateral trading system during the Doha process. Although there has been some positive planning in this direction and schemes that grant tariff-free entry to exports from the poor G-90 countries have been devised, thus far they have had little impact. These schemes include the Everything But Arms (EBA) initiative by the EU, and the Africa Growth Opportunity Act of the USA. They exclude the poor countries and populations outside the narrow group of countries identified by each scheme. Agricultural support in sugar, cotton and rice has the maximum anti-development and trade-distorting impact in a large number of G-90 economies. Stern (2003) contended that, 'A successful round that removed all trade impediments would mean 300 million fewer people would live in dire poverty by 2015 – a decline of 13 per cent. It is urgent to make progress in agriculture now, if the talks are to make sufficient progress.'

Another area in which the DDA can live up to its name is trade in services, a segment of world trade in which developing economies have increased their trade four-fold between 1991 and 2001. Their share of the global market in services increased from 14 per cent to 18 per cent over this period (WB, 2003). An increasing number of developing economies are carving out impressive niches in the global marketplace, and some conspicuous examples are: Barbados in data processing; China, India and the Philippines in computer software, supply-chain management and business-process services (BPS); and South Africa in telecommunications. Negotiations in services progressed rather slowly during the Doha Round, despite empirical studies concluding that services liberalization could result in three to four times larger gains for the developing economies than those in the merchandise trade sector (WB, 2003). If the OECD economies take appropriate liberalization measures in this area and developing economies become more proactive in negotiations in services, it might well help them in becoming competitive in several areas such as telecommunications, software, computer-enabled services, wholesaling and retailing, accounting, BPS and business and financial services.

Participation of developing economies in the Doha Round

The developing economies were active participants in the Doha process and their preparations for negotiating on modalities and targets in Cancún were of a reasonably high level. Several events happened for the first time in Cancún. The developing economies coordinated better among themselves and there were far less divisions in the stands taken by them than ever in the past. Trade in agriculture and the four Singapore issues were areas of their particular interest, and several middle-income developing economies in Latin America and low-income African countries were particularly focused on agricultural trade negotiations. The latter country group and the 49 LDCs were also concerned about the Singapore issues. Twenty-two developing economies were opposed to the inclusion of the Singapore issues in the DDA and they noted this in their pre-Cancún statement, although Mexico, Korea (Republic of) and Venezuela supported it.

The initiative to form a robust G-21 was taken by Brazil, China, India and South Africa before the Fifth Ministerial Conference started, and the four provided collegial leadership. Twenty members of this group had joined hands during the pre-Cancún period, while two more joined during the Conference. G-21 became a voice to reckon with in Cancún. This group represented half the world's population and two-thirds of its farmers; it also conducted itself in a well-organized and professional manner (*The Economist*, 2003). For negotiations in agriculture and the Singapore issues, developing countries coalesced into *ad hoc* coalitions.

The agenda on agricultural negotiations had three principal parts: domestic support, market access and export competition. For handling negotiations on each one of these, two ministers were chosen by the developing economies. 'Despite active efforts to split the group through specific offers to individual countries, the coalition remained together' until the end.[22] In the past, such efforts to split the developing economies had met with success, although not in Cancún. Another first was groups of developing countries taking a stand and participating together in negotiations. In the past, such group action was limited to agenda-setting or blocking coalitions.

Yet another first was the emergence of a noteworthy coalition of cotton exporting West African countries, which took a stand in favour of abolishing trade-distorting subsidies granted to cotton growers in the EU, the USA and China.[23] Their grievance was just. They were being crushed by the subsidies of the rich countries, particularly the annual $3 billion-plus that the USA was paying to its 25,000 cotton growers (*The Economist*, 2003). This subsidy helped in making the USA the world's biggest exporter of cotton. The subsidies tended to lower the world market prices of cotton by up to 40 per cent (WB, 2003), and therefore this country group demanded compensation for the three-year transition period when these subsidies would to be phased out. Although nothing came out of this proposal, it attracted a good deal of attention and support from the developing and industrial economies alike.

Market access for non-agricultural products

Elimination of 'tariff peaks, high tariffs and tariff escalation'[24] was an explicit objective of the Doha Round, and several recent studies have concurred that a number of important product lines of developing countries' exports face onerous tariff burdens.[25] Although they are most conspicuous in areas like textiles and clothing, transport equipment, leather and footwear, fish and fish products, they also exist in other areas. Second, developing economies have either bound their tariffs at relatively high levels or bound in only a few tariff lines,[26] and show more dispersion – as measured by the standard deviation – in their tariffs than do the industrial economies. However, the applied tariff rates of developing countries are far below their bound tariff levels. Third, LDCs have a low level of tariff bindings[27] and they benefit from preferences granted by industrial economies, which also grant preferences to developing economies other than LDCs and industrial economies under regional integration agreements (RIAs).

Based on a study of large import markets, that accounted for 85 per cent of total world exports, a market access analysis was conducted by Bacchetta and Bora (2003).[28] Market access can be impeded not only by tariffs and NTBs, but also by complicated structures of an import regime. Policy transparency and procedural simplification (or trade facilitation) go a long way in improving market access. Tabulation by Bacchetta and Bora (2003) showed that the variation in sheer numbers of tariff lines in each economy is exceedingly large. While most WTO members have tariff schedules in the range of 5,000 to 8,000 lines, some members (Brazil, Malaysia, Mexico and Turkey) have more than 10,000 tariff lines. This has a greater trade impeding or market restricting effect.

In general, non-*ad-valorem* tariff lines lead to complications, because they are not transparent. Their nuisance value in trade in agriculture is well-known. In industrial products, Switzerland and Thailand have the largest proportion of non-*ad-valorem* tariff lines, with Japan, Malaysia and the USA also having some, leading to problems in those trade areas to which they are applied. As regards binding of tariffs, while industrial economies have bound most of them and the members of the Quad (Canada, the EU, Japan and the USA) have the largest number of bound duty-free tariff lines, developing economies have a fairly large range in bound tariffs, from Turkey binding less than half of its tariff lines to several Asian countries binding over 70 per cent of them.

When binding of tariff lines is examined at a disaggregated level, it turns out that four categories of products face higher tariff averages than the other products in developing and industrial economies. They also have the highest standard deviation as well as the highest share of high tariffs in most countries (WTO, 2001b). The four categories facing maximum protection are: (i) textiles and clothing, (ii) leather, rubber, footwear and travel goods, (iii) transport equipment and (iv) fish and fish products. In eight countries in the sample of 18, textiles and clothing had the highest average tariffs.[29] In four sample countries the highest average tariffs were in the fish and fish-product categories. In these two sectors the largest tariff lines had bindings above 15 per cent, which is known as a tariff peak or a spike. Many sample countries have bound only a limited proportion of their tariff lines in the transport equipment category. In half the sample countries tariff spikes existed in textiles and clothing, while in the other sample countries (including the EU) the largest number of tariff spikes were found in the fish and fish-product category. In Japan, the largest number of tariff spikes existed in the leather, rubber, footwear and travel goods categories.[30]

Tariff slashing in non-agricultural goods would indeed go a long way in meeting the expectations of the developing economies under the DDA. Low technology, labour-intensive imports in the OECD economies not only face high tariffs and NTBs, but they also put up with significant rates of tariff escalation. This implies that as their level of processing rises, the tariff levels rise as well. Processed foods and textiles, for example, suffer from high degrees of anti-development tariff escalation, and numerous examples of tariff escalation with higher stages of processing can be found. Chilean tomatoes come into the USA with a 2.8 per cent tariff, while salsa and ketchup face 11.6 per cent tariffs. Likewise, tariffs and NTBs on Chinese cotton T-shirts in the USA are much higher than those exported from the other industrial economies (Stern, 2003). Thus, the Doha Round has a good deal of residual protection in the form of tariff peaks and tariff escalation to deal with. Furthermore, the WTO rules and reforms in the DSU are other areas which need to be addressed in the Doha Round for improving the multilateral trade regime in such a manner that the developing economies access to the OECD market improves.

Progress since the launch of the Doha Round of MTNs

Although there was no scarcity of expressed goodwill from the stake-holders, progress in negotiations was slow at best. Part of the problem was that different country groups had different interests and perspectives. Besides, the evolving agenda was not addressing the development-related issues, let alone concerns of the developing economies. For two full years after its launch, various subgroups in the developing economies seemed to believe that on many crucial issues the Doha

Round was moving in the wrong direction. Until the time members met in Cancún, serious disagreements had continued unabated.

Notwithstanding the disagreements and eventual breakdown in Cancún, some painstaking negotiations were successfully made after the launch of the Doha Round. The structure of negotiations was devised in January 2002, during the first meeting of the Trade Negotiations Committee (TNC). Seven negotiating bodies were set up by the TNC on (1) agriculture, (2) services, (3) non-agricultural market access, (4) the WTO rules, (5) trade and environment, (6) a multilateral register on geographical indications for wines and spirits and (7) reform of the DSP. Except for 5 and 6, all the other areas were of vital importance for the DDA. Additionally, a Special Session of the Trade and Development Committee (TDC) was set up to examine questions related to SDT for developing countries. Although member governments did not formally agree regarding the precise status of this group, the Chairman of the Special Session reported often to the TNC, along with the other seven chairs. Negotiations on SDT were taken up directly by the General Council in early 2003, and transparency in negotiations was emphasized by the TNC. Learning from the mistakes made in the Third Ministerial Conference in Seattle, the General Council[31] also mandated that minutes of meetings be circulated in all three WTO languages immediately to delegations and capitals of member countries, so that they would remain fully informed about progress in the negotiations.

During the ongoing Doha Round, participating members proposed various negotiating 'modalities' or approaches to reducing tariffs, NTBs and other barriers. Modalities of reduction of existing protection would indeed make a difference to WTO members, who *inter alia*, are addressing formulae for disciplining tariff peaks, high tariffs and tariff escalation in a flexible manner so that the constraints of all the members can be accommodated. Furthermore, taming anti-dumping measures became a critical priority of the negotiating blocs. Such measures were originally designed to thwart anti-competitive behaviour, but their unintended utilization 'to facilitate market cartelization' and increasing use for 'non-transparent and costly protection' became a nagging issue in global trade (WB, 2003).

Although members frequently missed the deadline for agreeing on modalities, agriculture negotiations did progress to some extent. Modalities were discussed and devised for reaching a final agreement by 1 January 2005, in the form of numerical and non-numerical targets as well as rules that members will use to achieve the objectives mandated by the Doha Ministerial Declaration. These modalities were intended to help members in making their commitments towards achieving the Doha objectives. However, members again missed the target of offering their commitments. The reason for the failure was that a large number and range of countries were involved in the agriculture negotiations, with a wide range of views and interests. Other than asymmetry in positions, the delegates lacked their governments' decisions at a political level. Should this not be read as a lack of governments' commitments? Towards the end of the negotiations, it was being hoped that in Cancún the participating ministers would be able to resolve the key differences at a political level and that final modalities and targets would be produced. They were not.[32]

In early 2000, negotiations started on specific market access commitments to further liberalize trade in services. During 2001, deliberations focused on members' proposals, which in turn revealed their interest and liberalization priorities in the specific services areas. By March, members had succeeded in achieving their objective of laying down negotiation guidelines and procedures. The guidelines that were agreed reflected the fundamental principles of the General Agreement on Trade in Services (GATS), namely, (1) members' right to regulate and to introduce new regulations on the supply of services in pursuit of national policy objectives, (2) their right to specify which services they wish to open to foreign suppliers and (3) the overarching principle of flexibility for developing and least-developed countries. After the Doha Ministerial Conference, GATS members continued negotiations on liberalization of a wide range of sectors as well as on movement of natural persons.[33] Member countries submitted close to 160 proposals covering sectors such as professional services, telecommunications, tourism, financial services, distribution services, construction services, energy services, maritime transport, courier services and environmental services. There were no proposals on health services, while there were four on education services. These negotiations prepared negotiations for intensive market access negotiations, which were to be started towards the end of 2002.

For further liberalization of trade in non-agricultural goods, a negotiating group on market access was created during the first meeting of the TNC. To be sure, negotiations covered a good deal of ground but missed the May 2003 deadline for agreeing on modalities for how tariffs should be reduced and how other market access issues should be handled. In the Tokyo Round (1973–79), participants had used an agreed-on mathematical formula to slash tariffs across the board. Similarly, during the Uruguay Round they negotiated tariff cuts using a variety of formulae. The tariff-cutting formula for the Doha Round needed studies and capacity-building measures, and the needs of this period were different from those of the earlier rounds. Following the eight rounds of MTNs, average tariffs are presently at their lowest. However, as noted above, tariff peaks, high tariffs and tariff escalation still continue to bedevil world trade. They *a fortiori* affect exports of developing countries. Although a draft on initial elements of modalities was prepared in May 2003, members disagreed regarding the comprehensiveness of the formula and its ability to meet all their needs.

The Doha mandate on TRIPS and public health was that it is important to implement the TRIPS Agreement in such a manner that it supports public health emergencies by promoting access to existing medicines and the creation of new medicines. The TRIPS Council considered a draft decision in December 2002, which allowed countries that can make drugs to export drugs made under compulsory licence[34] to countries that cannot manufacture them. This waiver is to continue until the TRIPS Agreement is amended. Almost all the members said that they could agree to the draft, but the USA found the draft 'too open-ended' to be acceptable. In early and mid-2003, the TRIPS Council took up the matter again, but consensus was not reached until the beginning of the Fifth Ministerial Conference.

The four Singapore issues are relatively new, and were added to the WTO agenda in December 1996. Foreign direct investment (FDI) is the first of these issues, which is presently governed by Bilateral Investment Treaties (BITs); approximately 2,100 of BITs are in operation at present. Under the Agreement on Trade-Related Investment Measures (TRIMs), the WTO has limited provisions on certain aspects of FDI. Over the last two decades, barriers to FDI have significantly declined, and consequently the volume of FDI flows increased several times until 2000, when it peaked. During the Doha Ministerial Conference, members recognized the need to create a multilateral framework to secure a 'transparent, stable and predictable' framework of laws for long-term cross-border investment. It was decided in Doha that an ambitious mandate on FDI should be negotiated after the next Conference in Cancún on the basis of the decisions to be taken on the modalities of negotiations. Discussions revealed widely differing sensibilities among the WTO member governments. Since the Doha Ministerial, the Working Group on the Relationship between Trade and Investment focused on clarifying various germane issues, like definitions and the scope of issues to be considered, transparency, non-discrimination, development provisions, consultation, dispute settlement, balance-of-payments (bop) safeguards, and how to deal with the FDI commitments. This was a tall list of issues for the Working Group, which has so far not completed its study. The developing economies have insisted that the BITs provide adequate legal protection to FDI and have expressed concern about WTO agreement adding to their obligations. In Cancún, the participating member governments had to decide whether there is an 'explicit consensus' on modalities that would allow the negotiations on TRIPs to progress in the future.

Competition policy is the next Singapore issue. Industrial economies and some 50 developing economies have instituted domestic competition laws,[35] which deal with the scourge of anti-competitive practices, including price-fixing, abuse of dominant market positions or monopolization, mergers that eliminate competition and 'vertical agreements' that foreclose markets for new competitors.[36] As in the case of TRIPS, the Doha Declaration provided that negotiations in this area should begin after the Fifth Ministerial Conference. In the run-up to Cancún, the Working Group on the Interaction between Trade and Competition focused on clarifying (1) core principles including transparency, non-discrimination and procedural fairness, and provisions on hard-core cartels, (2) modes of voluntary cooperation on competition policy among WTO members and (3) capacity-building support in the area of competition institution in the developing and transition economies. The Working Group focused on international hard-core cartels, firms that secretly fix prices. Such cartels increase costs to consumers by an estimated 40 per cent in the affected industries.[37] Two of the reasons for establishing a WTO framework in this area are fighting the hard-core cartels and supporting the national competition policies of WTO members. However, developing countries have expressed concern regarding the additional burden of a new WTO agreement on members that do not have competition in place in their economies. As in case of TRIPS, in Cancún the participating member governments had to decide whether there is an 'explicit consensus' on modalities that would allow the negotiations in the area of competition policy to progress.

A Government Procurement Agreement was first negotiated in the Tokyo Round and was updated in the Uruguay Round. It is a plurilateral agreement having 28 signatories so far. Its objective goes beyond mere transparency and extends to open international competition in government procurement. Intentions are to have general rules in this area and a schedule of national entities in each member country, whose procurement would fall under this agreement. Transparency in procurement is only one means of achieving this objective. A work programme on transparency in government procurement has been considered since the

Singapore Ministerial Conference, and in Doha ministers agreed to start negotiations on it after the Fifth Ministerial Conference on the basis of the decision to be taken by 'explicitly consensus' on the modalities of future negotiations.

While notable progress has occurred in the expansion of WTO discipline covering an increasing volume of world trade, traders justly complain of the vast amount of 'functionarism' or red tape that still persists in moving goods across borders. For instance, it still takes 11 days or more to clear goods from Indian customs. Such inefficiency and tardiness has high economic costs. In general, documentation requirement for customs clearance is large, opaque and with frequent duplication. Despite phenomenal advances in information technology over the last two decades, automatic data submission is far from commonplace. According to a recent UNCTAD study[38] the average customs transaction involves 20–30 different parties, 40 documents, 200 data elements, 30 of which are repeated, and the rekeying of 60–70 per cent of data at least once. The WTO has dealt with the issue of trade facilitation in the past, and its rules aim at transparency in this area as well as the setting of minimum procedural standards. WTO members have constructively debated on trade facilitation since the Singapore Ministerial, and a good deal of exploratory studies have been conducted in this area. Many members have proposed negotiating binding trade facilitation rules that should centre around commitments on border-related procedures to expedite the movement, release and clearance of goods. These new rules are expected to be built upon the existing WTO provisions and devised in accordance with Articles V, VIII and X of the GATT-1994. Like the other three Singapore issues, ministers agreed during the Doha Ministerial Conference that negotiations on trade facilitation should take place after the Fifth Ministerial Conference in Cancún on the basis of a decision to be taken by explicit consensus on modalities of the negotiations.

Negotiations on protection of trade in wines and spirits take place in the dedicated 'special sessions' of the TRIPS Council. Under TRIPS Article 23, wines and spirits are allowed a higher level of protection for geographical indicators than other products, which are protected under TRIPS Article 22. This reflects the multilateral agreement on protecting the wines' and spirits' names, even if there is no risk of misleading consumers. Under TRIPS Article 23.4, a multilateral register on geographical indications for wines and spirits needs to be negotiated. Work on a multilateral registration system for geographical indicators started in mid-1997 by the TRIPS Council. These negotiations came under the aegis of the Doha Round, which set a deadline for their completion of the beginning of the Fifth Ministerial.[39] Three country groups have submitted three sets of proposals, which argue in great detail the legal implications of the registration system and whether the register is to serve the purpose of 'facilitating protection'. An important issue is that of administrative and financial costs for individual governments, and whether they would outweigh the possible benefits. Furthermore, several countries have argued in the TRIPS Council to extend higher level of protection currently given to wines and spirits to other products, while others are opposed to it. Members are deeply divided on various key issues, although they are ready to continue discussions.

The TNC established a Negotiating Group on Rules in February 2002. In the Doha Declaration, 'rules' covered three principal areas, namely anti-dumping, subsidies and regional trade agreements (RTAs). As stated earlier in this chapter, that anti-dumping duties (ADD) are creating a serious bottleneck for exports from developing economies. During the initial phase of negotiations, participants indicated that they would like to clarify the WTO provisions, and over 100 submissions were made by the members in 10 meetings of the Negotiating Group on Rules. A number of discontented members opined that the present Anti-dumping Agreement should be improved to counter what they consider to be an abuse of the way the anti-dumping measures were applied in the past. They pointed to a growing incidence of dumping, and the rising trend in WTO disputes in this area. A polemical stand was taken by the USA, which stressed the importance of anti-dumping actions and countervailing measures for ensuring fair trade practices. The US delegation also proposed numerous improvements and clarifications of the present Anti-dumping Agreement. Negotiations on the Subsidies and Countervailing Measures Agreement progressed steadily, although they were not as important as those on the Anti-dumping Agreement. There were no deadlines to be reached in Cancún in this regard, ministers were only to review the progress in these negotiations.

The total number of notified regional trade agreements (RTAs) increased to 177 in December 2002.[40] Most WTO members are now party to at least one RTA, and many to several. Almost half of world trade is now conducted under RTAs (Das, 2004b). In February 1996, the WTO General Council set up a single committee – the Regional Trade Agreement Committee (RTAC) – to oversee all RTAs, replacing separate 'working parties', each dealing with a separate agreement. Issues in the ongoing regional debate are complex; some are primarily legal, while others are institutional. More importantly, several issues have an economic dimension. The RTA debate is concerned with the question of the impact of regional agreements on the future shape of world trade, given the large and increasing number of RTAs and their overlapping membership. In the foreseeable future, RTAs will be one of the biggest challenges facing the policy-making community. The relationship between regionalism and multilateralism has continued to be a critical systemic issue, and the Doha mandate on RTAs is to clarify and improve disciplines and procedures under the existing WTO provisions applying to RTAs. The Negotiating Group on Rules set up in February 2002, noted in the preceding paragraph, organized a seminar on regionalism in April 2002 in Geneva, that helped raise awareness of the significance of regional agreements in world trade. A listing of all the RTA-related issues raised in various WTO councils and committees was prepared in August 2002. The RTAC would aid the work of the Negotiating Group on Rules on RIAs, that decided to address the procedural issues (like transparency) first and the systemic issues later. Four systemic issues have been identified for early consideration.[41]

A good deal of work was to be done on trade and environment-related issues, and WTO members agreed to start negotiations on trade and environment linkage at Doha. It was decided that the future focus of these negotiations would be specific and cover the following four areas: (1) clarification of the relationship between WTO rules and specific trade obligations set out in the multilateral environment agreements (MEAs), (2) exchange of information between the WTO and MEA secretariats, (3) the norms and criteria for granting observer status to other international organizations and (4) liberalization of trade in environmental goods and services. These negotiations have been in progress in the special sessions of the Trade and Environment Committee (TEC) and were scheduled to be completed by 1 January 2005.

Members recognize that the Dispute Settlement Understanding (DSU) plays a pivotal role in the multilateral trading system. Therefore, more members participated in these negotiations than in any other negotiation, except that in agriculture. The mandate at Doha included 'improvements and clarifications of the Dispute Settlement Undertaking', and also stated that the negotiations on DSU should be squarely based on the work done so far. The objective was to conclude the agreement by May 2003. These negotiations were not to be a part of the 'single undertaking' and were not tied to success or failure of the other negotiations. A draft of the legal text was circulated on schedule in May 2003, which included members' proposals on enhancing third-party rights, introducing an interim review, clarifying and improving the sequences of procedure at the implementation stage, enhancing compensations, strengthening notification requirements for mutually-agreed solutions, and strengthening SDT for developing countries at various stages of the proceedings.

Causal factors behind the setback in Cancún

Different causal factors emerged from the press reports, including inapt chairmanship of the Ministerial Conference by Luis Ernesto Derbez, the Foreign Minister of Mexico. Some believed that the agenda for Cancún was 'overloaded', making it difficult for many WTO members to simultaneously negotiate issues before or during the Ministerial Conference. Some national negotiators were unwilling to go beyond the predetermined demands of the other delegations, and seriously negotiate with the other delegations. However, it would seem that negotiations on agriculture and the Singapore issues were the prime causal factors behind the 'Tequila sunset' in Cancún. These are described below.

Negotiations on the Singapore issues

The last day of the Fifth Ministerial Conference was entirely devoted to the Singapore issues. Different sub-groups of developing economies, including the members of the African, Caribbean and Pacific (ACP)[42] countries, the G-90 and the members of the African Union (AU) came to Cancún with a well-defined position of not supporting the launch of negotiations on the four Singapore issues. In this they had support from Malaysia, although other EMEs did not take a strong position because the industrial countries had scaled back the scope of these negotiations in a realistic manner before the Conference started. The G-21 took a defensive and intransigent position on the Singapore issues.

During the Ministerial Conference, the US position on the four Singapore issues was one of uncertainty, hesitancy and lukewarm, although it did have a strong desire to launch negotiations on trade and foreign investment-related issues. Since these areas are important in its economy, its interest in protecting it through WTO rules was natural. This observation is buttressed by the two recent bilateral trade agreements that the USA signed with Chile and Singapore, which included a clause on capital controls.

The principal proponents of the Singapore issues were the EU, Japan and Korea. In the EU, opinion on this issue was again divided. In several large EU economies, many firms did not support a strong EU stand on the Singapore issues. During the Ministerial Conference, the EU displayed foresight and flexibility by proposing to drop two of the four

Singapore issues (namely, competition and investment) from the nego-tiations, and to terminate the Working Group on this subject. Apparently the EU decision to make a retreat on the Singapore issues was made late, which turned out to be a tactical error.[43] Besides, Japan and Korea remained adamantly opposed to even the delayed EU pro-posal. Strong opposition from the ACP group, LDCs and AU countries in this regard persisted, although India proposed that the fourth Singapore issue (namely, trade facilitation) could be taken up for negotiations at Cancún. This was logical because all WTO members stood to gain from trade facilitation. However, given the diversity in positions, negotiations on the Singapore issues could not be launched.

One view was – and many WTO members seemed to share it – that the EU and Japan insisted on launching negotiations on the Singapore issues only to divert attention from their intransigence over agriculture, a politically sensitive area for the EU and Japan. Liberalized agricultural trade was, and was intended to be, an important focus of the Doha Round. These countries were aware of having some of the most illiberal, archaic and well-entrenched systems of agricultural protection in the world. They were hopelessly on the defensive from the launch of the Doha Round. Political acceptance of agricultural reforms in these countries seems beyond their governments. Therefore, intransigence of three groups of developing economies on the Singapore issues could easily be made a scapegoat for the failure at Cancún.

A post-Cancún view gradually emerged on the Singapore issues which emphasized taking them off the table.[44] While these issues have their developmental significance, in particular the fourth issue, they were not directly related to the core issue of market access, the *sine qua non* of the world trading system. These issues do not adhere to the 'tried-and-tested formula of improving economic welfare through trade negotiations that result in reciprocal reduction to impediments to international com-merce' (Evenett, 2003). In addition, negotiating and implementing any WTO agreement on the four Singapore issues would be both complex and expensive, further complicating the 'implementation-related issues' which concern the developing economies.[45]

Negotiations on agriculture

Trade in agriculture, which was originally outside the ambit of the multilateral trading system, continued to remain the most contentious area of negotiations in the MTNs; dividing negotiators both before and during the Cancún Conference. Through constant requests from the developing economies during the DDA, the EU and the USA jointly drew up a framework for the liberalization of farm trade in August 2003. It was a weak and limited plan, which ignored what was visualized at the time of the DDA's launch. This framework was criticized by 'the developing countries, correctly in our judgment, for ignoring their interests' as well as what was committed in the DDA (Stiglitz and Charlton, 2004). For instance, according to the August proposal, export subsidies – one of the principal bugbears – were not to be eliminated. The EU always and strongly resisted elimination of export subsidies.

Concurrently, as noted earlier, unilateral measures taken by the industrial economies were counter to what was being attempted multilaterally. For instance, the US Farm Bill of 2002, or the Farm Security and Rural Investment Act of 2002, increased the level of government support for farmers. The link between subsidies and production was made stronger than before. What was needed was its delinking.[46] A Japanese programme set an increased self-sufficiency goal in agricultural products of 45 per cent, implying higher production subsidies and trade barriers. Similarly, the EU's Luxembourg reform of the Common Agricultural Policy (CAP) declared in June 2003 was disappointing. According to this reform announcement, the EU was to shift farm support from the production-limiting 'blue box' to the 'green box' which is considered less trade-distorting.[47] The level of support to farmers was going to remain virtually the same; OECD (2004) projected it to decline from 57 per cent to 56 per cent. Partial decoupling of farm support was announced by the EU Agriculture Ministers, but this set of reforms appeared 'timid, uncertain, and easily reversible' (Francois, van Meijl and van Tongeren, 2003).

The complaints of the cotton-growing economies of West Africa were ignored in Cancún, and there was only a vague mention of them in the draft document that had emerged halfway through the Cancún conference. While the document mentioned a review of the textile sector, it did not touch upon the issue of eliminating the cotton subsidies, let alone the issue of compensation. Instead, the West African countries were advised to diversify their exports. Responding to the demand of national constituency, the US delegation led in rejecting the West African position on elimination of cotton subsidies. Such a move would not have gone well in the USA. Besides, the then (2003) chairman of the Senate agricultural committee in the USA is known to be an ally of cotton growers. Consequently, frustrated West African countries vented their anger by digging in their heels when it came to supporting negotiations on the Singapore issues.

As stated earlier in the chapter, despite repeatedly missed deadlines for agreeing on modalities, agriculture negotiations did progress to some extent, although, to be sure, the liberalization offer was nowhere near the mandate of the Doha Round. It was reported in the business press that the ministers were prepared to continue discussions on the last day in Cancún, when the chairman of the world-trade talks Luis Ernesto Derbez decided that the negotiations were not progressing and brought them to a formal closure. If they had not been ended abruptly, further progress in the area of trade in agriculture may have been plausible. With the breakdown of the Doha process, the progress of negotiations on other issues – including market access for services and industrial products, implementation-related issues, environment and some areas of intellectual property – stalled by default. It should, however, be noted that a weak final outcome on agriculture in the Doha Round would have added to the erosion of the WTO's institutional foundation. Ineffectually dealing with agriculture would have been sure to jeopardize the future operations of the entire multilateral trading regime.

The best thing about failure

Failure is an opportunity to identify errors and learn lessons. Several serious and avoidable errors were committed in Cancún, which led to failure. The first was to insist on negotiating on the Singapore issues until the last morning of the last day of the Conference. As noted above, an overwhelming majority of the WTO members eyed these issues with suspicion and did not consider them relevant or beneficial. The first three Singapore issues in no way gave an appearance of benefiting the developing country members of the WTO. In particular, negotiations on multilateral rules on trade and investment and trade and competition were considered issues that had little payoff for developing members of the WTO in terms of trade expansion and development. Reforms of the agricultural trade regime were long overdue and they were a crucial part of the DDA as well as a key to progress in the Doha Round. Linking them with the Singapore issues was 'counterproductive' (Hoekman, 2003), and this linkage made many developing countries question whether MTNs are in their interest at all.

Second, since the Uruguay Round the developing economies are no longer on the sidelines in the MTNs. Their active participation is a healthy institutional development because it strengthens the multilateral trading system. Members of G-21 were able to form a negotiating coalition and function, and although their negotiating positions did not always adhere to the demands of the respective national constituencies, they made accommodations for keeping the coalition together, which in turn displayed their maturity as negotiators. In hindsight, one suggestion that can be made to the G-21 is that of aiming for a Pareto-superior outcome by presenting a negotiable alternative by agreeing to the fourth Singapore issue, namely trade facilitation, which was in every member's interest. This could possibly avert failure of the Fifth Ministerial. A large number of developing members, if not all, need improvements in their customs procedures and other infrastructural areas. Efficiencies created by improvements in trade logistics would undoubtedly have benefited them.

Third, the negotiation modalities in Cancún did not require the LDCs to reciprocate and further liberalize their trade regimes. Also, under SDT other large developing economies were obliged to adopt only limited reciprocity. In order to harness reciprocity in the negotiations and impart dynamism to the MTNs, developing economies needed to change tack and make offers to the industrial economies in different areas so that the entire system could benefit from trade liberalization. Successful traders like China and the other EMEs can go a step further and offer the OECD countries *quid pro quo* in market-access negotiations in goods and services. In market-access negotiations, both developing and industrial economies bargain for eliminating poor trade practices, which have salutary systemic implications.

Fourth, it seems that during the post-Cancún period the old SDT concept needed to be revised and updated by making it more differenti-ated (Hoekman, Michalopoulos and Winters, 2003). The need for exempt-ing developing economies from reciprocity is no longer considered pressing for the higher-income sub-groups of developing economies like the NIEs and EMEs. While LDCs face genuine difficulties because of poor institutional capacity, other developing economies need to gradually advance towards progressively eschewing the SDT. That is, they can be graduated from the benefits of SDT. The large and successful traders among them need to take initiatives in this regard. Besides, developing economies are cognizant of the fact that not liberalizing their domestic trade regime has a boomerang effect on them, both individually and collectively. For starters, a short-term public policy objective should be to create domestic political support for such a change in the NIEs and EMEs.

Fifth, Hoekman (2003) has redrawn attention towards 'the gover-nance and procedures' of the WTO, which was intensely debated in the aftermath of the debacle in Seattle in 1999.[48] The large membership of the WTO has made consensus-formation both 'a major strength and weakness of the WTO'. Although successful improvements have been made in transparency of negotiations since the failure of the Green Room process in Seattle, transaction costs still remain exceedingly high. Cancún saw a move towards formation of negotiating coalitions, which led to some ease in negotiations because only the 'principals' participated for their respective groups. The flip-side of this coin was greater inflexibility and heightened probability of breakdown, particularly when negotiations take place against strict time deadlines.[49]

Retreat from intransigence

Both the replacement of the EU commission and the US presidential election were scheduled for November 2004, and therefore it was assumed that the EU and the USA would ignore vital multilateral issues, like the Doha process, and defer it for the next year. However, 31 July 2004 was a self-imposed deadline for agreeing to a negotiating framework and agenda of the Doha Round. As it drew near, the leading players and negotiating blocs became concerned about the stalemate in the MTNs, and the ambiance of criticism and recrimination gave way to grudging compromises and eagerness to break the impasse. The four principal negotiating blocs began to chip away at their old Cancún positions, switching to conciliatory stances. Deliberations among the four blocs began again, albeit in camera. The changes in the past positions and compromises that were on offer in mid-2004 vividly indicated a strengthening of political will to restart the stalled Doha process.

Much to the chagrin of the French, the EU made a fresh proposal in agriculture in May 2004, which was quite different from that made in August 2003.[50] This time export subsidies were not treated as a holy cow and their elimination was proposed. The developing economies welcomed it because export subsidies in the industrial economies do enormous damage to farmers in developing economies. Also, it was the first confession by the EU that such subsidies are unfair and therefore must go. If one takes a good look at it, this EU offer was not as dramatic as it *prima facie* appeared at first, because export subsidies accounted for a mere €3 billion ($3.6 billion). The EU annually lavished €45 billion on subsidizing its protected farmers. The EU offer was conditional upon Australia, Canada and the USA eliminating their own equivalents of export subsidies (*The Economist*, 2004a).

The EU also proposed that the G-90 economies be exempted from the requirement of lowering their trade barriers. According to this proposal, all the G-90 countries should be offered greater access to the non-G-90 markets. Many countries in this sub-group recorded a decline in their trade over the last two decades. Some developing economies dismissed this EU proposal as divisive, while others regarded it as a noteworthy move towards a promising consensus. To break the impasse, the EU modified its stand on the Singapore issues as well. The realization had dawned that emphasizing them so much that they had caused a complete collapse was a strategic mistake. The modified stand of the EU was that the Singapore issues be taken up one at a time and included in the DDA only after a consensus is arrived at among members, not otherwise (*The Economist*, 2004a). However, the EU pressed for trade facilitation to be retained in the DDA, without making it a sticking point. To be sure, there was a lot of wisdom in the modified stance of the EU.

At a time when the key players on the global stage were demonstrating flexibility and far-sightedness, as the July 2004 deadline approached some small, low-income, members of the ACP group took a recalcitrant, aggressive and short-sighted stand. These small economies had small and disparate demands, which could potentially stall the progress of the Doha Round once again. Small West African economies demanded that cotton subsidies in the industrial economies be negotiated as a separate issue, outside the agricultural trade negotiations. Reasons for this demand were far from convincing. Small economies of the ACP group that enjoyed preferential market access in the industrial economies wanted to ensure that a successful Doha Round would not reduce their preferential market access (discussed in Chapter 4). Some of the delegations of the ACP countries were vocal in expressing their concern, taking a myopic view that almost wished the MTNs to fail, an ignoble wish to say the least. The sugar and banana exporters in this country group reckoned that they were better off having preferential market access in a distorted global trading system. It would have been perverse and ironic if they had succeed in retarding, or stalling, the Doha Round because the DDA has been designed to benefit the developing economies.

Positions were revised by the other negotiating blocs as well. Earlier we brought out that developing economies have tended to have a great many tariff and non-tariff barriers in intra-developing country trade. Acknowledging this fact, in June 2004 the United Nations Conference on Trade and Development (UNCTAD) took the initiative and organized a conference for the developing economies, with the objective of reducing mutual trade barriers and thereby strengthening the negotiating position of the developing countries in the Doha process. China and Brazil were the leaders guiding this initiative. Developing economies reacted in two ways. Some were averse to it because they saw the UNCTAD initiative as a detracting force that could weaken the Doha process, while others believed that it would strengthen it and impart new momentum.

Negotiations around the Derbez Text

On 13 September, in Cancún, the Derbez Text was tabled by the WTO secretariat. Although prepared by the WTO secretariat, it was officially christened the Derbez Text in honour of Louis Ernest Derbez, the Foreign Minister of Mexico, who chaired the Fifth Ministerial Conference (WTO, 2003b). The decision of members to continue to negotiate around the Derbez Text was a positive one, and it became the basis for the July framework negotiations, discussed above. Tariff reductions for improving market access were larger in the Derbez Text than in the Uruguay Round Agreement on Agriculture (URAA). It also proposed to address the tariff peaks as well as devise a formula to rein in tariff escalation. In addition, a principle of a special safeguard mechanism was also accepted by the industrial economies.

After the Cancún failure, the issue of export subsidies was no longer untouchable, and the OECD economies that were regarded as highly protectionist and middle-of-the-road were willing to discuss it in a flexible manner. This was considered significant progress and a marked improvement over negotiations in the Uruguay Round. Offers to phase out export subsidies on products of interest to exporters from the developing economies were being deliberated, and an ambitious proposal in the Derbez Text was of negotiating a timeline and a final date for the elimination of all export subsidies. Although reasonable, this proposal was more than the Doha mandate. It was believed that the EU might not react favourably to this proposal, but it would at least be the beginning of negotiations that should have been achieved in the past (TCARC, 2003).

In addition, larger reductions in trade-distorting domestic subsidies were under consideration for the first time, which included the amber box and *de minimis* payments. As demanded by the G-21 economies, a capping of the blue-box payments was also on the cards. SDT for the developing economies was reaffirmed, which included lower reductions in the amber box support for them. In keeping with the accepted practice, developing economies were to be given longer implementation periods for agreements under the Doha Round.

Salvaging the Doha Round: The Framework Agreement

In the hope of rescuing the Doha Round after the Cancún failure, the WTO hosted a meeting of the General Council to negotiate a broad framework agreement for the future MTNs in the last week of July 2004. The General Council chairman Shotaro Oshima prepared a draft agreement and hoped that it would be finalized before the self-imposed 31 July deadline. The initiative to formulate, negotiate and finally come to the so-called 'July Package' – also referred to as the framework agreement – was taken by Australia, Brazil, the EU, India and the USA. After intense all-night negotiations a broad framework agreement was reached in principle, albeit a small number of finer details were left for the future negotiating sessions. This has been seen as a victory for multilateralism. The July Package is a non-binding frameworks agreement, which succeeded in reviving the stalemated MTNs. As it was negotiated in Geneva, it is also called the Geneva agreement.

The broad framework agreement was a meaningful achievement in the life of the Doha Round. It marked the end of seemingly interminable deliberations and negotiations about what and how to negotiate in the Doha Round. Although it has its weak spots, it is expected that intense negotiations around the July Package will enable members to come to a binding agreement in due course of time. The Zen of free trade is *Quand on s'arrete, on tombe*, or when one stops, one falls. The July framework rescued the MTNs from coming to a full stop and therefore collapse.

While the role of the five member countries, named above, was positive, the framework agreement was reached because of clear and positive thinking and responsible action by all the other leaders. The leader of G-21, Celo Amorim, the Foreign Minister of Brazil, emerged as a pivotal figure with Pascal Lamy and Rober Zoellick. The G-21 acted firmly and refused to move forward with trade negotiations until the USA, the EU and Japan agreed to reduce their agricultural subsidies. The G-21 blamed farm subsidies in the developed countries for stimulating overproduction of agricultural products and driving agricultural commodity prices below the costs of production, harming farmers in developing and least-developed countries. Even the G-90 played a constructive role, with Rwanda taking the lead. Once again France had sought the right to block the deal, claiming it was contrary to European interests, but its objections were brushed aside by the other EU economies. A lot was riding on the success of the framework agreement. Failure would have meant the end of MTNs for an indefinite period, reducing the WTO to a glorified court for resolving multilateral trade disputes. Success in reaching the framework agreement affirmed that the WTO provides a workable forum for developing global trade policy for its 148 members. The Doha Round is back on the rails, although it still has a long way to go. Despite the breakthrough, it only clears the way for the long-delayed start of a marathon to come (de Jauquières, 2004).

The most conspicuous achievement of the Geneva agreement, or the July Package, was a seven-page 'framework for establishing modalities in agriculture', making agriculture the most important part of the July

Package. According to this document, the industrial economies are to eliminate all of their export subsidies which are acknowledged to be highly trade-distorting, although the date has not been finalized. The G-21 countries succeeded in persuading the industrial economies to make deeper cuts in their domestic production subsidies. That a commitment to negotiate an end date for export subsides by the EU is now agreed on paper is a major achievement, which would underpin multilateral trade in agriculture. However, this concession was made in the face of stiff resistance from France, which managed to harden the EU's line and subordinate elimination to the CAP reform timetable. In practice this means that the removal of export subsides will not take place before the end of the current period of reform which will end in 2013. The long-term French opposition to liberalization of the CAP is not logically well-founded. Empirical estimates using the Global Trade Analysis Project (GTAP) version 5.2 database show that the impact of agricultural liberalization under the Doha Round would be positive for France as well as the EU (Francois, van Meijl and van Tongeren, 2003). As discussed in Chapter 6, for France, the largest set of gains would follow from the elimination of remaining domestic support measures. Although the issue of the cotton subsidy was not taken out of the general deliberations on agriculture, it was decided that the subsidy to US cotton farmers would be dealt with 'ambitiously, expeditiously and specifically' (*The Economist*, 2004b).[51]

In the area of tariffs on industrial products, one of the most contentious areas, attempts are being made to cut tariffs drastically, and particular attention is to be paid to high tariffs and tariff spikes. The July Package text in this regard is a carry over from the Derbez Text, which was strongly opposed in Cancún by all the groups among the developing economies. In turn, they had proposed a non-linear formula for tariff reductions, sectoral negotiations and weak special and differential treatment. Tariff reduction in industrial products continues to be a volatile issue even after the framework agreement, and modality negotiations in 2005 may face serious disagreements and friction.

A new deadline of May 2005 was set for negotiations in trade in services in the July Package. Members have been asked to submit high-quality offers to achieve progressively higher levels of liberalization with no *a priori* exclusions of any service sector or mode of supply. Also, new rules would be framed on the 'movement of natural persons' which could affect both migrant workers' rights as well as outsourcing (WTO, 2004). In a pragmatic manner, members agreed to begin reviewing 'trade facilitation', with a view to fast-tracking goods across borders. The push for expedited customs procedures was led by the USA, which revealed the trade *über alles* agenda of the WTO. Trade facilitation has large implications for food-safety issues. However, improvements in customs regulations would certainly require a whole new layer of technological infrastructure for tracking and inspection, and low-income developing economies and LDCs are sure to find it a difficult area to comply with (WTO, 2004). On the behest of the developing economies, the July Package dropped the first three Singapore issues for the present, but they will have to be taken up in the future.

To be sure, there are some loopholes such as the USA managing to exclude its 'counter-cyclical' payments to farmers when prices are depressed. Exemption given to low-income G-90 economies from the requirement of lowering tariffs was well-received. This country group considered it a coup that would protect its nascent industrial sector for a longer period, although consumers in these countries will be required to pay higher amounts for a longer period. The framework agreement also left the door open for the rich countries to protect some 'sensitive' (or politically sensitive) products. No doubt such loopholes would go a long way in slowing the MTNs down as well as in diluting the achievement of the Doha Round.

The Sixth Ministerial Conference is scheduled for December 2005 in Hong Kong SAR. The Doha Round is sure to continue beyond this time point as well because there are whole swathes of areas where the WTO has made little progress so far. Several finer issues were left for future negotiations in the July Package, and negotiations on them may potentially become tricky. The size of the differences in positions between many negotiating groups and individual members are still significant. For a continuance of the negotiations on the lines of the July Package, the completion of the Doha Round has been moved to mid-2007, which coincides with the expiry of the US Trade Promotion Authority, also known as the 'fast-track' authority. More gridlocks and missed deadlines can be taken for granted.

Conclusions and summary

The possibility of a north–south divide was apprehended well before the Fifth Ministerial Conference started in Cancún. The sizeable divergence in positions of developing and industrial economies existed on several significant issues, and the gap was not bridged. However, not all the developments in Cancún – and in negotiations that were undertaken before the beginning of the Fifth Ministerial Conference – were negative.

Some movements were made in reaching partially agreed positions and a formula-based approach in issues like trade support to the agricultural sector. Market Access for Non-Agricultural Products is an area where the Doha Round can do a lot of good work leading to strengthening of the multilateral trading system. Elimination of 'tariff peaks, high tariffs and tariff escalation' was an express objective of the Doha Round. It is widely perceived that a successful conclusion of the Doha Round is sure to benefit the developing economies.

Notwithstanding the disagreements and eventual breakdown in Cancún, some painstaking negotiations were made since the launch of the Doha Round. Seven negotiating bodies were set up by the TNC on (1) agriculture, (2) services, (3) non-agricultural market access, (4) the WTO rules, (5) trade and environment, (6) a multilateral register on geographical indications for wines and spirits and (7) reform of the DSP. A Special Session of the Trade and Development Committee (TDC) was also set up to examine questions related to special and differential treatment (SDT) for developing countries. Although negotiations moved slowly and several self-imposed deadlines were missed, varying degrees of progress were achieved in these areas.

Unlike in the past, developing economies were active participants in the Doha Round and their preparations for negotiating on modalities and targets in Cancún were of a high level. Also, unlike in the past, as a group they coordinated better among themselves and there was far less division in the stands taken by them. Trade in agriculture and the four Singapore issues were areas of their particular interest. They took an initiative to form a Group-of-Twenty-One (G-21) before the Fifth Ministerial Conference, with Brazil, China, India and South Africa providing collegial leadership. Three large groups of developing economies came to Cancún with a well-defined position of not supporting the launch of negotiations on the four Singapore issues. At constant requests from the developing economies during the Doha Round, the EU and the USA drew up a framework for the liberalization of farm trade in August 2003. It was a weak and less ambitious plan than was visualized at the time of the launch of the Doha Round. That the Cancún Ministerial failed need not surprise anyone. The silver lining behind the failure in Cancún is that it has left several valuable lessons in its wake. If learned, they should benefit the global trading system.

Due to serious, albeit avoidable, errors of judgement and the negotiating stands taken by the large trading WTO members wheels did come off the cart of the multilateral trading system in Cancún. During the post-Cancún period, the participating members and the four active country groups continued negotiations. Wisdom to learn from the failure of the past prevailed and the negotiating groups adopted much-needed flexibility in their positions in the third quarter of 2004. The new positions of the members were more realistic, and consequently the framework agreement was reached. It was a meaningful achievement and revived the Doha Round and helped put it back on the tracks.

4
The Doha Round and the Developing Economies

The multilateral trade regime and the developing economies

Definitions of the multilateral trade regime and the World Trade Organization (WTO) were given in Chapter 1, clarifying that the WTO is not a development institution. That being said, efforts to enhance the development relevance of the WTO have constantly been made. There are certain facets of its mandate that decisively influence developmental endeavours of countries consciously striving to climb the ladder of growth, development and industrialization. The two quintessential functions of the WTO regime are: (1) negotiating commitments for improving market access, and (2) establishing a rule-based trading system that leaves no element of unpredictability in multilateral trade. These are two critically important dimensions and the developing economies can benefit from both of them. First, a domestic policy stance of openness is associated with brisk growth and poverty alleviation as noted in Chapter 1. If the WTO ensures market access for the developing economies, the ones that have reformed and liberalized their domestic policies and put compensatory policy structures in place are sure to experience acceleration in their growth performance. Tariffs and non-tariff barriers (NTBs) work as a tax on development. This observation applies to both developing and industrial economies (Das, 2001).[1] Secondly, developing economies are relatively weaker players in the multilateral trading system. By conceiving, designing and establishing a rule-based multilateral trade regime the WTO protects the interests of developing economies, particularly the smaller traders that have little ability to influence the policies of the dominant players in the world trade arena. A system of common rules and a mutually agreed code of conduct among WTO members can reduce uncertainties among trading patterns by placing boundaries on the policies adopted by members.

This in turn helps in promoting domestic investment at lower risk. It has been observed that the private sector shies away from investing if a rule-based trade discipline and commensurate domestic reforms are in doubt, because investors perceive it as a high-risk situation. A framework of multilateral agreements renders the domestic policy measure more credible. Such a framework also renders domestic policy reversal or back-sliding impossible because for all appearances they are locked in with a multilateral agreement.

Although not the naissance, the evolution of the multilateral trade regime took place in an oblique and prejudiced manner during the General Agreement on Tariffs and Trade (GATT) era. As the developing economies were not significant traders and did not actively participate in MTNs, the multilateral trade regime evolved to reflect the perceived interest of the industrial economies. Many early GATT rules reflected the practices that were being followed in the industrial economies; heavily subsidized production and export of agricultural products in the industrial economies and distortion in trade in agricultural products was considered acceptable because it suited the interests of the industrial economies. The same logic applies to binding trade in textiles and apparels in quotas, an anathema according to the GATT rules. This was not only true of the past practices but has also persisted until the present. Many recent laws adopted in the WTO reflect the interests of and practices followed in the industrial economies. For instance, the WTO rules on the protection of intellectual property rights are the very same laws that are followed in the industrial economies. This implies that while the developing economies are obliged to create a new regulatory framework on intellectual property rights, the status quo continues in the industrial economies. No changes are required by the WTO in their intellectual property rights regulations (WB, 2002).[2]

During and after the Uruguay Round, as developing economies became active participants in the multilateral trade regime, the old GATT mindset had to change. They also became more proactively involved in multilateral trade. Consequently, in the space of just the 1990s, the average trade-to-GDP ratio for the developing economies soared from 29 per cent to 43 per cent (Ingco and Nash, 2004). With the progressive involvement of the developing economies, a new goal needed to become part of the WTO deliberations and negotiations, namely economic growth and development. The implications of the new WTO rules need to be carefully evaluated. They should be so designed that they proactively lead a member developing economy to the new target. Economic growth is indeed a difficult mataprocess, which *inter alia* requires active and educated involvement of the developing economies in the multilateral trading system.

In the recent past, the developing economies have been more successful in exporting manufactured goods than agricultural products, partly due to the idiosyncrasies of the multilateral trading regime. During the two decades ending in 2001, multilateral trade growth in agriculture and manufacturing trade took place at similar paces. Table 4.1 shows that exports of agricultural products from developing economies rose in the 1990s, as did the growth rate of manufacturing products. However, these statistics conceal an important difference. During the period under consideration, developing countries' exports of agricultural products to other developing economies more than doubled, while those to industrial economies stagnated. Consequently, the share of developing countries' agricultural exports to other developing countries increased from 9.5 per cent to 13.4 per cent during the 1980–2001 period. Over the same period, their share of agricultural exports to industrial economies declined from 25.8 per cent to 22.9 per cent. Conversely, their share of manufactured goods exports to industrial economies soared from 12.7 per cent in 1980–81 to 15.2 per cent in 1990–91, and further to 21.1 per cent in 2000–01. This set of simple statistics portend to the fact that trade barriers have been more effective in stifling agricultural exports from the developing economies than manufacturing exports.

Participation of the developing economies in the multilateral forum is progressively becoming more consequential. The Group-of-Twenty-One (G-21) which was born in Cancún, played an important role both at the Cancún Ministerial Conference and at the WTO meeting in Geneva, held in the last week of July 2004, which put together the July Package or the framework agreement.[3] The members of the G-21 should endeavour

Table 4.1 Export growth rates in constant (1995) dollars

	World export growth rates (%)		Developing countries' export growth rates (%)	
	1980–90	*1990–2001*	*1980–90*	*1990–2001*
Agriculture	4.5	3.6	3.5	4.8
Manufacturing	5.9	4.8	7.6	8.9

Source: Computed by Ingco and Nash (2004) from COMTRADE date tapes.

to ensure that to avoid later frustrations they approach future ministerial conferences, MTNs and other important WTO meetings only with well beefed-up teams of trade economists. For the most salutary outcomes, their degree of preparations for future negotiations should be on the lines of the delegations of the Quadrilateral (or Quad) countries.[4]

A developmental round: abiding by the basic principles

As the Doha Round is intended to be a development round, development concerns have formed an integral part not only of the Doha Ministerial Declaration but also of the subsequent July Package (31 July 2004), or the framework agreement as discussed in the previous chapter. The General Council rededicated the WTO members to fulfilling the development dimension of the Doha Development Agenda, which places the needs and interests of developing and least-developed countries at the heart of the Doha Work Programme. The Council reiterated the 'important role that enhanced market access, balanced rules, and well targeted, sustainably financed technical assistance and capacity building programs can play in the economic development of these countries' (WTO, 2004).

For the developing economies, gains from trade integration are acknowledged to be far larger than any probable increase in external assistance flows. A pro-development outcome of the Doha Round is sure to provide developing economies an opportunity and incentive to use trade integration proactively as a growth lever. To ensure that it remains a Development Round, the WTO members need to run some checks and balances over what is currently transpiring in the MTNs. Stiglitz and Charlton (2004) devised four litmus tests of whether the negotiations, agreements and decisions are pro-development or not. These four principles are: (i) the agreement's future impact on development should be assessed objectively, if there are possibilities of it being negative, then it is unfit for inclusion in the DDA, (ii) the agreement should be fair as well as (iii) fairly arrived at and (iv) the agreement should be confined to trade-related and development-friendly areas, and not venture outside into non-trade-related areas because they have an indirect bearing on trade.

Little economic analysis was done in the past for the potential impact of individual WTO agreements on member country or country groups. Analytical studies that were attempted did not penetrate into the core of negotiations, which largely remained based on prevailing orthodoxies.

They were also influenced by lobbying from strong interest groups. For quantifying the potential impact of each agreement, computable general equilibrium (CGE) exercises can be very useful. Modelling frameworks like the Global Trade Analysis Project (GTAP) and its variations have been in frequent use by scholars and professional economists to this end. The GTAP project is coordinated by the Centre for Global Trade Analysis, which is housed in the Department of Agricultural Economics, Purdue University. The Centre undertakes applied general equilibrium (AGE) modelling, and provides services to other AGE modellers as well as supranational organizations. The objective of GTAP is to improve the quality of quantitative analysis of global economic issues within an economy-wide framework. Since its inception in 1993, GTAP has rapidly become a common 'language' for many of those conducting global economic analysis. Economists at the University of Michigan and Perdue University have a great deal of experience, over a decade, in running these comprehensive simulation exercises. Given the availability of this technique, the WTO Secretariat could be assigned the responsibility of conducting general equilibrium incidence analyses, with the help of academic scholars in this area, to quantify the impact of different proposals on different countries or country groups. However, it should be ensured that the CGE and AGE models used remain sensitive to this differentiation.

The fairness of agreements is as important as it is problematical, and conflict-ridden. It is a somewhat tricky concept. The economic circumstances of each one of the 148 WTO members are different, and therefore each WTO agreement impacts upon each of the members in a different manner. In terms of net gains measured as a percentage of GDP, if any agreement that hurts one country group benefits another, it is considered unfair by the one that is hurt. Fairness also has an element of being progressive, that is, the largest benefits of an agreement should accrue to the poorest group of member developing countries. So defined, fairness has not been a part of the multilateral trading regime thus far. This concept of fairness applies to the entire package of WTO agreements, not to individual agreements. The package has to be viewed and adjudged in its entirety. In the case of individual agreements, there necessarily has to be leeway in give and take; one agreement may give more to one group of members, while another may give more to another group. This effect of the WTO agreements is inevitable, and therefore one needs to look at the bottom line in this regard and reckon which country is benefiting or losing on balance.

Procedural fairness or justice is the principle that deals with the transparency of the negotiations process. Historically, transparency has not been part of the culture of the GATT system, which is known for its lack of transparency and as reflected in the Green Room process. Its lack of transparency became one of the destructive features during the Seattle Ministerial Conference. It is apparent that setting an agenda will have a large bearing over the final outcome of the MTNs, and therefore it is essential that participating members have a say in the agenda-making. As many opinions and stances as possible need to be taken into account before the agenda of an MTN is finalized. A lack of transparency often allowed the large and powerful trading economies to ride roughshod over the system. After the debacle at Seattle, transparency in the WTO system has made visible and impressive strides. The 'July Package', a framework agreement, finalized on 31 July 2004, was posted on the website of the WTO soon after finalization.

The fourth principle relates to defining and limiting the policy space to trade-related areas during the MTNs. Over the last two decades, particularly during the Uruguay Round, there was a strong tendency to expand the mandate of the WTO to include all kinds of assorted areas, ranging from intellectual property rights to labour standards and pollution control. Any international issue which was not formerly covered by any other supranational organization was considered right for the WTO. Attempts were made to include in the ambit of the WTO even those issues for which there were specialized or United Nations organizations, like the environment and labour issues. Stiglitz and Charlton (2004) contend that policy-makers employed the prefix 'trade-related aspects of' somewhat liberally in the past. The WTO deals with a difficult and important area of multilateral economic life; it cannot possibly be made into a negotiating forum and enforcement mechanism for all and sundry areas. There is a price for expanding the policy space of the WTO. First, inclusion of many tangentially related issues tends to confuse and overload the WTO system, which has expanded considerably following the Uruguay Round and thereafter. Second, it also stretches the analytical and negotiating resources of the member developing economies. Third, the industrial economies negotiate from a higher platform in the WTO. Expansion of the WTO boundaries gives them an opportunity to use their superior bargaining strength in trade negotiations to exploit the developing economies over a larger range of issues. The inclusion of the Singapore issues in the Fifth Ministerial Conference at Cancún is a case in point. Therefore, expansion of the WTO mandate should strictly follow the principle of conservativism, and not include issues that do not have a direct relevance to multilateral trade flows.[5]

Special and differential treatment

The WTO does not have a definition of developing economies, although some supranational institutions, like the World Bank, not only provide a closely worded definition, but also of their various sub-groups (see Chapter 1). A WTO member decides and declares its status itself. Over the years, the traditional approach of the developing economies has been to seek benefits under special and differential treatment (SDT). The term SDT captures the WTO provisions that grant preferential access to markets to certain subsets of developing economies and gives them exemptions from certain rules, or gives them extra time to comply. The history of SDT is as old as the GATT/WTO system; SDT has existed since the inception of the GATT, and has had a significant history in the multilateral trading system.

Raul Prebisch and Hans Singer were the intellectual fathers of the concept of SDT. They argued that the exports of the developing economies were concentrated in the area of primary products and commodities, which were characterized by volatile prices and declining terms of trade. They therefore (along with Ragnar Nurkse) propounded the strategy of import-substituting industrialization (ISI), supported by high rates of protection for the developing economies. Although the infant industry argument is accepted by economic theory, this group of economists applied it a little too comprehensively. Consequently, in the economies that followed the ISI strategy, the infant industries remained infants for decades – until many of them touched their middle age. This strategy was avidly followed by South Asian and Latin American economies in the 1950s and beyond, who also promoted the notion of preferential market access for developing economies in the industrial country markets through instruments like SDT.

In the initial stages SDT was limited to the provisions of Article XVIII of GATT-1947, which allowed developing economies to void or renegotiate their commitments.[6] The second defining moment in SDT came during the Kennedy Round (1962–67), when Part IV on the benefits to and obligations of the developing economies was introduced in the Articles of Agreements of the GATT-1947. Article XXXVI of Part IV acknowledged the wide income disparities between the developing and industrial economies, and emphasized the need for rapid economic advancement in the developing economies by means of 'a rapid and sustained expansion of the export earnings of the less-developed contracting parties'.

The third important moment in the life of SDT came during the Tokyo Round (1973–79), when the Enabling Clause was introduced which established that the developing economies were exempted from Article I (the most-favoured-nation, MFN, clause) of GATT-1947.[7] The Enabling Clause meant that the developing countries should receive more favourable treatment without having to reciprocate to the other signing contracting parties (CPs). The reciprocity was limited to levels 'consistent with development needs' and the developing economies were provided with greater freedom to use trade policies than would otherwise be permitted under the GATT rules. These objectives are covered by Article XVIII of GATT-1947, and subsequently GATT-1994. Article XVIII not only permits the developing economies to use their trade policies in pursuit of economic development and industrialization, but also imposes a weaker discipline on them than on the industrial economies in several areas of GATT regulations. It also exhorts the industrial countries to take into account the interests of the developing economies in the application of the GATT discipline. The Enabling Clause made SDT a central element of the GATT system. With prescience, the Enabling Clause also required that, as economic development gathers momentum, the developing economies would try and improve their capacity to gradually reciprocate concessions. This was christened the process of 'graduation'. Subsequently, several preferential trade agreements (PTAs) were created under the Enabling Clause.[8]

To maximize the benefits of WTO membership, developing economies sought to expand the reach of SDT, whose benefits span three important areas, namely, (i) preferential access to the industrial economies' markets without reciprocation, (ii) exemption from some WTO obligations, many of which are transitory and some permanent and (iii) technical assistance and help in institution-building so that WTO obligations can be fulfilled and negotiated and decisions implemented.

The SDT is a system of preferences, which by definition are discriminatory. Historically, efforts to operationalize SDT centred on preferential market access through the Generalized System of Preferences (GSP). Theoretically the concept of SDT is unarguably noble, but in reality it did not generate substantial benefits to the developing economies. There were several causes behind this failure. The preferential market access schedules under SDT were designed voluntarily by the industrial economies, which chose the eligible countries and products for their schedules. It was observed that, first, the selected countries and products generally lacked capacity to export and, secondly, countries and products with export potential were excluded from the schedules. Furthermore, when market preferences were granted, the preference schedules were laden with restrictions, product exclusions and administrative rules. Also, the overall coverage of these schedules was only a tiny part of developing country exports, and the eligible countries were able to utilize only a small part of the preference granted to them. The exports of countries that enjoy the GSP under various preferential schemes form a very small part of the EU and US imports; over the preceding three decades, they have ranged between 0.9 per cent and 0.4 per cent of the total annual imports of the EU and USA. In addition, the preference schedules were characterized by trade diversion, that is they diverted trade with the ineligible developing countries. And finally, the preferential market access schedules did not benefit the target group called the absolute poor of the world;[9] they could not reach this target group at all (WB, 2004).

There has been a long-standing trend of unilateral discriminatory liberalization, or offering tariff- and quota-free market access to the small and poor least-developed countries (LDC).[10] If fully implemented, this could certainly make the SDT more effective than it was in the past. This kind of unilateral market access cannot be offered to the developing economies that do not fall under the LDC category, because it is a political impossibility. Therefore, the absolute poor of the global economy cannot benefit from it because a large proportion of them live in South Asia and sub-Saharan Africa. While all of these economies come under the category of developing economies, not all of them are LDCs. This means that the absolute poor can only benefit if trade liberalization is made multilateral and non-discriminatory. Such reforms would allow the developing economies to exploit their comparative advantage, and, besides, many benefits of free trade accrue to the exporting economy through reform of the domestic macroeconomic framework. That being said, as expected by the Enabling Clause, consistent with their development needs the middle-income – both lower and upper – developing countries should explore the feasibility of exchanging reciprocal concessions with the industrial economies under the WTO framework, and promote the normal trade liberalization process.[11]

Beneficiaries of special and different treatment

The SDT has operated for small, low-income developing economies for many decades. Although there have been a good number of recipients of SDT's benefits, not all of them have in practice benefited from it. The foremost group to benefit from SDT was a small sub-set of the relatively more advanced developing economies. The supply-side scenario in this small group was better developed than in the other small, low-income developing economies, and the rents generated were put to good use by them. This group not only had the wherewithal to export the products, but also met the administrative requirements of the GSP-granting countries. Preparation of the documents required by the preference-granting countries was efficiently met by them. It was observed that liberal rules of origin (ROO) were a critical factor for eliciting a strong response from the potential beneficiary economies, particularly in products like textiles and apparel.[12]

According to the statistics compiled by the World Bank (2004), in 2001 there were 130 countries eligible for SDT, and 10 of them accounted for 77 per cent of the United States (US) non-oil imports under its GSP. The same 10 countries accounted for 49 per cent of all GSP imports from all the industrial countries that were providing GSP. Occasionally a small developing country did benefit substantially from preferential market access where domestic prices were raised above the world market prices by tariffs, subsidies or other trade-distorting mechanisms. For instance, Mauritius which exports sugar and enjoys preferential access to EU markets benefited a good deal from this opportunity. However, these benefits to Mauritius came at a high cost to EU taxpayers and consumers (WB, 2004).

Recent performance of the GSP beneficiaries has also indicated that a small number of small developing economies that developed their supply-side capabilities have succeeded more in exploiting the market access that was provided to them under the GSP. A comparison of countries that were eligible for the US GSP, and those that were recently graduated from it, revealed that the latter category outperformed the former in terms of export performance. Countries that were no longer on the GSP eligibility list had a higher ratio of exports to GDP, as well as higher export growth rates in real terms. One explanation of the success of countries that graduated from the US GSP-eligible list that seems rational is that it appears that GSP provided a stimulus to their export industries. Causality must be carefully attributed, but GSP seemingly helped the graduating countries in engendering supply-side capabilities, which strengthened with the passage of time and turned them into successful trading economies. The flip-side of the coin is that GSP by itself cannot turn them into successful exporters; reforming their macroeconomic policy structure must have played a decisive role in this endeavour.

Special and differential treatment in the Doha Round

The Doha Development Agenda (DDA) again reaffirmed the importance to the SDT for the multilateral trade regime and referred to it as 'an integral part of the WTO agreement' in the Doha Communiqué. The SDT figures at several places in the Doha Communiqué, and the objective of the DDA in this area is clearly laid down in paragraph 2, as

> we shall continue to make positive efforts designed to ensure that developing countries, and specially the least-developed among them, secure a share in the world trade commensurate with the need of their economic development. In this context, enhanced market access, balanced rules, and well-targeted, sustainably financed technical assistance and capacity-building programs have important roles to play. (WTO, 2001)

Recognizing that SDT has not imparted a lot of benefits to the target group of beneficiaries, in paragraph 44 participating members called for a review of the SDT schedules so that their provisions can be strengthened 'making them more precise, effective and operational' so that it is able to fulfil its objectives (WTO, 2001). As noted above, the benefits of SDT are provided through three different channels. A good case exists for rethinking all of the three channels so that the benefits can be targeted more precisely for the target groups that need them most. In paragraph 14, the Doha Communiqué provided a deadline for reestablishing the new modalities of the SDT; the deliberations and dialogues on this issue continued all through 2002, but without a consensus or decision. Members were not only divided on important SDT matters, but also had opinions that were significantly far apart from each other.

In view of the fact that the SDT did not spawn large benefits for the target groups, academics and policy-makers have debated over what shape the SDT should take in future so that it is able to meet the expected goals.[13] The ongoing Doha Round negotiations give an additional relevance to this debate, because this is an opportunity to refine the SDT system. There is some degree of agreement among researchers on the new shape of STD and their comprehensive recommendations are summarized as follows:

- First, the industrial economies need to slash all MFN tariffs on labour-intensive exports from the developing economies to 5 per cent by 2010, and 10 per cent on agricultural exports. The target year for the Millennium Development Goal is 2015; by this time all tariffs on exports of manufactured products should be eliminated.
- Second, likewise developing economies on their part should reduce their tariff barriers on the basis of the adopted formula approach.

This would be their reciprocation to the measures taken by the industrial economies.

- Third, industrial economies should make binding commitments in trade in services to expand temporary excess of services providers by a specific amount, say 1 per cent of the workforce.
- Fourth, industrial economies need to unilaterally expand market access for LDCs, along with simplification of the ROO requirements.
- Fifth, an affirmation by the WTO should be made regarding core disciplines about the use of trade policy, which should apply equally to all members.
- Sixth, feasible channels of meeting the special institutional development needs of small developing economies and LDCs should be replaced.
- Seventh, there are some WTO agreements that are required to be adopted in such a manner that they become supportive of development.
- Eighth, meeting the trade-related technical assistance needs of the small and low-income developing economies should be attempted.[14]

Although none of these proposals are novel and revolutionary, these or similar changes in SDT have been discussed in the past. However, if they are deliberated, promoted and adopted during the Doha Round, the final outcome would indeed be supportive of development in the low-income developing economies and LDCs. The name DDA would then ring true. Although numerous academics have addressed this issue, a Group of Wise Men, like the famous Leutwilder Group of eminent persons appointed by the GATT in 1985, could be appointed once again to analyse these issues and provide objective and functional recommendations that would bring the multilateral trading system closer to the DDA mandate.

The July Package and the SDT

After the failure of the Fifth Ministerial Conference, the framework agreement was arrived at during the last week of July 2004 (discussed earlier in Chapter 3). In the framework agreement the General Council reaffirms that provisions for SDT are an integral part of the WTO agreements. The Council not only reaffirmed the DDA objective of strengthening them, but also making them more precise, effective and operational. The Council instructed the Committee on Trade and Development (CTD) to expeditiously complete its review of all the outstanding Agreement-specific proposals regarding SDT, and report to the General

Council with clear recommendations for a decision by July 2005. The CTD, within the parameters of the Doha mandate, intends to address all other outstanding work, including the cross-cutting issues, the monitoring mechanism and the incorporation of SDT into the architecture of WTO rules.

The Council instructed all WTO bodies to expeditiously complete the consideration of these proposals and report to the General Council, with clear recommendations for a decision, as soon as possible and no later than July 2005. In doing so these bodies will ensure that, as far as possible, their meetings do not overlap so as to enable full and effective participation of developing countries in these discussions.

The General Council reviewed and recognized the progress that has been made since the beginning of the negotiations of the Doha Ministerial Conference in expanding Trade-Related Technical Assistance (TRTA) to developing and low-income countries in transition. In furthering this effort, the Council affirms that such countries, and in particular the LDCs, should be provided with enhanced TRTA and capacity-building, to increase their effective participation in the negotiations, to facilitate their implementation of WTO rules, and to enable them to adjust and diversify their economies. In this context the Council welcomed and further encouraged the improved coordination with other agencies, including under the Integrated Framework (IF) for TRTA for the LDCs and the Joint Integrated Technical Assistance Programme (JITAP) (WTO, 2004). This gives the impression that SDT is being taken up for serious review and at the end of the Doha Round should emerge stronger than in the past.

Hierarchies of beneficiaries and preferential market access

In the hierarchy of beneficiaries from preferential market access, the most preferred countries are those that are part of a regional integration agreement (RIA) with the preference-granting economy. Trade partners in an RIA commonly have close trade and economic ties, and this relationship is usually reciprocal in nature. The LDCs, which enjoy unilateral preferences or free market access, come next. Other small developing economies with which the preference-granting economies have GSP relationships are the last. The GSP is unilateral in nature and devised for large country groups of beneficiaries; GSP status does not provide free market access, but only reduction in tariff rates to the exporting economy in the GSP arrangement.

Several unilateral preferential market access programmes were devised as GSPs by the industrial economies as well laid out, structured and customized programmes that were intended to be carefully implemented. Each of them had characteristic features regarding eligibility criteria, product coverage and administrative rules, in important areas like ROO. Together these criteria determine which developing countries are excluded and which can benefit from the customized unilateral preferential market access schedule. The programmes devised and implemented by the USA include the African Growth Opportunity Act (AGOA), the Caribbean Basin Initiative, the Andean Trade Promotion Act, as well as several unilateral and reciprocal trade agreements with Israel and Jordan. Likewise the principal EU programmes include the Cotonou convention which includes the African, Caribbean and the Pacific (ACP) countries, and the Everything-But-Arms (EBA) initiative targeting the LDCs. The EU has also entered a large number of unilateral and reciprocal trade agreements with the North African, Middle Eastern and Mediterranean economies.[15]

The characteristic features of the unilateral and reciprocal trade agreements differ in several important respects. Several sectors (such as textiles and apparel, processed foods, etc.) are treated as 'sensitive' and usually excluded from the GSP. They are designed for large numbers of potential beneficiaries. These sensitive sectors of trade are included in the unilateral and reciprocal trade agreements. For instance, by 2009 the EBA initiative will cover all the exports of the target group of countries, and all protectionist measures will be eliminated for imports into the EU economies from the 50 LDCs. However, an unseen restriction in this is that the products that matter most to LDCs (rice, sugar and bananas) will not be liberalized until after 2006. Their liberalization will begin in 2007 and end in 2009. Secondly, under the unilateral and reciprocal trade agreements administrative requirements tend to be more relaxed in comparison to the more comprehensive GSP schemes, particularly regarding the ROO.

Despite recent improvements in the implementation of these programmes, as alluded to earlier, the overall imports into the industrial economies under various preferential schemes have continued to remain diminutive, almost insignificant. An exception in this regard is in textiles and apparel exports from small African economies that came under the AGOA to the USA, which recorded significant gains. In 2001, imports by the Quad countries from the GSP beneficiary economies amounted to $588 billion, of which $298 billion were subject to normal trade and non-trade restrictions, while $184 billion came under various preferential trade programmes. That is, the coverage of these programmes was 38.9 per cent of the eligible exports, which in turn received market access preference. In 1991, this proportion was 51.1 per cent. Thus the proportion of coverage of eligible exports declined during the decade of the 1900s (Inama, 2003). A similar quantitative study by Haveman and Shatz (2003) produced comparable, although slightly different, evidence of coverage.

Small developing countries in the Doha Round

A large number of small and low-income developing countries and LDCs are now members of the WTO; together they dominate its membership. Although a majority of them belong to the LDC category, there are some that do not such as the Kyrgyz Republic, Surinam, Guyana, Tajikistan and the like. Cambodia is one such country which became the 148th member of the WTO. With growing numbers, this category of countries has acquired a good deal of influence in the multilateral trade system and its decision-making process. As noted in Chapter 3, during the Fifth Ministerial Conference in Cancún, and the subsequent WTO meeting in Geneva in July 2004, this group held together as the Group-of-Ninety (G-90) and was led by Rwanda.

Two interesting characteristics of small and low-income developing countries and LDCs tend to stand out. First, their economies and trade volume are small, if not tiny. By definition, each one of them accounts for 0.05 per cent, or less, of multilateral imports of goods and services. Realistically, such a small trader has little to offer in terms of market-access concessions to its trading partners during the MTNs. This eliminates this group of small developing countries from any serious reciprocal bargaining, which is considered central to the WTO operations. Second, the interests and trade-related requirements of this group of WTO members are imperfectly aligned with the extensive agenda of the multilateral trade system. In addition, as these small economies enjoy preferential market access to industrial country markets, further multilateral liberalization in the Doha Round would in many cases erode rather than enhance the market access of these countries. Many of them would reap few benefits from broadening the WTO mandate. If anything, they might incur substantial costs.[16] Owing to these two characteristic differences from the principal trading economies, small and low-income developing economies stand out as an unusual and exclusive group in the multilateral trading system.

As alluded to earlier, the contemporary intellectual and political environment strongly favours a 'fair' Doha Round outcome for this country group. In such a *mise-en-scene* the multilateral trading system is faced with the challenge of equilibrating two important and seemingly incompatible issues. Accommodating the interests and needs of this country group on the one hand, and ensuring rapid, efficient and expeditious progress in the Doha Round on the other. Stiglitz and Charlton (2004) noted that the primary principle of

> the Doha Round should be to ensure that the agreements promote development in the poor countries. To make this principle operational the WTO needs to foster a culture of robust economic analysis to identify pro-developmental proposals and promote them to the top of the agenda. In practice this means establishing a source of impartial and publicly available analysis of the effects of different initiatives on different countries. This should be a core responsibility of an expanded WTO Secretariat.

The other objective of this analysis would be to reveal that if any WTO agreement 'differentially hurts developing countries or provides disproportionate benefits to developed countries', it should be regarded as unfair and be considered inappropriate for and incompatible with the DDA (Stiglitz and Charlton, 2004). In the final analysis, the DDA should promote both *de facto* and *de jure* fairness.

To be sure, the MFN liberalization route is considered both efficient and innovative for the Doha Round (see the following section), but the multilateral trading system 'faces the classic conflict between efficiency and distribution' (Mattoo and Subramanian, 2004). If the MFN-based liberalization is the most efficient for reallocation of global resources, it also leads to adverse distributional effects on economies that have been granted the benefit of preferential market access. As the WTO has followed the GATT tradition of arriving at decisions by consensus, this situation is further deformed and exacerbated by the fact that the small, low-income WTO member countries in this group have as much say in ensuring the progress of the Doha Round and creating an efficient multilateral trading system as a large industrial economy member. Without this say, the multilateral trading regime could not be egalitarian. To resolve this knotty, if paradoxical, situation Mattoo and Subramanian (2004) proposed devising a transfer mechanism for compensating the small and low-income WTO members that stand to lose by further liberalization of the multilateral trade regime.

A word about consensus in the GATT/WTO system is relevant here. Although the legal requirement of the Marrakesh Agreement (or the

GATT-1994) establishing the WTO is of a two-thirds or three-fourths majority, depending upon the decision being made, some decisions can only be made by consensus, giving the small member economies *de jure* powers to block any agreement in those areas. In the Doha Round negotiations, this power can be exercised in some categories of issues, while it cannot be exercised on others. For instance, it can be exercised in issues like inclusion of the four Singapore issues and deepening the WTO rules, which requires a two-thirds majority. The latter category covers areas like anti-dumping and subsidies agreements, and strengthening the framework of the GATT-1994 and the General Agreement on Trade in Services (GATS).

However, these *de jure* powers can have less influence over further market access liberalization negotiations. Members that mutually agree can proceed and exchange market access concessions without countenance or interference from other members, who are less concerned in these areas. Thus, in a lot of areas in the DDA, agreements can be reached without the apprehension of small developing countries blocking them. In addition, this country group has come to acquire *de facto* powers, which stem from the fact that during the Uruguay Round they were required to take on numerous obligations, which they subsequently found demanding, intricate and costly to implement. Delivering on those commitments seemed beyond the institutional and budgetary capabilities of these economies. These obligations were in areas like liberalization of trade, institutional up-gradation and protection of intellectual property rights. The small and low-income members argue that if they are expected to take on arduous obligations, they should also have a commensurate influence over WTO affairs. Basically, this is fallacious logic because, first, small developing economies and the LDCs were not the only economies that were asked to take on costly obligations, all the participants were. Second, in acknowledging their special set of circumstances they were given significant latitude and more time than other members for fulfilling demanding and stringent WTO obligations.[17]

To be sure, a transfer mechanism such as that proposed by Mattoo and Subramanian (2004) would be difficult to devise. Even if it was devised, it would be politically infeasible to implement. If so, then the system would gravitate towards what is feasible, albeit less desirable. As regards the question, what is desirable?, it is logical to say that if this country group consents to let the multilateral trading system move forward with the broad liberalization agenda in the DDA, they would be offered a *quid pro quo* in the form of improved non-preferential market access and increased technical and financial assistance. Both are valuable and have long-term significance for this country group. At the present time, the favourite systemic response to this knotty riddle that is emerging is as follows: As the financial assistance and market access response is seemingly infeasible, small member economies are being relieved of WTO obligations which they see as an imposition, in the process eliminating their opposition and antagonism to the continuance of multilateral trade liberalization under the DDA.

MFN-based liberalization: a possible Doha Round innovation

Experience with the GSP programmes so far has been that they have produced only limited results. In spite of the goodwill of the donor economies, the target groups are not receiving benefits, that is the absolute poor in the world population have not been benefiting from the various GSP schemes. The target of achieving the Millennium Development Goals (MDGs) in this regard is not likely to be met unless the delivery vehicle is thoughtfully changed. As a large proportion of the absolute poor live in the People's Republic of China (hereinafter China), South Asia and sub-Saharan Africa, economies in these geographical regions cannot be granted zero tariffs under GSPs, for all their exportables, because it would be a political impossibility. However, there is a possibility of granting zero tariffs to the sub-Saharan economies because their export volumes are tiny.

To this end, an ambitious and innovative modality could be considered during the ongoing Doha Round. The old approach – before the GSPs were created under the GATT – was that MFN-based liberalization is the best route to underpinning economic growth. It was believed that, first, as noted above, it is efficient, and, second, it will *inter alia* eliminate reverse SDT. Reverse SDT refers to the opt-outs and exemptions made by the industrial economies due to political expediency or pressure from the domestic interest groups. They are made at the expense of the exporting developing countries. Elimination of agricultural subsidies as well as protection of the textiles and apparel sector would be not only beneficial to the developing countries, but also benefit consumers in the industrial economies. The same observation can be made regarding the removal of tariff peaks, both international and national on the one hand, and tariff escalation on the other.[18] This will advance trade policy reform process in the developing economies and liberalize their macroeconomic structure.

Over the last half century, several United Nations (UN) commissions committed to promotion of growth and development globally, and two of the notable commissions were headed by Lester B. Pearson and Raul Prebisch. Both developing and industrial economies were part of these commitments to economic development. The final outcomes of many of these Commissions were creations of worthy institutions like the Food and Agriculture Organization (FAO) and the United Nations Conference on Trade and Development (UNCTAD). The most recent endeavour of this kind is the Millennium Development Goal (MDG), which also committed the international community to an expanded vision of global development. Many of the targets were first set out by international conferences and summits held in the 1990s, and subsequently adopted as the MDGs. In a similar vein, the policy objectives of poverty alleviation by means of an ambitious programme of trade-policy reforms could be adopted together by the developing and industrial economies. To be sure, such a reform programme would necessarily encompass decoupling of agricultural support, including abolition of export subsidies, significant tariff-slashing on the MFN-basis on labour-intensive products, which are of interest to the exporting firms from developing countries. This comprehensive reform programme could cover all WTO members, both developing and industrial economies. Such a reform programme has immense potential to become a source of welfare gains to the former country group, and the absolute poor in it.

As for the negotiating modality for such a comprehensive MFN liberalization, two steps are essential for WTO members. First, setting up benchmarks of tariff reduction and product coverage; and, second, setting up a precise timetable and having an accepted schedule for the implementation of various measures. To this end, identifying 'reciprocal commitments that make economic sense and support development' would be a challenging and time-consuming task for the members (WB, 2004). In such negotiations, the old norm of non-reciprocity can become a disadvantage for the developing economies; hindsight reveals that non-reciprocity was overly used in the past, resulting in reductions in gains from trade by way of domestic trade-policy liberalization. Besides, 'non-reciprocity is ... a reason why tariff peaks today are largely on goods produced in developing countries' (WB, 2004). However, since the Uruguay Round this policy mindset in the developing economies has undergone a sea change, and besides, an impetus to domestic trade liberalization would also be instrumental in stimulating intra-developing country trade.[19]

Intra-developing country trade and the Doha Round

Historically, developing economies reluctantly traded with other developing economies and maintained high tariff and non-tariff barriers against each other; they preferred to focus on opening up access to industrial country markets. This represents a missed opportunity by the developing economies and LDCs, since export-market diversification is one of the most important benefits of intra-trade among developing economies. Not only the growth rate of intra-trade among developing economies was low, it grew in fits and starts as these economies went through their stop–go cycles. Intra-trade was also dominated by primary products, and accounted for 6.4 per cent of multilateral trade in 1990. During the decade of the 1990s, developing economies grew at a faster rate than the industrial and transition economies. The growth rate of intra-developing country trade was twice as fast as that of world trade during the 1990–2001 period, during which its value soared from $219 billion to $640 billion. Recent long-term forecasts show that the developing economies will continue to grow faster than the industrial and transitional economies during the coming decade (2003–15).[20] Higher GDP growth performance during the 1990s was the principal reason leading to doubling of the share of the intra-developing country trade in the total multilateral trade in 2001, and therefore a possibility of this performance being repeated during the first decade of the twenty-first century is strong.

As continuance of high GDP growth rate is forecast for the medium term for the developing economies, further liberalization under the DDA could provide an impetus to their intra-trade, and diversify their exports further. To this end, the Doha Round provides an apt opportunity to the developing economies for making concerted efforts to slash both tariffs and NTBs.

The two factors described, namely an above average real GDP growth rate and substantial trade and investment liberalization, led to dynamic growth in trade expansion in the developing economies, and intra-trade benefited from it. Notwithstanding the liberalization of trade regimes since the mid-1980s, the developing economies still have higher tariffs and non-tariff barriers (NTBs) than the industrial economies. One measure of tariff barriers is the ratio of tariff revenue collected *vis-à-vis* the value of imports, and this ratio has been computed for the selected developing economies. It recorded a decline from 12 per cent in 1985 to 4.5 per cent in 2000. Also, average applied tariffs fell from 25 per cent to 15 per cent over the same period. However, wide differences still persist in levels of protection, both among the developing economies and the product categories. The dollar value of total import duties collected in the developing economies in 2000 was $83 billion, almost 65 per cent of the total global import duty collection.[21]

Using the Global Trade Analysis Project (GTAP) 6.3 database (or GTAP 2004 database), Fugazza and Vanzetti (2004) computed the trade-weighted applied average tariffs in merchandise trade for different country groups against each other. Their calculations, shown here in Table 4.2, show the trade-weighted tariffs levied by industrial countries, developing countries and LDCs. The data show that in the area of merchandise trade the industrial economies levy 2.1 per cent tariffs on imports from the other industrial economies, 3.9 per cent on imports from the developing economies and 3.1 per cent from LDCs. The most significant sectors contributing to higher tariffs on developing country exports are petroleum and coal products and textiles and apparel. Industrial economies face higher tariffs (9.2 per cent) when they export to developing economies than do the other developing economies (7.2 per cent). This is partly explained by the composition of trade and partly by preferential agreements among groups of developing economies. Agricultural trade presents a different picture, where average tariff rates are higher in both industrial and developing economies for exports from both the country groups. However, in this sector industrial economies provide greater access to LDCs (2 per cent) than to developing economies (12 per cent). The reason is that various GSP schemes exist, which applies to all the industrial economies.

Fugazza and Vanzetti (2004) also examined the potential for gains from liberalizing intra-developing economies trade. The GTAP 6.3 database had 86 countries and 65 sectors, and they estimated that the static annual welfare gains to developing countries were $50 billion from intra-developing country trade liberalization. As against this, liberalization of

Table 4.2 Trade-weighted average tariffs by stage of development (%)

Exporting country group	Industrial countries	Developing countries	Least-developed countries
Industrial economies	2.1	9.2	11.1
Developing economies	3.9	7.2	14.4
Least-developed countries	3.1	7.2	8.3
Total	2.9	8.1	13.6

Source: Fugazza and Vanzetti (2004). Computed from WITS/TRAINS (2004) database.

industrial economies resulted in estimated annual gains of $24 billion to the developing economies. Estimates show that all the developing regions gain from liberalization of trade among the developing economies. However, the largest beneficiaries were Korea (Republic of), Taiwan, Mexico, China, and the Association of Southeast Asian Nations (ASEAN) region. Conversely, Latin American economies and sub-Saharan Africa turned out to be net losers. The negative effects were derived from the negative terms-of-trade (TOT) effect in the manufacturing sector. As the TOT effects add up to zero globally, these negative effects have a positive impact through lower import prices for the other developing economies.

Trade in textiles and apparel and the Doha Round

Several developing economies and LDCs have strong comparative advantage in the textiles and apparel sectors, and are among the major exporters in both. According to the COMTRADE database, in 2002 China ($16.9 billion) was the largest exporter of textiles, followed by the USA ($12.4 billion). Other sizeable developing country exporters included Korea ($11.2 billion), Taiwan ($9.9 billion) and India ($4.8 billion). In apparel trade, again China ($41.0 billion) was the largest exporter, followed by Italy ($14.1 billion). The other large developing country exporters included Turkey ($8.9 billion), Mexico ($8.5 billion), Hong Kong SAR ($8.3 billion), India ($7.0 billion) and Bangladesh ($5.1 billion). The last named country is an LDC. Over the 1980–2000 period, apparel exports from developing countries increased by a factor of seven and textiles exports by five. The corresponding figures for the industrial economies were three and two, respectively. During this period, textiles and apparel were the second most dynamic products in the world trade, with an average annual growth rate of 13 per cent. Electronics and electronic goods was the only sector which surpassed this growth performance, with an average annual export growth rate of 16 per cent. In 2000, the developing economies accounted for 60 per cent of world exports in apparel and 46 per cent of the world textiles exports. Two decades ago these figures were 8 per cent and 9 per cent, respectively. These statistical data convincingly establish that textiles and apparel are not only two of the most important sectors of exports for the developing economies, but that they also have comparative advantage in these two sectors and have strengthened their position in the global trade arena.

Two of the latest trends in trade in textiles and apparel are the emergence of transnational intermediaries and concentrations of retailers. Both of these new trends have had a discernible impact on production and trade in textiles and apparel. Firms from East Asia have moved up from mere manufacturing and assembling of cut fabric to more complex operations that entail coordination, supply of machinery and finance, and managing a network of global sub-contractors. These firms have now started operating as transnational intermediaries, receiving large orders from retailing chains in the industrial economies, sub-contracting them to a network of globally spread manufacturers, and selling the final output to the retailing chains. Besides, markets in textiles and clothing have become highly concentrated in the industrial economies. For instance, 29 large retailers cater for 98 per cent of the US apparel market, and the EU economies show the same trend. Furthermore, high-volume discount chains in the industrial economies have developed their own brands and outsourced all their textiles and apparel needs, instead of manufacturing them at home (Gereffi and Memedovic, 2003).

The Uruguay Round Agreement on Textiles and Clothing (ATC) expired on 1 January 2005, ending the 30-year long regime of the Multifibre Arrangement (MFA), which was a well-honed system of import quotas. From point in time these important sectors of multilateral trade will come under WTO discipline. The original objective of the MFA was to protect the textiles and apparels industries in the industrial economies, but it unintentionally benefited the textiles and apparel industries of several developing economies that otherwise would not have been competitive in these sectors. The expiry of the MFA quota system threatens the positions of small developing economies in these sectors of multilateral trade. A number of these small exporters are fearful of losing their export markets overnight to China and other large exporters that have strong comparative advantage in textiles and apparel.[22]

Numerous empirical studies are available that have tried to estimate post-ATC textiles and apparel trade, most of them utilizing the Global Trade Analysis Project (GTAP) model. These simulation exercises conclude that while Asian exporters will benefit from the expiration of the ATC, other exporters that have gained their market shares through regional integration agreements (RIAs) are likely to lose. Also, economies specializing in assembly and export of low-value-added garments will face intense competition in the post-ATC era (Spinanger, 2003).

Trade in textiles and apparel was not identified as one of the 20 issues in the DDA. However, during the Doha Round negotiations, the Negotiating Group on Market Access for non-agricultural products (NAMA) was attempting to reduce or eliminate tariffs in textiles and apparel. Trade in textiles and apparel presently suffers from all the three problems of tariff spikes, high tariffs and tariff escalation, that were being addressed under the Doha Round along with the NTBs in these two sectors.[23] Negotiators are to take into consideration the needs of the developing economies, particularly those of the LDCs. Also, in keeping with the provisions of Article XXXVIII *bis* of GATT-1994, less than full reciprocity has to be applied in exchanging liberalization commitments.

The modalities in this regard have not been finalized. However, in the so-called July Package, or the framework agreement of 1 August 2004, the General Council decided that Annex B is to be the basis of future negotiations in this area. WTO members have agreed to include textiles and apparel in sectoral negotiations, the benefit of which is that rapid full liberalization of trade – which implies elimination of tariff and non-tariff barriers – in the selected sector becomes a reasonable possibility. This is expected to be undertaken according to a pre-stipulated timeline. Some developing economies have proposed that participation in sectoral negotiations must be made voluntary, because full liberalization in this sector at a rapid pace may create serious domestic adjustment problems for them (UNCTAD, 2004).

The Doha Round and global poverty alleviation

As alluded to earlier, one of the expectations of the Doha Round is to achieve the Millennium Development Goal (MDG) of cutting down income poverty by a half by 2015. It is the first of the eight MDGs, articulated by the United Nations General assembly in 2000. The long-term trend is that the number of absolute poor in the world has been rising. During the nineteenth and twentieth centuries the number of poverty-stricken people in the world constantly rose (Bouguignon and Morrisson, 2002). There was a small reversal in this trend after 1970, and the number fell by a little over 200 million. Measured in 1985 PPP terms, the number of poor had declined by 350 million (Sala-i-Martin, 2002). Impressive as this achievement seems, there were still 1.2 billion in the world, or one person in five, still living in poverty (Collier and Dollar, 2002).

It should be noted that while the linkage between poverty alleviation and social-sector reforms – for example in education, health, land reform, micro-credit, infrastructure development and governance – is direct, trade and poverty alleviation are not directly linked. However, economic theory suggests that trade can certainly favourably affect the poor through its positive effect on GDP and per capita income in an economy. We saw in Chapter 1 that trade liberalization and expansion has both static and dynamic impacts over the economy and creates optimal conditions for rapid growth through flows of better ideas, technology transfer, goods, services and capital. More importantly, trade expansion underpins growth through better resource allocation in the domestic economy. However, it cannot be ignored that growth is a necessary, not a sufficient, condition for poverty alleviation. Even when trade liberalization and expansion lead to rapid GDP growth, it does not and cannot ensure improvement in income inequality in the economy. But higher GDP growth decisively enhances the probability of poverty alleviation. As wage inequality decreases as a consequence of trade expansion, the poverty level declines. Liberalization of multilateral trade in line with the mandates of the DDA is widely expected to contribute to alleviating poverty and achieving the MDGs.[24] In the Asian economies, the wage gap between the skilled and unskilled workers narrowed in the decades following trade liberalization in Korea, Taiwan, Singapore and Malaysia, although evidence in the Philippines was mixed.

The Stolper–Samuelson theorem can provide meaningful guidance over trade liberalization leading to poverty alleviation. In the medium and long term, increases in the return to labour and capital employed in one sector – one having comparative advantage – should logically attract more resources to that sector. It would also raise gains for labour and capital going to this particular sector. If this sector of the economy is relatively labour-intensive, a rise in the prices of the output of this sector is sure to raise the economy-wide wages of labour. This would benefit all wage-earners, skilled and unskilled, and also those directly or indirectly employed in the sector in question. This is more likely to be the long-term impact of trade liberalization. While this holds as a generalization, empirically linking multilateral trade liberalization to poverty requires a multi-region approach. As most household surveys are country-specific, they are not the most ideal tools for multi-region models used for trade policy analysis (Reimer, 2002). To circumvent this problem, most empirical studies that quantify the impact of trade liberalization over poverty focus on the impact on the average or per capita income.

According to the most recent estimates made by Chen and Ravallion (2004), 1,039 million people live below the poverty line globally if the reference poverty line is defined as $1.08 dollars a day, and 2,736 billion if it is defined as $2.15 a day. The largest proportions of populations living below the poverty line are found in South Asia (31.3 per cent) and sub-Saharan Africa (36.9 per cent). China has made the most impressive strides in reducing the proportion of population living below the poverty line; between 1981 and 2001, this proportion declined from 63.8 per cent to 16.6 per cent.[25]

To analyse the impact of multilateral trade reform at a global level, applied general equilibrium (AGE) models have been found to be useful tools in the past. Whally (1985) and Martin and Winters (1996) put such tools to good use in the context of the Tokyo Round and the Uruguay Round, respectively. AGE models capture the detailed interactions across the many agents of an economy, which includes producers, consumers, public entities, investors and exporters. Despite their level of representation, they present a stylized representation of an economy. For instance, the version of model used for WB (2002) represented economic activity by only 20 goods and services sectors. This analysis decomposed the world economy into 15 regions and 20 economic activities, and the model was calibrated to the latest release of the Global Trade Analysis Programme (GTAP) dataset with a 1997 base year.

According to World Bank (2002) estimates, success in the Doha Round would lift 320 million out of absolute poverty. That is, it could cut the number of people living in poverty by 8 per cent by 2015. Besides that, it can potentially lift global income by $2.8 trillion by 2015, of which $1.5 trillion would accrue to the developing economies.[26] Hertel *et al.* (2004) developed a micro-simulation model to assess the impact of trade liberalization on household income. They posited that 'in the short run household incomes will be differentially affected by global trade liberalization, depending on their reliance on sector-specific factors of production'. Their methodology was applied to an assessment of the consequences of global trade liberalization in the following sectors: merchandise tariffs, agricultural export subsidies, and quotas on textiles and apparel. This study focused on Indonesia and concluded that the national headcount measure of poverty declines following global trade liberalization both in the short and long term. In the long run the poverty headcount in Indonesia falls for all strata of poverty. The increased demand for unskilled workers lifted income for the formerly self-employed, some of whom moved into the wage-labour market. Thus viewed, successful rounds of MTNs do have a discernible favourable impact over the incidence of poverty.

Conclusions and summary

As the Doha Round is intended to be a development round, development concerns form an integral part not only of the Doha Ministerial Declaration but also of the subsequent framework agreement or the July Package. To ensure that the Doha Round remains a Development Round, the WTO members need to run some checks and balances over what is currently transpiring in the MTNs. This chapter focused on four possible tests of whether the negotiations, agreements and decisions are pro-development or not.

Although the WTO is not a development institution, its operations have definite development relevance and consequences. There are certain facets of its mandate that decisively influence developmental endeavours of countries. The system of ruled-based conduct provided by the WTO reduces uncertainties in the multilateral trade arena, which in turn helps in promoting multilateral trade and domestic investment at lower risk. For a long time the developing economies remained inactive participants in the multilateral trading system. For the first time, during the Uruguay Round, and thereafter, developing economies became active participants in the multilateral trade regime. The old GATT mindset changed. They also became more proactively involved in multilateral trade. Since then, participation of the developing economies in the multilateral trade forum has progressively become more consequential. The Group-of-Twenty-One (G-21) developing economies, which was born in Cancún, played a consequential role both at the Fifth Ministerial Conference in Cancún and at the WTO meeting in Geneva held in the last week of July 2004 which put together the so-called July Package or the framework agreement.

Special and differential treatment (SDT) was devised exclusively to assist the small and low-income developing economies. In the initial stages SDT was limited to the provisions of Article XVIII of GATT-1947, which allowed developing economies to void or renegotiate their commitments. The SDT underwent several fundamental changes in the Kennedy Round (1962–67) and the Tokyo Round (1973–79). The SDT has operated for so many decades. There were a good number of recipients of SDT benefits, but not all of them benefited from it. It is widely acknowledged that the preferential market access schedules did not benefit the target group called the 'absolute poor' of the world.

Therefore, the WTO members participating in the Doha Round called for a review of the SDT schedules so that their provisions could be strengthened making them more precise, effective and operational so that they are able to fulfil their objectives. The ongoing Doha Round negotiations give an additional relevance to this debate, because this is an opportunity to refine the SDT system. In the framework agreement, the General Council not only reaffirmed the DDA objective of strengthening the SDT but also making them more precise, effective and operational. A large number of small and low-income developing countries and LDCs are now members of the WTO; together they dominate its membership. The contemporary intellectual and political environment strongly favours a 'fair' Doha Round outcome for this country group. In such a *mise-en-scène*, the multilateral trading system is faced with the challenge of equilibrating two important and seemingly incompatible issues: accommodating the interests and needs of this country group on the one hand, and ensuring rapid, efficient and expeditious progress in the Doha Round on the other. The primary principle of the Doha Round should be to ensure that the final agreement promotes development in the poor countries. To make this principle operational the WTO needs to foster a culture of robust economic analysis to identify pro-developmental proposals and promote them to the top of the agenda.

Historically, developing economies reluctantly traded with other developing economies and maintained high tariff and non-tariff barriers against each other. Consequently, intra-developing country trade remained low in volume and value. The developing economies customarily preferred to focus on opening up access to industrial country markets. This penchant underwent a transformation in the 1990s. Developing economies grew at a faster clip than the industrial economies and transition economies. The growth rate of intra-developing country trade was twice as fast as that of world trade during the 1990–2001 period. Recent long-term forecasts show that the developing economies would continue to grow faster than the industrial and transitional economies during the coming decade. It is a realistic expectation that the intra-developing country trade would also continue to grow in the medium term at a more rapid pace than multilateral trade.

Several developing economies and LDCs have strong comparative advantage in both textiles and apparel sectors and are among the major exporters in both the sectors. Trade in textiles and apparel was not identified as an issue in the DDA. However, during the Doha Round negotiations, the Negotiating Group on Market Access for non-agricultural products (NAMA) attempted to reduce or eliminate tariffs in textiles and apparel.

Success in the Doha Round can certainly influence the absolute poor of the world. An empirical study estimated that it would lift 320 million out of absolute poverty. That is, it could cut the number of people living in poverty by 8 per cent by 2015. Besides, it could potentially lift global income by $2.8 trillion by 2015. Of this, $1.5 trillion would accrue to the developing economies. Thus viewed, successful rounds of MTNs do have a discernible favourable impact over the incidence of poverty.

5
Trade in Services and the Doha Round

Trade in services

The services sector is the largest sector of the contemporary global economy, accounting for 60 per cent of total output, and it also accounts for a comparable share of employment, in some countries even a larger share. In the industrial economies services has been the single largest sector for a long time, and in the developing economies its share in total GDP has recorded considerable expansion in recent years. It has become the largest of the three economic sectors in many developing economies, making the maximum contribution to GDP and employment. As a rule of thumb, the services sector contributes 40 per cent to 60 per cent to the GDP in developing economies, and 60 per cent to 80 per cent in the industrial economies. As it is such a large sector, developing economies need to identify their comparative advantage in this sector as well as their export markets. They would logically have comparative advantage in one or more labour-intensive service industries. Many developing economies are known to have reasonably large reservoirs of semi-skilled and in some cases skilled labour forces, and consequently they may have comparative advantage in the labour-intensive industries that deploy their labour resources.

Sizeable multilateral trade exists in commercially tradable services, and in the recent past it has ranged between one-fifth and one-fourth of total merchandise trade. It amounted to $1,350 billion, or 20.2 per cent of total merchandise trade in 1999; it rose to $1,435 billion in 2000, or 23.2 per cent of merchandise trade. After a decline in 2001, trade in services increased to $1,570 billion in 2002, or 25.3 per cent of the total merchandise trade, and to $1,763 billion in 2003, or 24.2 per cent of the total merchandise trade.[1]

Technological progress has greatly enhanced the scope for trade in conventional services. The onward march of globalization and global economic integration, facilitated by technological advancement, have led to a continuous expansion in the range of traded services.[2] International transactions that would have been impossible or prohibitively expensive in the past have now become commonplace because of the ease with which people can move, communicate and transfer goods across national borders. Thus, expansion in trade in services reflects more than mere quantitative expansion. An amber signal is necessary here. The statistics provided in this paragraph understate the true value of trade in services, because a good deal of it is conducted by expressly created corporate establishments in their export markets. Therefore, this trade in services is not recorded in the balance-of-payments (bop) statistics. In addition, invisibility and intangibility of many services imply that when they are delivered to a trade partner, their passage is often not recorded by the customs department.

Therefore, statistics on trade in services are not entirely reliable; they even tend to be volatile. Problems in measuring trade in services are not new. Constant endeavours have been made to improve and harmonize the measuring and reporting systems. A newly defined statistical framework for measuring trade in services has been devised by the World Trade Organization (WTO), the European Commission, the International Monetary Fund (IMF), the Organization for Economic Cooperation and Development (OECD), the United Nations Conference on Trade and Development (UNCTAD) and the United Nations (UN). It has been named the *Manual on Statistics of International Trade in Services* (2002), jointly published in partnership by six supranational institutions as a manual.[3] This well-researched manual sets out an internationally agreed framework for the compilation of statistics of international trade in services to meet the need for having comparable and comprehensive statistics on services trade. The recommendations in the manual, which will be promoted by the six organizations, will enable countries to progressively expand and structure information on trade in services in an internationally comparable manner. Following the convention established by the related supranational organizations, the manual conforms with and explicitly relates to the *System of National Accounts 1993* (published by the UN) and the fifth edition of the International Monetary Fund's *Balance of Payments Manual*.

During the decade 1990–2000, the simple average annual growth rate of merchandise trade was 6 per cent and that of trade in services 7 per cent. Over the 15-year period 1985–99, the compound annual growth rate for services exports on a bop basis – which covers cross-border supply abroad – was 9 per cent per annum, compared to 8.2 per cent for merchandise exports (WB, 2002). During this 15-year period, trade in services trebled in size to $1,350 billion in 1999, growing faster in developing economies than in the industrial economies. Consequently, their average annual share in world services exports increased from 14 per cent in 1985–89 to 18 per cent in 1995–99 (WB, 2002).

According to the World Trade Organization (WTO) classification, there are 12 principal services sectors:

1 Business services, which include professional services, computer and related services, research and development services, real estate services, rental and leasing services.
2 Communications services, which include postal and courier services, telecommunication services and audiovisual services.
3 Construction services, which include general construction work for building, installation and assembly work.
4 Distribution services, which include commission agent's services, wholesale trade services, retailing services and franchising.
5 Educational services.
6 Environmental services.
7 Financial services, which include insurance and banking.
8 Health-related and social services.
9 Tourism and travel-related services, which include hotels and restaurants, travel agencies and tour operators.
10 Recreational, cultural and sporting services, which include entertainment services, news agency services, libraries, archives, museums and other cultural services.
11 Transport services, which include rail and road transport, maritime transport services, air transport services, space transport.
12 Other services.

These 12 services sectors comprise 160 sub-sectors. The WTO General Agreement on Trade in Services (GATS) defines four ways in which services are traded. These are popularly known as the four 'modes of supply', which are as follows: The first mode is services supplied from one country to another, officially named 'cross-border supply', like an international phone call. The second mode of supply entails consumers of one country consuming the services provided by another country, like tourism, higher education, health tourism and advanced medical services such as open-heart surgery. In this case the consumers of services move to the supplier, and therefore this supply mode is known as 'consumption abroad'. The third mode is a firm from one country setting up branches or a subsidiary in another country to make its services available in the importing country, like Citicorp setting up branches in Mexico or a subsidiary in the Republic of Korea (hereinafter Korea). This mode of movement of services suppliers is known as 'supply via commercial presence' or 'supplying services via the presence of natural persons'. The fourth mode of supplying services is to travel to another country to supply services, like a Chinese visiting professor at the Wharton School of Business. Transnational corporations (TNCs) are known to move their personnel around at short notice as they move their special-purpose project teams globally. In WTO parlance, this is formally known as 'temporary movement of natural persons' and has recently become a source of a great deal of debate and deliberations. The GATS agreement provides WTO members a choice to commit to providing market access or national treatment in any number of the WTO-identified sectors and sub-sectors. The scope of issues covered under the fourth mode of supply transcends the WTO, and entails organizations like the International Organization for Migration (IOM), the Organization for Economic Cooperation and Development (OECD), the UNCTAD as well as the World Bank.

Trade in services has been traditionally dominated by the industrial economies, with the United States being the largest market player. According to the 2003 WTO statistics, the USA was the largest exporter of services exporting $282.5 billion worth, and accounting for 16.0 per cent of the total services trade. The United Kingdom (UK) was next with $129.5 billion of services exports, which was 7.3 per cent of the total services trade. Germany exported $111.7 billion worth of services, accounting for 6.3 per cent. The fourth and fifth places were held by France (5.6 per cent) and Spain (4.3 per cent), in that order.[4] The five largest exporters of services accounted for 39.5 per cent of the total trade in commercial services in 2003. In the same league table, the next five largest services traders are Italy, Japan, the Netherlands, the People's Republic of China (hereinafter China) and Hong Kong SAR, in that order. The second tier of five services exporters of commercial services accounted for 12.7 per cent of the total trade in commercial services. The combined share of the 10 largest services traders was more than half (56.2 per cent) of the multilateral trade in services. In this category, there were only two developing economies, namely China ($44.5 billion) which was in ninth place, while Hong Kong SAR ($43.2 billion) was tenth.[5] As regards regional distribution, trade in services is the highest in Western Europe, followed by North America and Asia, in that order.

Together these three regions account for 88 per cent of total exports in services.

Some stylized facts about trade in services

Market access in services and their supply modes are not only different from market access in goods, they are also more complex. Simple reduction or elimination of tariffs would improve market access for trade in goods. Conversely, for trade in services, enhancing market access requires reducing government policy interventions, which are often invisible. The barriers to trade in services may be applied after the services suppliers have entered the domestic market. These measures are generally in the form of government policy measures and regulatory structures that are basically intended to meet domestic policy objectives, rather than trade policy objectives.

In general, trade in services is more heavily protected than trade in manufactured products. On average, developing economies have more restrictive barriers *vis-à-vis* trade in services than industrial economies. The developing economies are a heterogeneous group in themselves and protect their services sectors in a diverse manner and to dissimilar extents. In most countries market segmentation in services is large. Notwithstanding advancing globalization, several important services sectors – retailing, retail banking, insurance, domestic air transport – are overwhelmingly dominated by domestic services suppliers.

Unlike the developing economies, the industrial economies provide evidence of being more liberal markets in trade in services. There are several reasons for this, including large cross-country foreign direct investment (FDI), mergers and acquisitions (M&As), and foreign services providers buying out domestic services providers in their areas of activity. Also, governments have higher levels of market-access commitments. More open and transparent markets in the industrial economies are helping in the growth of market integration in the numerous services sectors. Conversely, in the developing economies much less market integration and cross-market penetration has occurred in the past, although this ambiance is presently changing (McGuire, 2002).

Liberalization of trade in services

Liberalization of trade in services under the sponsorship of the Doha Round (discussed in more detail later in the chapter) is sure to have far-reaching ramifications for the multilateral trading system, trade in services and the domestic economies in the WTO member states. As elaborated below, services play an essential and basic role in an economy and underpin its production structure. The performance of an economy, including that of its traded-goods sector, is favourably influenced by the efficiency of its services sector. In principle, the economic rationale behind liberalization of multilateral trade in services under the GATS is not different from the rationale that has driven the liberalization of merchandise trade in the latter half of the last century. Market liberalization is expected to encourage quality improvement as well as product and process innovation. It reduces the scope for wasteful utilization of productive resources as well as rent-seeking behaviour. It removes constraints over individual economic operators.

Restrictions on trade in services have costs in terms of higher prices for businesses and consumers in the domestic economy. By limiting domestic and international competition, a barrier-ridden environment in services lowers efficiency and increases transaction costs. Barriers on competition allow the incumbent services suppliers to charge prices above the competitive market price level. These costs cannot be taken frivolously, since high transaction costs can work as impediments to economic growth. Some analysts go so far as to consider them the most serious hurdles. Collier and Gunning (1999), for example, found that they were the most significant bottleneck to growth endeavours in Africa.

An overarching objective of liberalization of trade in services is to give market forces a freer reign in fixing their prices in a competitive manner, and with that determining production, trade and investment patterns. Liberalization of trade in services moves an economy 'towards competitive prices, aligning them more closely with prevailing international levels, and additional emphasis being placed on positive adjustments via product and process innovation' (WTO, 1998a). In this context, multilateral liberalization can be seen as an invaluable strategy to capture benefits of competition in the services sector. Competition enhances price declines. Although empirical studies in this area have been attempted, many have limited coverage and focus on a narrow range of economies. Majority of the empirical studies focus on the liberalization and deregulation of one sector, namely, financial services.

Some services are more important for the domestic economy than others, in that they constitute the infrastructural backbone of any contemporary economy and contribute to improved economic performance. Financial services, health, education, telecommunications and transport (land, air and ocean) services squarely fall in this category. These basic services not only have a significant impact on growth, they also provide the bulk of employment and income. They facilitate production of other goods and services in the economy and work as vital inputs for the production of goods. The international competitiveness of traditional sectors in developing economies is heavily dependent on access to services at a reasonable price, preferably at world-market prices. For instance, a smoothly functioning financial services sector transforms savings into investment, in the process ensuring that the resources are deployed where they have the highest productivity. An efficiently operating financial sector also benefits the economy by improved opportunities for risk-sharing in the economy.

Thus viewed, efficiency in the services sector is essential for the efficiency of the user industries throughout the domestic economy as well as for enhancing general economic performance. Empirically capturing the entire impact of the services sector over the economy is not possible. Liberalization and regulatory reforms in this sector commonly produce competition-enhancing price declines, but to quantify the impact of lower prices and more efficient services inputs on the user industries and economic activity in the liberalizing economy is exceedingly difficult. Isolating the links in empirical studies frequently proves to be onerous because reform-oriented economies concurrently move on a variety of fronts. Liberalization and reforms are not implemented under controlled laboratory conditions.

One of the ways in which a trade partner may improve welfare in the economy of its foreign trade partner is by establishing a commercial presence there. It is the third mode of supply of services noted earlier, and is one of the important means of trade in services. In this mode, a foreign services supplier makes FDI in its trade-partner country, so that a personal contact may be established between the service provider and the foreign clientele. Restrictions on FDI or inward movement of professionals may restrict services trade like tariffs and non-tariff barriers (NTBs). However, if FDI and movement of personnel are smoothly permitted, the trade partner economy receives capital, skilled personnel and technology, which in turn upgrades productivity in the domestic economy of the recipient economy. As alluded to above, financial, communications and professional services are key intermediate inputs into production in all sectors, and therefore price declines and technological improvements in these sectors can potentially upgrade overall productivity in the economy (Konan and Maskus, 2004).

Timeliness of provision of services, providing institutional support, and sequencing of domestic deregulation and external liberalization are key issues in many services industries. In the telecommunications industry the deregulation of the domestic sector generally comes first and international liberalization second. It has been felt that reversal of this sequence could undermine, even endanger, the incumbent firms' position in the domestic market. They may find that competition from foreign operators is too much for their profitability, or even survival. Poorly timed or premature liberalization of financial services – that is, financial liberalization before adequate institutional development has taken place and regulatory and supervisory norms have been developed – can lead to a spurt in capital inflows, macroeconomic instability, exchange rate volatility, capital flight and eventually a financial crisis. The recent economic crises in Asia, Latin America and Turkey testify to this fact. In contrast, properly sequenced liberalization – under effective supervision and supported by appropriate institutions – leads to smooth and profitable development of the financial sector (Das, 2004b).

Proper supervision and institutional support of the liberalization measures is equally essential. Properly supervised financial services liberalization results in micro-level benefits to the economy. Consumers tend to benefit from a wider array of banking schemes and services, lower service fees and higher interest rates on deposits. In general, liberalization and deregulation leads to consumer welfare. Evidence is available to show that in many services sectors post-deregulation price reductions, quality improvements and widening product variety lead to significant consumer welfare, although there can be exceptions to this generalization, as in the US aviation industry where deregulation resulted in higher airfares and rising business concentrations. This was explained by the economies of scale, scope and density. That is, in the aviation sector there is commercial advantage in having bigger firms (WTO, 2000).

Liberalization and deregulation in minor services areas like business services – which include accounting and legal services – also result in competition-enhanced price declines, which in turn reduce transaction costs in the economy. As alluded to earlier in this section, higher transaction and other costs feed into the economic system, impeding growth. The contribution made by the general acceptance of standardized accountancy principles in the financial development of industrial economies has been rated highly. Summers (1999) identified them as the single most important innovation in the financial history of US financial markets. Another service sector, which can no longer be called small and has begun to have enormous economic impact globally, is information and communication technology (ICT). A strong ICT sector became the foundation of modern knowledge and the information-based economy. It is the initiator of the so-called New Economy paradigm.[6] This is an economy in which ICT plays a significant role, which in turn enables producers of both tangible products (from computers to shoes) and intangibles (the range of services, R&D, ideas) to compete efficiently in global markets.

The impact of trade liberalization in services

As set out earlier, developing economies maintain higher barriers to trade in services in general, and particularly in areas like telecommunications, banking and the financial sector than do the industrial economies. Economies with higher barriers gain more by liberalizing than do those with lower barriers. Therefore, the Doha Round-induced liberalization should benefit the developing economies more than the industrial economies. In the short term gains may be small, or there may even be losses due to the costs of adjustment to new regulations and lower trade barriers. An appropriate policy framework can reduce the costs of adjustment; by paying attention to nature, pace and sequencing of liberalization, adjustment costs may be kept under control.

Existing models have attempted to quantify the impact of trade liberalization in services sectors. The computable general equilibrium (CGE) modelling of liberalizing trade in services provides insights into the projected real-income gains from an efficient allocation of resources, and such exercises can assist in establishing priorities in multilateral negotiations when the negotiators can compare gains from liberalization in services with those in other major sectors, like agriculture and manufactures. The CGE exercises that have attempted to determine the impact have produced wide-ranging, even contradictory and somewhat confusing, conclusions. These exercises have entailed numerical simulation, using global general equilibrium models. Conclusions of some of the noteworthy studies are as follows. Using a Global Trade Analysis Project (GTAP) model, Dee and Hanslow (2000) showed that liberalization of services sectors in the Uruguay Round was exceedingly beneficial to some countries. According to their results China's gains were as high as 14.6 per cent of GDP and that of Indonesia 5.1 per cent. They also concluded that more than a half of the global welfare gains from liberalization originated in the services sector.

As opposed to these conclusions, Robinson *et al.* (1999) used a similar GTAP model and estimated China's gains as small as 0.34 per cent of GDP. The ten ASEAN economies stood to gain 1.29 per cent of GDP and South Asia 1.13 per cent. A third exercise by Verikios and Zhang (2001) went as far as suggesting losses to Malaysia from liberalization in the telecommunication sector. According to this study, Indonesia was also going to lose from its financial-sector liberalization, while China was to register minor gains. In a recent computation, Brown *et al.* (2003) found large welfare gains from the liberalization of trade in services in the Doha Round. They were of the tune of $574 billion per year, with $413 billion originating in the services sector. A dominant part of these benefits were estimated to go to the developing economies.

Wide variations in estimates are as conspicuous as they are jarring. One factor may be that all these simulation exercises took considerably different approaches in their modelling, coverage and assumptions. Another reason for the wide variation in estimates was that modelling in services trade was relatively new and there was little agreement on the methodology and the set of initial barriers to be taken among the modellers. For instance, Dee and Hanslow (2000) covered only the third mode of supply of services liberalization in their exercise. As opposed to this, Robinson *et al.* (1999) did not differentiate between modes of supply. One commonality among the results of CGE modelling exercises, however, was that liberalization of trade in services was found to increase real global income. This is where the similarity in estimates ended. The distribution of gains among countries and regions was dependent upon the specifications of the individual modelling exercises, and evidently varied significantly.

Multilateral liberalization: detrimental or rewarding

Since the early 1980s, the developing economies have been sceptical regarding the multilateral liberalization of trade in services. Led by Brazil and India, they tenaciously opposed inclusion of trade in services as an agenda item in the GATT Ministerial Meeting of 1982 held in Geneva. Their scepticism stems from their perception that the services sector in the developing economies is inherently inefficient and therefore cannot compete with the highly competitive and resourceful services suppliers from the industrial economies, much less with the global leaders. This view held sway in spite of the widely known economic rationale behind the benefits of liberalization. Their caution and concern regarding multilateral negotiations was based on the perception that future negotiations in services are likely to be *de facto* one-sided, and would produce nothing that would benefit the developing economies. In addition, they perceived that following negotiations in trade in services, developing economies would be required to make large adjustments in their domestic economies. The domestic adjustment costs of liberalization commitments were believed to be a drain on their budgetary resources, not matched in terms of returns.

The reason why policy-makers in the developing economies believed that negotiations and liberalization commitments would be one-sided, is that because of the strong bargaining position of the industrial economies during the MTNs, the industrial country services firms would certainly and easily gain improved access to markets in the developing economies, while the reverse is not likely to happen. If it does, it would only be in a symbolic manner. This assumption of asymmetry in the respective positions during the MTNs is largely based on the experiences of the developing economies during the MTNs. For instance, after the completion of the Uruguay Round many developing economies not only believed that they overcommitted, they also felt that they unwittingly became a part of an uneven and detrimental covenant.

Other than the heavy budgetary cost of adjustment, large liberalization commitments would call for multifaceted modifications and fine-tuning in the developing economies. An important dimension is adjustment to foreign ownership or majority ownership of domestic services firms, which may have security and cultural implications. With the advancing liberalization of trade in services, domestic bank ownership by foreign banks is sure to grow. Foreign banks come to have knowledge regarding financial details and records of domestic corporate entities, which is resented in some countries. The entertainment industry is another similar example. Most countries resent foreign ownership in their audiovisual industry because most societies tend to see it as a part of their national cultural identity. Foreign ownership in the movie, television or broadcast industries is seen as an unacceptable intrusion and evokes an emotional response from the populace. Developing countries also find the influence of liberalization over the domestic labour market difficult to adjust to in the short term. For instance, if foreign banks or airlines begin to dominate the domestic financial and aviation sectors, they can potentially create large unemployment in labour-intensive services areas.

To be sure, these are valid concerns and ways are being found to address them. For instance, regulatory reforms are being made in the regulatory structure of industrial economies so that market access by services providers from the developing economies can be allowed. However, these reforms are yet to be reflected in the scheduled commitments of the GATS. They can indeed be part of the current negotiations in the Doha Round in sectors and modes of interest to the developing economies.

The cost of reform and liberalization for an economy can be controlled. Adoption of an appropriate policy framework is sure to reduce the adjustment costs of liberalization and reforms of trade in services.

The nature, pace and sequencing of reform measures is crucial in this respect; they need to be carefully conceived, calibrated and implemented. The GATS also emphasizes the need for caution in planning the liberalization and reform measures. It advocates inbuilt flexibility and promotes progressive and sequential liberalization. In most developing economies creating an appropriate framework for the reform of the services sectors – and then for enforcing it – calls for considerable institution-building (Neilson and Taglioni, 2004).

Escalating services trade from the developing economies

An increasing number of developing economies, in particular the emerging-market economies (EMEs) and the newly industrialized economies (NIEs), are becoming active players in the arena of trade in services. While all the four modes of supply are used by them, many are increasingly investing in other countries for the purpose of exporting services. As noted earlier in this chapter, this is known as 'supply via commercial presence' or 'supplying services via the presence of natural persons'. For instance, in the recent past Malaysia has made large investments in environmental services and South Africa in the telecommunications sector for the purpose of supplying the corresponding services. Rapid advances in the ICT sector since the 1980s have enhanced the scope and feasibility of export of services in a wide range of ICT-enabled activities and professions. These advances made it possible for the Philippines to turn into a successful exporter of software and Barbados a centre for providing global data processing services. Approximate estimates are available to indicate that the size of the potential market for the developing country exports for long-distance services could be of the order of 1 per cent to 5 per cent of the total employment in services sectors in the Group-of-Seven (G-7) economies. This could mean annual services exports worth $100–120 billion from the developing economies that have comparative advantage in ICT-enabled activities (WB, 2002).

Of late, the developing economies have become active traders in new service areas like the audiovisual industry, tourism, health services, construction, courier services and maritime transport.[7] Other labour-intensive sectors like data processing and business-process outsourcing (BPO) are increasingly becoming important export revenue earners for a group of developing economies having well-educated, inexpensive, English-speaking workforces. This group of countries is expanding and their exports have been moving towards the higher-skill end of the chain. As elaborated below, India has emerged a successful exporter of

ICT-enabled services. Other developing and transition economies that have entered this export market include China, Hungary, Jamaica, the Russian Federation and the Philippines. The last named country has also become a prominent hub for financial and accountancy services. Mexico is rapidly becoming an information technology and engineering outsourcing economy for a large number of medium-sized and large US firms. Tourism is another area of successful involvement of the developing economies. It is the largest employing industry, employing almost 10 per cent of the global workforce. There are also regional differences in growth rates in trade in services; during the 1990s, in Asia the growth rate of trade in services was higher than that in merchandise trade. In contrast, in the Latin American economies the reverse held.

An oft-cited example of successful services export from a developing economy is that of Indian software and BPO. Expanding global trade in services created new opportunities for India in a small segment of its economy, and expansion of Indian exports of software since the mid-1980s has been nothing short of spectacular. Over 200 of the Fortune 500 corporations outsource their software from Indian firms, generating several billion dollars in export revenue for them. India first found comparative advantage in software and computer programming, and second it found a profitable niche in back-office outsourcing of business services and call centres. India became the world's largest recipient of US outsourcing in the ICT sector, while Canada took second place (Scoffield, 2004). Indian exports in these services were $225 million in 1992, soaring to $1.75 billion in 1998 and further to $6.22 billion in 2000. Their current (2003) level is $9.86 billion. The USA was the largest ($6.69 billion) market for Indian software exporters in 2003, followed by the European Union ($2.10 billion) and Japan ($193 million).[8] Indian exports of ICT-enabled services to Asia and Latin America were also significant; the growth rate of these exports was close to 50 per cent per annum. One direct outcome of this success was the steadily rising level of foreign exchange reserves. They doubled in 2002 and again in 2003, reaching $103 billion in early 2004, creating pressure on the rupee to appreciate beyond what the fundamentals could justify. The Reserve Bank of India, which is the central bank, had to purchase huge quantities of dollars to keep the rupee from appreciating.

Business-process outsourcing (BPO) firms in India have been expanding the range of work that can be performed remotely, with virtually endless applications. There were some 3,000 BPO firms and a large number of outsourcing jobs in 2004. Revenue from BPO alone grew by 50 per cent in 2003 to $3.6 billion. Four kinds of firms were scrambling to perform these white-collar jobs. First, large Indian software firms like Infosys and

Wipro, which aspired to be full-service providers to their clients. Second, the specialist third-party outsourcing firms like Evalueserver, Cognizant and Daksh, which provided narrowly specialized services to their clients. Of these ICT firms, Daksh was set up in 1999, and its turnover doubled every year since its establishment. Third, large captive units created by transnational corporations (TNCs) particularly by financial services TNCs like GE Capital, American Express, HSBC, Citigroup and Standard Chartered. Fourth, the establishments created by the gigantic global professional-services consultancies, like IBM, Ernst & Young and Accenture (*The Economist*, 2003b). India's thriving BPO industry faces two major uncertainties, namely, growing protectionism in its important markets, particularly the USA, and the usual meddling of an incompetent and parasitic government. Besides, competition from other countries (such as Barbados, Brazil, Bulgaria, China, Malaysia, Mexico, the Philippines, Rumania, Russian Federation, South Africa and Vietnam) is likely to start making inroads and challenge the Indian ICT-enabled services and BPO industry in the near future (Das, 2005).

Indian ICT and software firms only cater for half a per cent of the world software market. There are large differences across countries in the cost of software development. The average cost per line of code in India is $5, in Italy and Ireland it is $10, in the USA it is $18 and in Germany $22. The same observation applies to software support operations. The global market of software services is large, with the USA alone having a market size of $58 billion. The other large markets are the EU ($42 billion) and Japan ($10 billion) (WB, 2002). Trade in software services is sure to rise, and result in cost savings.

Accord on trade in services

The WTO was established as a successor of the General Agreement on Tariffs and Trade (GATT). Built upon a broader legal and political base than the GATT, it can be correctly described as the mutated GATT. The WTO covers numerous trade agreements,[9] one of the most important being the WTO General Agreement on Trade in Services (GATS).[10] This accord came into force in January 1995.[11] It is the first and only set of multilateral rules that cover trade in services, with a broad scope and coverage of all traded services. The GATS accord has two parts – first, the framework agreement containing general rules and disciplines; and second, the national schedules of commitments which list each member country's individual commitments regarding market access by foreign suppliers of services.[12]

If a service sector is listed in the national schedule, it implies that the listing economy has liberalized its domestic market in that sector for trade and is ready to offer market access to foreign suppliers. It applies to all the members on a non-discriminatory basis in the selected services area. The GATS accord is fairly flexible as noted earlier, and members have complete freedom in choosing services as well as the degree to which foreign services suppliers can operate in their domestic markets. For instance, if a member country chooses financial services and commits to open its domestic banking sector for foreign suppliers, it is also free to limit market access by limiting the number of licences it grants. Additionally, it may predetermine the number of foreign bank branches it is going to allow to operate in its territory. Thus, the services agreement, unlike the WTO, provides for both market access limitation and national treatment limitation.

As the trade in commercial services expanded, *pari passu* a need for a legal framework in trade in services emerged. Its absence would have been both abnormal and anomalous because, as stated earlier, the potential benefits of liberalization of trade in services are as substantive and consequential as they are in the case of merchandise trade. Unlike merchandise trade, multilateral trade in services did not have a multilateral liberalization movement; it was set in motion only after the GATS came into force. The reason for traditionally ignoring services in international trade negotiations was that they were initially, albeit incorrectly, perceived as non-tradable. This perception was underpinned by legal and institutional factors. For instance, in many countries public-sector monopolies were ubiquitous in core services sectors like telecommunications and transport. Economic and technical constraints also promoted the same misperception of non-tradability. For instance, in some services industries the simultaneous presence of producers and consumers was considered necessary. In many other sectors transmission technologies were not available, perpetuating the belief that services are non-tradable. However, the present services scenario is radically different. As alluded to at the start of this chapter, over the past two decades technological breakthroughs in ICT and transport technologies not only dispelled this misperception but also added to the importance of many services sectors in multilateral trade, enhancing the potential gains from their smooth and innovative liberalization.

The Doha Round and services negotiations

The GATS committed member governments to undertake negotiations on specific issues and to enter into successive rounds of negotiations to progressively liberalize their trade in services. According to Article XIX of the GATS, the first round had to start no later than five years from 1995. Accordingly, services negotiations started afresh officially on 1 January 2000 under the sponsorship of the Council for Trade in Services. In March 2001, the Services Council fulfilled a key element in the GATS negotiating mandate by establishing the negotiating guidelines and procedures. Thus, the negotiations on services were already almost two years old when they were incorporated into the Doha Development Agenda (DDA). The Doha Declaration endorsed the work already done under the Council for Trade in Services, reaffirmed the negotiating guidelines and procedures, and established some key elements of the timetable including the deadline for the conclusion of the negotiations as part of a Single Undertaking. It implies that every item of negotiation is a part of a whole and indivisible package and cannot be agreed in parts or separately. The meaning of the Single Undertaking has undergone some transformation and is open to debate and interpretation among academics and policy-makers alike.

Paragraph 15 of the Doha Communiqué stated that

> The negotiations on trade in services shall be conducted with a view to promoting the economic growth of all trading partners and the development of developing and least-developed countries. We recognize the work already undertaken in the negotiations, initiated in January 2000 under Article XIX of the General Agreement on Trade in Services, and the large number of proposals submitted by members on a wide range of sectors and several horizontal issues, as well as on movement of natural persons. We reaffirm the Guidelines and Procedures for the Negotiations adopted by the Council for Trade in Services on 28 March 2001 as the basis for continuing the negotiations, with a view to achieving the objectives of the General Agreement on Trade in Services, as stipulated in the Preamble, Article IV and Article XIX of that Agreement.

In this Paragraph, Ministers agreed that participants shall submit initial requests for specific commitments by 30 June 2002 and initial offers by 31 March 2003. The word 'initial' was of course indicative of the reality of the negotiating process, which was a succession of requests-and-offers operations. The timeline provided by the participating ministers represented their political commitment to the liberalization process. To this end, each participating member submits an initial request which does not have to be exhaustive. In the initial request a participating member does not necessarily have to think of every conceivable item it wishes to request of the other participants. In order to keep to the predetermined schedule, members tend to avoid seeking perfection which might cause delays.

Stress-free negotiations

Contrary to the WTO, the GATS accord has not been a source of controversies and contentious debates; negotiations under the GATS are relatively easy to conduct. The reason is the remarkable flexibility of the GATS accord, that permits member governments to determine the level of market liberalization obligations that they would like to assume. This flexibility stems from four idiosyncratic features of the GATS accord. First, member countries identify the sectors and sub-sectors for making commitments to foreign services suppliers. Although members have a schedule of commitments, there is no minimum requirement in this regard. Members have liberty to identify as small a part of one sector for guaranteeing the rights of foreign suppliers to provide services as they please. Second, having identified the sector(s), member governments have a right to set limitations on market access and the degree of national treatment they are willing to guarantee. Third, developing country governments frequently limit their commitments to one or two 'modes of supply' through which services can be traded. Furthermore, if they see it is reasonable and appropriate, they may withdraw or renegotiate commitments. Fourth, in order to provide favourable treatment to certain trading partners, governments are at liberty to make deviations from the most-favoured-nation (MFN) principle, which applies for a period of 10 years. This *modus operandi* has rendered the GATS accord adaptable and accommodating.

The accord comprises a number of general obligations which apply to all services sectors, and, to be sure, the MFN principle is the most significant of the general rules applicable to the accord. Other than the general obligations, each member defines its own rules in its own specific obligations through the commitments in its national schedule. As a rule of thumb, the GATS accord accepts that the developing economies would liberalize fewer services sectors and types of transactions than the industrial economies. Accordingly, the commitments of developing economies are relatively less extensive. Due to this flexibility in the scheduling of commitments the probability of north–south controversy in the operation of the GATS accord has been effectively eliminated.

Adopting modalities for the treatment of liberalization measures

In March 2003, the Council for Trade in Services took a significant step towards fulfilling the DDA mandate by adopting modalities for the treatment of liberalization measures taken unilaterally by members since the previous multilateral negotiations. This issue was fraught with possibilities of disagreements and antagonism among the members. Dr Supachai Panitchpakdi, Director General of the World Trade Organization, noted that 'A significant part of the negotiating mandate has been achieved' and hoped that this agreement would inject new dynamism in the services negotiations. The timely display of flexibility and political will by the members was expected to provide momentum in the ongoing process of request-and-offer operations. By establishing agreed criteria for granting credit for autonomous liberalization in services, negotiators could engage more confidently in their bilateral negotiations for specific commitments on market access.

These agreed modalities were established pursuant to Article XIX: 3 of the GATS, Paragraph 15 of the Doha Ministerial communiqué, and Paragraph 13 of the Guidelines and Procedures for the Negotiations on Trade in Services. For the purposes of these modalities, definitions were agreed. For instance, a 'liberalizing member' is a member seeking credit for an autonomous liberalization measure, and a 'trading partner' is a member from whom credit is being sought. An 'autonomous liberalization measure' is a measure which is subject to scheduling under Part III of the GATS, and leading to the termination of an MFN exemption, and compatible with the MFN principle. The liberalization should be undertaken by the liberalizing member unilaterally, in accordance with Article XIX of the GATS, and applicable to any or all service sectors.[13]

Criteria for assessing the value of autonomous liberalization were established and accepted by members, and pragmatism was accepted as a key principle for the application of the agreed approaches. In applying them, a member is required to take into account the level of development and the size of economies of individual members as well as size and development in individual sectors. The application of modalities may be advanced bilaterally, plurilaterally or multilaterally. The granting of credit for autonomous liberalization measures is to be advanced through bilateral negotiations.

A liberalizing member has to make the autonomous liberalization measure for which credit is being sought known to its trading partners. The liberalizing member may also choose to notify such a measure to the Special Session of the Council for Trade in Services. It was agreed that such a notification neither guarantees any right for credit, nor implies any obligation on the part of the liberalizing member to bind the notified measure. In addition, an autonomous liberalization measure notified or made known to a trading partner should contain information based on the relevant criteria set out in Part II of these modalities, and specify the credit being sought.

In keeping with the objectives of the GATS, as stipulated in the Preamble, Article IV, and Article XIX: 2, and in line with Paragraph 2 of the Doha Ministerial Declaration, these modalities would be used *inter alia* as a means of promoting the economic growth and development of developing countries and their increasing participation in trade in services. In the application of these modalities, and in recognizing and granting credit pursuant to these modalities, members should take fully into account the flexibility provided for individual developing country members under the provisions referred to in Paragraph 13 above, as well as the level of development of developing country members in relation to other members. Special consideration shall be given to the least-developed country (LDC) members.[14]

Fourth mode: temporary labour mobility for supplying services

Under the fourth mode of supplying services, a services supplying firm or skill-possessor from one WTO member country temporarily moves to the territory of another member for the express and predetermined purpose of supplying services. The underlying conditions of the fourth mode are that services suppliers gain entry to another country only for a prespecified purpose as a self-employed professional or as an employee of a service-supplying firm. Their status is not that of immigrants. Therefore, unlike immigrants the services suppliers stay confined to the sector for which they had ostensibly entered the host country, and do not become a part of the general labour force.

The issues related to the movement of workers and professionals under the fourth mode of the GATS are a narrowly, if incompletely and imprecisely, defined subset of issues related to temporary migration of labour. As the movement of natural persons is more than a mere trade issue, The *WTO Annex on Movement of Natural Persons* specifically and cautiously excluded coverage of access to the labour market, citizenship and permanent employment. Owing to its direct relationship and relevance to trade and immigration, policy-makers and practitioners in these two areas are involved in preparing the host-country policy framework on the movement of natural persons under the fourth mode of the

GATS. Workers and professionals, who move and stay, do so within the regulatory framework of host governments on migration, not under the fourth mode of supply of labour under the GATS. However, when during the MTNs governments take on commitments related to the movement of natural persons under the fourth mode, their implementation is the function of the immigration departments and immigration managers in the government systems.

Most importantly, their entry to the host country has to be temporary and, having supplied the contracted services, they have to return to their country of origin. The term 'temporary' has so far not been defined by the GATS, but it ranges from five weeks to five years, depending upon the country and services sector under consideration. The level of skill has also not been specified by the GATS, but the working assumption is that only higher-level skills, such as managers, executives, subject-area specialists and other professionals are considered under the GATS. The fourth mode is an interface between immigration issues and trade in services issues, which renders it conceptually complex.

Professionals that possess higher-level skills make a material long-term impact over the host economy. Evidence is available to show that high-level skill-holders, particularly in sciences and engineering, have favourably impacted upon the rate of innovation and productivity growth in the USA (Basu *et al.*, 2003; Borjas, 2004; Hall, 2004). The community of highly skilled immigrants is considered a significant contributor to the innovating potential of the US economy, which is ranked the highest in the world. This hypothesis was empirically tested by Chellaraj, Maskus and Mattoo (2004) by estimating the innovation production function in which highly-skilled immigrants and foreign graduate students are an input into the development of new ideas. This econometric study concluded that an increase in the presence of these two groups of contributors has a positive and significant impact over US patent applications as well as grants of patents. This applies to grants of patents to both universities and private firms.

The fourth mode under the GATS, which does not have mere developing country versus industrial country dimension, has emerged not only as a major issue in the Doha Round but also in trade in services *per se*. With advancing global economic integration the new trends in labour integration are developing and movement of services suppliers, under the fourth mode, is not limited to movement from developing to industrial economies. Flows of services suppliers between industrial economies are significant, as they are between the developing economies; however, these flows from industrial to developing countries are not known to be large.

As the product cycles have been increasingly shortening, labour mobility for supplying services is becoming an important issue for the industrial economies as well. With shortening product cycles, TNCs, large manufacturing firms and services suppliers in the industrial economies need to move professionals and technicians having different kinds of skills, for shorter periods, at shorter notices, to the economies that are consumers of their products and services. With advancing globalization, they are required to move professionals to more countries. Therefore, a significant range of business firms in the industrial economies have joined hands with the developing economies for progress on this issue during the Doha Round. They see the need of clear, harmonized and easily understandable regulations in this area.

To be sure, liberalization in the fourth mode of services will neither be easy nor trouble-free. The importing country is likely to have numerous concerns and will be required to devise appropriate regulatory infrastructure for the temporary inward movement of professionals and technicians. It is widely acknowledged that the problems associated with the fourth mode labour mobility are obstinate, but they are not beyond resolution. They call for new levels and systems of policy coordination between trade, labour and immigration authorities in the importing countries, and endeavours will have to be made at the national and international levels for reaching functional decisions and workable solutions.

Statistical dimensions of fourth mode services trade are difficult to determine because so far no reliable data compilation practice exists. Skilled workers moving temporarily to another country for the purpose of supplying services have not become a part of any enumeration exercise. Movement of people under the fourth mode is not separated from other broad categories of migrants. Even when professional categories of migrants are available, it is not possible to determine to which sector they belong. Also, trade data in services is never disaggregated according to the four standard modes of supply. Often proxies are used to gain an approximate idea of the dimension of this trade. One of the commonest proxies is remittances from foreign workers, which includes professionals that cannot be included in the fourth mode of services trade. Thus reasonably accurate statistics in this regard may only be available in the medium term. Available statistics suggest that there has been a steady increase in the number of fourth-mode services suppliers. The highest growth sector is in the three to six months' movement for services suppliers (OECD, 2003b). Comparative advantage of the developing economies most often – albeit not always – lies in providing low- and semi-skilled labour services to the industrial economies. The developing economies are therefore eager to move low- and semi-skilled workers for supplying labour. Imperfect statistics in this area suggest that the developing economies are net exporters of labour services and the industrial economies net importers (WTO, 2001b).

Empirical studies to compute the impact of liberalization of trade in services under the fourth mode was initially neglected because this area of intellectual curiosity does not fall squarely in any neatly demarcated economic sub-discipline. As alluded to above, it straddles two disciplines, namely migration and trade in services. In addition, no methodology has been developed for quantifying the impact of workers' mobility under the fourth mode. Their movement is not migration because, having provided the required services, they return to their home country. It does not come under the category of trade as measured by the balance of payments (bop).

The WTO (1998b) attempted to quantify the value of trade under the fourth mode and concluded that between 1980 and 1990, mode-four exports of industrial economies increased at a much faster rate than those from the developing economies. They were computed in terms of labour income, remittances and migrant income transfers. Developing countries exported labour services worth $45.95 billion in the 1990s, up 57 per cent from their 1980 level. As opposed to this, their imports of labour were only worth $9.25 billion in 1990, up 13 per cent since 1980. In the case of the industrial economies, the value of labour exports was $25.19 billion, up 93 per cent from their 1980 level. Their labour imports were also large at $50.33 billion in 1990, up 106 per cent since 1980.

Using the proxy series of world income in compensation of employees that participated in trade in services deploying the fourth mode of supplying services, Karsenty (2000) estimated that the value of this trade was $30 billion for 1997. It was 1.4 per cent of total services trade. Thus, mode four was merely 4 per cent of total trade in services, while modes one and three accounted for 80 per cent of the total trade in services. Of the four modes of supply, mode four was found to be statistically the least significant. It should, however, be borne in mind that all these computations were based on inadequate statistics (Cattaneo and Nielson, 2003).

The effect of liberalization of labour mobility under the fourth mode was computed by Winters (2002), who asserted that increased labour mobility can result in total gains worth $300 billion per annum; however, this number was arrived at under certain assumptions. Two other studies concluded that increased labour mobility from developing to industrial economies by 3 per cent of the industrial country labour force would result in aggregate gain of $150 billion per annum, which is 0.6 per cent of the global income. These two studies also pointed out that both developing and industrial economies would benefit from the movement of low-skilled labour under the fourth mode, because these workers are spread more thinly over the economy than highly-skilled workers, whose contribution is sector-specific (Winters and Walmsley, 2002; Winters *et al.*, 2002).

The liberalization of merchandise trade has reduced the price differential between developing and industrial economies to a ratio of 2:1 (Rodrik, 2001a). However, the price differential in services is much higher between the two country groups, and can differ by a factor of 10, often even more. Therefore, liberalization of trade in services, particularly in the temporary movement of labour, can be reasonably expected to result in far greater gains than that in merchandise trade. An empirical exercise modelled labour movement based on GATS visas, and entailed labour movement from the developing economies as large as 3 per cent of the total labour force of the industrial economies. These developing country services-providers were to remain in the industrial economies for three to five years, and were to be replaced thereafter by another similar wave of services-providers. Such a system of labour mobility would result in a gain of $200 billion per annum (Rodrik, 2001a).[15]

The Doha Round and the fourth mode
of trade in services

Given the development focus of the Doha Round, attempts are under way for the opening-up of trade in services in areas of interest for developing economies. Temporary movement of services providers in areas like ICT, business services, construction services, health-related services and the like is a crucial issue for these economies. Sending services supplies, under the fourth mode of the GATS, to lucrative markets is seen as one of the principal areas of negotiations during the Doha Round by many developing economies. The present level of commitments under the fourth mode made under the GATS accord is limited, and it is also the mode of supply in which the smallest number of commitments were made under the Uruguay Round. As the gains from liberalization under the fourth mode are significant, the expectations of the developing economies are high in this regard. Some of them have even offered a *quid pro quo* between investment in services areas in their domestic economies for meaningful progress in the Doha Round in the movement of semi-skilled workers and professionals as suppliers of services. Negotiations on mode four of the GATS are being considered a litmus test for the DDA. To some this will be the final determinant of whether the development promise of the DDA is being adhered to.

After the commencement of the Doha Round of MTNs, members took stock of the work done under the GATS negotiations since January 2000. The six proposals put forth by members were examined, and the negotiations on the fourth mode were the subject of some uncertainty. Pursuant to the Doha mandate, participants in the services negotiations have been exchanging bilateral initial requests since 30 June 2002. Between 31 March 2003 and 30 October, 39 Members submitted initial offers: Argentina, Australia, Bahrain, Bolivia, Bulgaria, Canada, Chile, China, Chinese Taipei, Colombia, the Czech Rep, the EU, Fiji, Guatemala, Hong Kong, Iceland, Israel, Japan, Korea, Liechtenstein, Macao, Mexico, New Zealand, Norway, Panama, Paraguay, Peru, Poland, Senegal, Singapore, the Slovak Republic, Slovenia, Sri Lanka, St Christopher & Nevis, Switzerland, Thailand, Turkey, the United States and Uruguay. A close analysis of these offers indicates that the developing and industrial economies tabled two different kinds of proposals. While the former group was eager to negotiate on increasing market access, the latter preferred negotiations on improving the effectiveness of existing market access norms and practices. The developing economies' proposed channels of augmenting market access were the issuance of time-limited GATS visas and sector-specific commitments instead of blanket permission for fourth mode entry. As opposed to this, the industrial economies emphasized having commonly agreed definitions as well as greater clarity and transparency in members' commitments. These were proposed as the principal means of improving the efficiency of current imperfect practices followed under the fourth mode.

Programmes for labour movements under the fourth mode

Since presently the planning and implementation of policies related to the temporary movement of labour and professionals is the function of the immigration departments and immigration managers in the government systems, one needs to have a clear notion of the status of the policies, administrative structures and implementation mechanisms of the various host-country governments. These policies reflect the interests of both the countries of origin of the workers as well as the countries of destination. While they have important ramifications for both sets of economies, there is no comprehensive system at the international level governing this specific kind of migration. Most countries have primarily designed and followed unilateral, bilateral or regional strategies in this area. As it entails allowing non-nationals to enter the country it is a complex policy area, involving fundamental attributes of state sovereignty, which partly explains the reluctance of states to enter into a binding multilateral agreement regarding the fourth mode of supply of labour.

One of the special agencies of the UN system, the International Labour Organization (ILO), recently took a great deal of interest and initiative in this area. It designed the ILO Plan of Action for Migrant Workers in 2004, which proposed the development of a non-binding multilateral framework for a rights-based approach to labour migration which takes into account labour-market needs in the host country. The ILO plan proposed guidelines and principles for policies based on best practices and international standards. Another comprehensive and goal-oriented ILO study analysed this issue in the background of the presently emerging global economic scenario.[16]

Current demographic trends which include ageing populations and falling birth rates in many industrial economies, combined with structural labour deficits in specific sectors like the ICT, healthcare and domestic work portends to a growing future for foreign workers. Many industrial countries are presently changing or planning to change their legislation to facilitate the entry of skilled foreign workers (McLaughan and Salt, 2002), given the need for mobile human resources.

Employment-related immigration programmes in the countries of destination are generally of two kinds. The first set is based on long-term economic development goals, while the second is based on temporary migration policies which reflect short-term labour-market needs. Some countries operate both sets of programmes discreetly, while in others both programmes are at some point joined, and a temporary entrant can become an applicant to be a permanent immigrant, or at least allowed to stay for an extended period. These programmes have country to country variations. For instance, Korea and Singapore which have a long tradition of importing temporary workers and professionals, now allow permanent settlement of their highly-skilled temporary migrants. A majority of OECD economies plan their temporary labour entry based on labour-market realities; market demand that cannot be met locally is filled with the help of a temporary intake of foreign workers.

As protecting domestic labour market has a high policy priority in the destination countries, they assess and establish an annual number or quota for foreign temporary workers needed by the economy. Based on the so-called economic needs tests (ENTs), the number is revised annually and accordingly short-term permits, which have different names in different destination economies, are issued to the temporary workers.

The ENTs have become commonplace in the countries of destinations, and Australia, Canada, Kuwait, the UK and the USA have applied them for the longest period. The permits issued to short-term foreign workers specify the length and conditions of stay, including conditions related to permit renewals and the possibility of employment mobility. Administrative structures exist for monitoring temporary workers' obligations to their employers.

Some destination countries operate visa and permit systems together for their temporary workers. The former permits entry while the latter sets out the conditions of employment in intricate detail. In other countries visas have several categories and the category of visa performs both functions. The government bodies issuing the relevant papers and performing these tasks can be immigration authorities, labour ministries, *ad hoc* bodies which function in coordination with several local ministries, or central employment boards. The annual quotas estimated by these bodies can be applicable to the country as a whole, or they are divided region or state-wise, or for specific sectors of the economy. This quota regime has been found helpful and easy to operate by most countries of destination, and has been operating in Italy, Germany, Switzerland, South Africa, the United Kingdom and the USA, among others. One limitation of this system is that governments are found to be slow in perceiving changes in the needs of their labour markets. An alternative to this system is that employers can be given the right to hire a foreign worker, if he demonstrates that the short-term worker will neither take a job away from native workers nor will affect domestic wages and employment conditions adversely (Doudeijns and Dumont, 2003).[17]

Conclusions and summary

The services sector is the largest sector of the contemporary global economy. Sizeable multilateral trade exists in commercially tradable services. In general, trade in services is more heavily protected than trade in manufactured products. On an average, developing economies have more restrictive barriers *vis-à-vis* trade in services than the industrial economies. Liberalization of trade in services under the sponsorship of the Doha Round is sure to have far-reaching ramifications for the multilateral trading system, trade in services and the domestic economies in the WTO member states.

As the economies with higher barriers gain more by liberalizing than do those with lower barriers, the Doha Round induced liberalization in trade in services should logically benefit the developing economies more than the industrial economies. In the short term gains may be small, or there may even be some losses due to the costs of adjustment to new regulations and lower trade barriers. Attempts have been made to empirically estimate the welfare implications of liberalization of trade in services. One commonality among the results of CGE modelling exercises was that liberalization of trade in services was found to increase real global income.

An increasing number of developing economies, in particular the emerging-market economies (EMEs) and the newly industrialized economies (NIEs), are becoming active players in the arena of trade in services. While all the four modes of supply are used by them, many are increasingly investing in other countries for the purpose of exporting services. As the trade in commercial services expanded, *pari passu*, a need for a legal framework in trade in services emerged. Its absence would have been both abnormal and anomalous.

The GATS comprises the legal framework governing the multilateral trade in services. It committed member governments to undertake negotiations on specific issues and to enter into successive rounds of negotiations to progressively liberalize their trade in services. According to Article XIX of the GATS, the first round had to start no later than five years from 1995. Accordingly, the services negotiations started afresh officially on 1 January 2000 under the sponsorship of the Council for Trade in Services. In March 2001, the Services Council fulfilled a key element in the GATS negotiating mandate by establishing the negotiating guidelines and procedures. Thus, the negotiations on services were already almost two years old when they were incorporated into the Doha Development Agenda (DDA). The Doha Declaration endorsed the work already done under the Council for Trade in Services, reaffirmed the negotiating guidelines and procedures, and established some key elements of the timetable including the deadline for the conclusion of the negotiations as part of a Single Undertaking.

In March 2003, the Council for Trade in Services took a significant step towards fulfilling the DDA mandate by adopting modalities for the treatment of liberalization measures taken unilaterally by members since the previous multilateral negotiations. These agreed modalities were established pursuant to Article XIX: 3 of the GATS, Paragraph 15 of the Doha Ministerial communiqué, and Paragraph 13 of the Guidelines and Procedures for the Negotiations on Trade in Services.

The fourth mode of supplying services has become a focus of recent attention by both policy mandarins and academics. Under the fourth mode, a services-supplying firm or skill-possessor from one WTO member country temporarily moves to the territory of another member for the express and predetermined purpose of supplying services. The underlying conditions of the fourth mode are that services suppliers gain entry to another country only for a prespecified purpose as a self-employed professional or as an employee of a service-supplying firm. Their status is not that of immigrants. As the movement of natural persons is more than a mere trade issue, *The WTO Annex on Movement of Natural Persons* specifically and cautiously excluded coverage of access to labour market, citizenship and permanent employment. Owing to its direct relationship and relevance to trade and immigration, policy-makers and practitioners in these two areas are involved in preparing the host country policy framework on the movement of natural persons under the fourth mode of the GATS.

Liberalization of trade in services, particularly in temporary movement of labour, can be reasonably expected to result in far greater gains than that in merchandise trade. Given the development focus of the Doha Round, attempts are under way for opening up trade in services in the areas of interest of the developing economies. Temporary movement of services providers in areas like ICT, business services, construction services, health-related services, and the like, is a crucial issue for the developing economies. Sending services supplies, under the fourth mode of the GATS, to lucrative markets is seen as one of the principal areas of negotiations during the Doha Round by many developing economies. The present level of commitments under the fourth mode made under GATS accord is limited, though expectations of the developing economies are high in this regard. To some this will be the final determinant of whether the development promise of the DDA is being adhered to.

6
Trade in Agriculture and the Doha Round

Dimensions of trade in agricultural products

World trade in agricultural and agro-industrial products was $547 billion, or 9.1 per cent, of total merchandise trade in 2001. It increased marginally to $583 billion in 2002, or 9.3 per cent of total merchandise trade. Although trade in agricultural products has been increasing in absolute terms, its share of total world trade declined steadily during the twentieth century. Until now this trend has shown no sign of abating, which is logical and easy to comprehend. As a share of merchandise trade, trade in agriculture declined from 17 per cent to 10 per cent over the 1980–97 period.

According to 2002 statistics published by the WTO in 2003, Western Europe was the largest exporter, followed by Asia and North America in that order. Exports of agricultural products from Western Europe stood at $248.7 billion, which was 42.7 per cent of total agricultural exports. Asian exports stood at $106.2 billion, or 18.2 per cent, and those from North America $101.4 billion, or 17.4 per cent. The Latin American economies accounted for $67.5 billion, or 11.6 per cent of total agricultural exports.[1] There also was significant intra-regional trade in agricultural products. Intra-Western Europe agricultural trade was the largest and stood at $189.3 billion; intra-Asia agricultural trade stood in second place at $64.6 billion, while intra-North America trade was third ($34.0 billion). Trade flows between North America and Asia were also significant and valued at $32.8 billion.[2]

The Doha Round negotiations are expected to advance multilateral agricultural trade liberalization, and thereby expand trade in agricultural and agro-industrial products. As decided in the July Package or the framework agreement signed on 1 August 2004, multilateral trade negotiations (MTNs) are likely to succeed in achieving reductions in high tariffs, export subsidies and domestic support of agriculture in the Organization for Economic Cooperation and Development (OECD) economies. Consequently, exports of sugar, beef, fruits and vegetables from the developing economies to the OECD economies would rise, which should lead to two immediate beneficial consequences for the economies involved. First, increasing trade volume *per se* would be beneficial. Second, trade expansion in agriculture would dampen world market price volatility in agricultural products. Thinness of the markets is partly responsible for the large and unpredictable price volatility in agricultural products.

Trade statistics for the 1980–2001 period show that the developing economies have been more successful in exporting manufactured goods than agricultural products. This is partly due to the idiosyncrasies of the multilateral trade regime. Statistical data show that exports of agricultural products from developing economies rose in the 1990s, as did the growth rate of manufacturing products. However, these statistics conceal an important difference between the two rates of acceleration. During the period under consideration, developing countries' exports of agricultural products to other developing economies more than doubled, while those to the industrial economies stagnated. Consequently, the share of developing countries' agricultural exports to other developing countries increased from 9.5 per cent to 13.4 per cent during 1980–2001. Over the same period, their share of agricultural exports to industrial economies declined from 25.8 per cent to 22.9 per cent. As opposed to this, developing countries' share of manufactured goods exports to industrial economies soared from 12.7 per cent in 1980–81 to 15.2 per cent in 1990–91, and further to 21.1 per cent in 2000–01. This set of simple statistics show that trade barriers have been more effective in stifling agricultural exports from the developing economies than manufacturing exports (Ingco and Nash, 2004).

The lingering tradition of excessive protectionism

Trade in agriculture has always had a difficult political chemistry, and a high level of protection has been its hallmark. High tariffs and non-tariff barriers (NTBs) as well as subsidization have been age-old chestnuts in agricultural trade. A historical search in this regard yields only one solitary example of liberalization of trade in agricultural products during the last three centuries, namely the repeal of the Corn Law in Britain in the middle of the nineteenth century.[3] The agricultural policy structures of the

European Union (EU) and the USA are squarely based on their design in the 1930s. The EU farm policy structure is essentially based on the French farm policies of that period, and represent 'dinosaurs' of contemporary trade world, irrelevant to the needs of a modern multilateral trade regime.

Since the 1950s, agricultural protection increased substantially in the industrial economies, and the newly industrialized economies (NIEs) followed the same trend. Protection of agriculture and agro-industrial products further worsened in the 1980s (Anderson, 1995). Liberalization of trade in this sector was and continues to be a politically difficult task, and therefore governments have a strong penchant to ignore it. Multilateral negotiations or regional trade agreements are considered an effective instrument for liberalizing trade in the agricultural sector because in a multilateral trade negotiations (MTNs) setting, liberalization concessions are reciprocally traded by the participating economies. It is an easier way out, which does not mean that it is easy.

During the regime of the General Agreement on Tariff and Trade (GATT), little progress was made in liberalizing agricultural trade. If anything, it was ignored during the first five rounds of MTNs because it was considered too contentious and politically sensitive to be approached.[4] This was because there were two principal country groups having opposite mindsets and contradictory sets of agricultural policies. The first group comprises the Cairns Group[5] and several developing economies, which are exporters in the world agricultural product markets and have lightly protected trade regimes. As opposed to this, the second group is made up of the industrial economies of Western Europe, Japan, the Republic of Korea (hereinafter Korea) and some food-importing developing economies. The second group stringently protects its agriculture. In any negotiations both of these country groups always took strongly conflicting positions. Their views were considerably at variance from each other and they remained obdurately intransigent. When liberalization of multilateral trade in agricultural products was taken up for the first time in the Uruguay Round (1986–94) of MTNs, strong differences in positions and disagreements in views were to be expected. However, inclusion of trade in agriculture was necessary in the Uruguay Round because agricultural trade policies had continued to be increasingly protectionist, and became highly distorted by the mid-1980s. There were indications that more countries would adopt a protectionist stance on agriculture if it is not restrained through an MTN (Anderson, 2003; Baker, 2003).

Agricultural trade regimes are presently markedly more complex and distorted than those of trade in manufactured products, as will be discussed in the next section. Heavy traditional subsidization of agriculture by the industrial economies has led to ineffable distortion of multilateral trade regime. Kym Anderson (2003) contended that 'agricultural trade policies remain by far the most costly of all goods market distortion in world trade'. They massively disrupt international markets in agricultural products. Often a public-good argument is put forward to justify protection, that is, the agricultural sector not only provides foods but also public services like a pleasing and scenic countryside, environmental benefits and biodiversity. This justification is superficial and spurious because government support for these public goods can be made directly, without subsidizing agricultural production. Also, environmental degradation can be taxed or regulated at source. Another justification that is frequently given by the European Union is that withdrawal of agricultural support would lead to a dwindling of the agricultural sector, which is totally unfounded (as we shall see later in the chapter).

It is a widely acknowledged fact that trade in agriculture remained virtually outside the multilateral trade discipline. Developing economies are also known to maintain high average rates of tariffs on agriculture, higher than those in the industrial economies. This state of affairs did not change appreciably after the Uruguay Round Agreement on Agriculture (URAA), which is justly considered an important milestone in agricultural trade. The structure of protection in these economies was so high and non-transparent that it influences global trade in agriculture highly adversely. The developing economies, many of which have comparative advantage in trade in agricultural commodities and products as well as in agro-industrial products, were directly hurt by this kind of protectionism. Several African countries could potentially become successful exporters of groundnut and cotton, while Southeast Asian economies could become potentially significant exporters of rice. Members of the Cairns Group and India have shown serious interest in the export of wheat and dairy products, while several developing economies from Africa, Asia and Latin America have a potential to be strong exporters of sugar. Other impending export products from the developing economies are fruits and vegetables, cut flowers, fisheries and seafood, and wheat. Excessive protection did not allow these potential exports to materialize.

Protection of trade in agriculture *inter alia* 'compounds the losses associated with inefficient domestic policies' in the industrial economies (OECD, 2003a). Trade partners are forced to forgo the benefits that can potentially accrue from comparative advantage, which represents a shortsightedness of policy-makers. There is a gradual but growing recognition in the industrial economies regarding the need for fundamental reforms in their agricultural policies, including agricultural trade policies. They acknowledge that the twenty-first century calls for radical reforms in this policy area. The principles of reform were first profiled by the OECD ministers in 1987; acting on them and strengthening them is the need of the hour. The central idea in the reform principles is to eliminate or reduce those forms of agricultural support that distort international markets. Policy-makers do realize that at this point in time they need to examine afresh why agriculture in the OECD economies requires protection. Is there a logical explanation at all? Notwithstanding the existence of goodwill and sound and sagacious ideas, tangible progress in this direction has so far been modest. Although reforms have been attempted, they were not only inadequate but significant differences existed in the pace of reforms between countries. Before the launch of the Doha Round of MTNs, many developing economies thought that this was the opportune moment to give an impetus to liberalization of trade in agriculture and reduce distortions.

A distorted and non-transparent trade regime

Many of the protectionist measures used in agricultural trade are complex, non-linear and difficult to calculate, even comprehend. Average non-agricultural tariffs worldwide are 4 per cent, while average agricultural tariffs in the industrial economies are 45 per cent. Besides, 28 per cent of the agricultural imports in the OECD economies are protected by tariff-rate quotas (TRQs), which are two-tier tariffs formulated and adopted at the end of the Uruguay Round as an instrument for providing greater market access in the industrial economies' markets having high tariffs and NTBs. In the TRQ system, an import quota is first determined, and then one tariff rate is set for imports inside the quota, and another for those outside of it. A limited volume of imports is allowed at the lower tariff inside the predetermined quota, and all subsequent imports are charged at much higher rates. If the demand for imports at the low tariff is greater than the volume allowed by the TRQ, then imports are rationed. Of the many rationing methods currently allowed by the WTO, some are more likely than others to bias trade in an unwarranted manner. TRQs cannot be easily converted into tariff equivalents.

Notwithstanding the adoption of the URAA, tariff barriers in agriculture remain extremely high even after the Uruguay Round. Recent estimates indicate that average agricultural tariffs are approximately six times as high as industrial tariffs (Gibson *et al.*, 2001). Although TRQs have replaced the NTBs in agriculture, out-of-quota tariff rates have remained prohibitive in numerous cases. When they are not prohibitive, they are exceedingly high. Also, in-quota tariff rates are frequently so high that the quotas cannot be fully utilized. Tariff rates of 50 per cent or higher exist for 60 tariff lines in Canada, 71 tariff lines in the European Union, 14 in Japan and 8 in the United States (McCulloch, Winters and Cirera, 2001). In addition, specific tariffs are rampant in agriculture trade. They are also regarded as non-transparent and more distortional than *ad valorem* tariffs. Until the present period, over 40 per cent of the tariff lines in agriculture in the EU and the USA have contained specific duties. Many of these tariff lines change with product prices and seasons, rendering it difficult to estimate the average rate of tariffs because prices keep varying constantly. This tendency obscures the real level of protection in the importing economies.

Exports of sugar from the developing economies face tariff rates of 129 per cent or above in the USA and 162 per cent or above in the EU. The agriculture sector is also well-known for tariff peaks, which are sometimes as high as 500 per cent against agricultural exports from the developing economies. Furthermore, tariff escalation impedes exports of processed foods and agro-industrial products in the EU and in US markets. Tariff escalation also affects exports of processed tropical products, obstructing exports of high value-added farm products from the tropical countries. There are various schemes of preferential trade which facilitate market access for the logarithm of income developing economies, but they fail to compensate for the continued high levels of protection. In the USA, merely 34 per cent of the agricultural exports from the developing economies come under the generalized system of preferences (GSP) and only 26 per cent of these imports benefited from the GSP.[6]

Long-enduring export subsidies is another instrument of acute distortion of agricultural trade in several agricultural commodities. The EU has had a long tradition of heavily subsidizing its agricultural exports, which frequently results in depression of world market prices. Over the 1995–98 period, global agricultural subsidies amounted to $27 billion per annum, and the EU was the source of over 90 per cent of these subsidies (Elbehri and Leetma, 2002). Price distortions created by export subsidies prevent economies having comparative advantage from exporting their products. Their exports are rendered less competitive by the subsidized products in the world marketplace. To be sure, importers reap short-term benefits due to lower prices, but this leaves detrimental long-term effects on the agricultural sectors of both the importing and exporting economies.

A highly protected agricultural sector weighs heavily on the budget of the protecting country, and leads to a high cost to both taxpayers and consumers. In the OECD economies, subsidies provided from the budget and transfers from consumers created by high tariffs were $250 billion per annum during 1999–2001. This was in spite of a decline in protection from 62 per cent of farm revenue during 1986–88 to 49 per cent in 1999–2001. In 2002, the level of financial support provided to OECD farmers was close to $220 billion, which represented 31 per cent of the total farm revenue in this country group. Output-based support and input subsidies accounted for 76 per cent of total support to farmers in 2002. The cost of farm support measured in terms of proportion of percentage of GDP is also high. For the EU economies and Japan it was 1.4 per cent of GDP in 2001, and for Switzerland it was 1.9 per cent. For the USA and Canada it was comparatively lower at 0.9 per cent and 0.8 per cent, respectively (OECD, 2002).

As specified below, the larger part of the cost of current support to agriculture is met by consumers by paying higher prices associated with border protection, and the balance comes from budgetary resources in the form of direct subsidies. Owing to various subsidies and supports, prices received by farmers in the OECD countries are 31 per cent higher than world market prices. Conversely, in the developing economies tariffs are often the only instrument of protection and farm price support.

While the incidence of cost of agricultural support falls on taxpayers and consumers, the distribution of benefits is paradoxically regressive. It is instructive to identify the groups that benefit most from agricultural support in the OECD economies. First, the poor in the economies that support their agriculture spend a far greater proportion of their income on food than do the rich. Second, the smaller farmers receive a disproportionately smaller proportion of farm subsidies. According to OECD (2003b) data, the largest 25 per cent of EU farmers receive 75 per cent of the farm support. Third, in at least three EU economies (France, Denmark and the Netherlands) the average income of farm households is significantly – 50 per cent or more – higher than the average income of non-farm households. Similarly, farm households earn more in Australia, Belgium, Finland, Japan and the USA also.

A hierarchy has gradually emerged among the economies that protect their trade in agriculture. The OECD countries that provide the largest support to their farm sector, measured as a percentage of GDP, are Korea, Japan, Norway, the EU, Hungary, Poland, the Czech Republic and Switzerland. A large proportion of this support is provided as subsidies, and their agricultural trade regimes are highly protectionist. The second tier comprises the USA, Canada, Turkey and Mexico. This group is considered to be middle of the road in this regard. At the opposite extreme are Australia and New Zealand, which are the only two OECD countries that have achieved substantive agricultural reforms, with New Zealand liberalizing far more than Australia.[7] They deserve their reputation as free traders in the world agricultural markets. These two Asia-Pacific economies provide a gleaming example of how reforms can make agriculture a dynamic and efficient sector, a situation that does not exist in several West European economies.

If the objective of subsidizing and supporting the agricultural sector is to provide assistance to low-income agricultural households in the industrial countries, more appropriate policy instruments are needed to meet the objective. The appropriate policy measures would be to, first, define the poor agricultural households, and second to channel benefits to them directly rather than provide blanket support to the entire agricultural sector, which includes a significant proportion of large and wealthy farmers. If income support to a targeted group of farm households is the objective, present policies in the industrial economies are inefficient. Turning to the developing economies, they also must eliminate their trade barriers and integrate with global agricultural markets. They can achieve this objective in a WTO-consistent phased manner, and the ultimate consequence would be the creation of much vaunted free agricultural markets.

Measuring OECD financial support

Estimates of agricultural support and subsidies have been provided in the preceding section. However, their quantitative dimensions have become controversial, and precise estimates of how much money is transferred to farmers in the industrial economies by way of agriculture policies has become a contentious issue, with differing claims made by different organizations.[8] Tangermann (2004) delved into this issue to bring order and precision to it. He found that the principal channels of support to farmers in the OECD countries consist of domestic price support provided behind tariff walls and through export subsidies, and in addition support by way of public expenditure going directly to them. Together these are called producer support estimates (PSE). The second, indirect, channel of support is in the form of general services support, which includes research and development (R&D), advisory systems and food inspection-related support. The third route for cash to flow to farmers is the associated budgetary support, called the General Services Support Estimate (GSSE). Other than these three large channels of support to farmers, in some countries governments also transfer finances to poor consumers through food subsidies. Together, the producer support, general services support and the taxpayer transfers to poorer consumers represent the OECD's Total Support Estimate (TSE). This became a standard indicator of financial support to the farm sector and has been published annually since the mid-1980s by the OECD secretariat.

In 2002, the TSE in OECD countries was over $318 billion. Of this, $55 billion was used for GSSE as outlined above. Another $28 billion of taxpayer money was channelled to poorer consumers, mainly through the food-stamp programme in the USA. But the lion's share was support going directly to farmers (under the PSE), which amounted to $235 billion, of which $148 billion came from high prices resulting from tariffs and export subsidies, and $87 billion was transferred by taxpayers through government payments to farmers. Thus viewed, the most affluent economies of the world are paying a high price for supporting the farm sector.

Total support – as against payments made by governments – needs to include all that goes to the farming communities. Out of the €107 billion producer support going to EU farmers in 2002, €61 billion came from consumers' pockets to pay for the high prices caused by tariff protection and export subsidies, and €46 billion from tax transfers. In the USA, total support to farmers was $40 billion, of which $15 billion came from consumers and $25 billion from taxpayers. In Japan, farm support amounted to ¥5,500 billion, of which ¥5,000 billion originated from consumers and ¥500 billion from taxpayers.

Agricultural policy-related farm support may go to farmers in different forms, but its net result is the same. That is why the OECD's producer support estimate adds up both parts of government payment to farmers, often referred to as 'subsidies', and farm support provided through high prices. For example, in the USA, support to wheat farmers comes through a government payment per tonne of wheat produced, which raises the price farmers receive without raising the price paid by consumers. In contrast, Japan applies import tariffs which raise the price paid by consumers and received by farmers. In both cases, the net result is that farmers receive higher prices than the market would generate. A given price increase, whether it is through a government payment or a tariff, has exactly the same effect on domestic production, trade and farm income.

However, not all forms of government expenditure are as distorting. For instance, some countries now make fixed payments to farmers, irrespective of what they produce. These payments result in less expansion of production than payments per tonne of wheat or milk produced. It is important to understand the difference between policies that primarily distort markets and policies that interfere less with market forces, while also offering a better chance of achieving other important policy objectives in an effective way. The problem in 30 OECD countries has been that three-quarters of total support still goes through the most market-distorting policies, such as price support and payments per unit of production. Some progress has been made in reducing market-distorting and inefficient support, both in the EU and elsewhere, but it is far too slow (Tangermann, 2004).

One recent development is that in the industrial economies direct subsidies have been delinked in a small way from the level of production, which reduced incentives to overproduce. The decoupling of direct subsidies has been on the rise. They declined by 9 per cent during 1996–98, and further by 20 per cent during 1999–2001.[9] This picture of decoupling is only partially correct because some crops, such as cotton, are kept outside this classification, although they are highly subsidized. Cotton prices in the EU and the USA are the same and are less than half the cost of production.

Long-standing irrational French antagonism

It is well-acknowledged that France has had a long-term antagonism to multilateral liberalization of agricultural trade. Since the early 1980s, France took the most inflexible and illogical stand on reform of the Common Agricultural Policy (CAP) and multilateral agricultural trade.[10] One of the two reasons for the failure of the GATT Ministerial Conference of 1982 was the French adamant refusal to have trade in agriculture on the agenda in any form. It repeatedly succeeded in either scuttling or foiling attempts of other WTO members to liberalize multilateral agricultural trade, and whenever the EU proposed even limited reforms of the CAP, France either successfully blocked them or tried to dilute them (see Chapter 3). In an attempt to provide an impetus to agricultural negotiations in the Doha Round, the EU announced weak and disappointing reforms of the CAP in June 2003.[11] France played a decisive role in the formulation of these reform proposals and succeeded in keeping them as limited as it possibly could.

The highly protected French agricultural sector produces approximately 120 per cent of domestic consumption. Grain production is 200 per cent of domestic consumption, while sugar production is 130 per cent. Using an applied general equilibrium model of the global economy known as Global Trade Analysis Project (GTAP) version 5.2 database, Francois, van Meijl and van Tongeren (2003) estimated the impact of liberalization of the agricultural sector in France under the sponsorship of the Doha Round. The GTAP is an applied general equilibrium model of the global economy.[12] They concluded that the overall impact for France and the EU would be favourable. Elimination of domestic support measures would be the largest source of gains for France. In the short term they would result in annual gains ranging from €2.6 billion to €4.1 billion. In the long term this range would expand to €8.1 billion to €15.5 billion annually. Despite these strong possibilities of gains to the French economy, France's opposition to market-access reforms under the Doha Round has continued unabated.

During the formation of the framework agreement during the last week of July 2004, the EU agreed to substantive reforms in its agricultural policy, which was expected to underpin multilateral trade in agriculture. However, these concessions were made in the face of stiff resistance from France, which eventually managed to harden the EU's line and subordinate elimination to the CAP reform timetable. In practice this means that the removal of export subsides will not take place before the end of the current period of CAP reforms which will end in 2013.[13]

The Uruguay Round agreement on agriculture

The URAA prohibited quantitative restrictions (QRs) and other NTBs,[14] and signatory countries also agreed to convert existing QRs and NTBs into TRQs first and then reduce those tariffs. This was considered a feasible and acceptable mode of taming high tariff rates in agricultural trade. Member nations that had bans and quotas in place at the time of signing the URAA were allowed to adopt TRQs as a transitional instrument, with the intent that all TRQs would be eventually transformed into tariffs, which are simple to comprehend and easy to deal with in a trade liberalization endeavour. Under the URAA, OECD countries were obliged to provide a minimum level of market access in products that were previously protected by stringent QRs and NTBs.

To be sure, the URAA represents a turning point in the way agriculture was treated under the multilateral trade regime. It established the first-ever framework for a long-overdue transformation in the agricultural trade regime. Bringing trade in agriculture under multilateral discipline is considered a momentous achievement of the Uruguay Round. The URAA attempted to create a tariff-based regime to improve market access to the industrial economies, which became known as the 'tariffication' process, leading most industrial economies to bind their agricultural tariffs. However, the paradox was that while the objective of tarrification was to improve market access, the industrial economies bound their tariffs at excessively and unjustifiably high levels. That is, they did go through the tariffication process, but made sure that market access was not improved, or not improved meaningfully. While the current average for the OECD is 60 per cent, tariff peaks of 200 per cent are commonly found in most OECD countries. It was pointed out earlier that *vis-à-vis* some agricultural exports from developing economies, tariff peaks as high as 500 per cent existed.

Under the URAA, signatory countries also agreed in principle to substantially reduce agricultural support and protection in important areas like barriers to market access, reduction of export subsidies as well as reductions in trade-distorting domestic support. The arbitrariness and unpredictability in trade in agricultural products was further reduced, first, by the Agreement on the Application of Sanitary and Phytosanitary (SPS) measures, which established rules to prevent countries from using unjustifiable health and environmental regulations as disguised barriers to trade in agricultural products. The Technical Barriers to Trade (TBT) Agreement was another step in the same direction. It covered legally binding technical requirements relating to SPS measures, such as product-content requirements, processing methods and packaging.

Dirty tariffication and the illusory decline in agricultural support

There is a flip-side of this coin. Although a watershed agreement, the URAA did not succeed in influencing high levels of subsidies, agricultural support and protection in any manner. Indubitably some progress was made in global agriculture and trade-policy reforms, but the measures remained fragile and failed to liberalize agriculture trade. Domestic policy reforms and trade liberalization were difficult to achieve both in the industrial and developing economies, and the Doha Ministerial Declaration reflected a widespread dissatisfaction of the developing economies with the URAA. Many agreements under the URAA remained agreements in principle and were never practised. Asymmetries in the implementation of the URAA were *inter alia* the consequence of industrial economies 'adopting a more adroit interpretation of the rules and thereby limiting the impact of their commitments' (Brooks *et al.*, 2004). The first source of asymmetries in the implementation of the URAA between the industrial and developing countries was the fact that industrial countries provided far more support to their farm sectors than did the developing countries, and the URAA institutionalized this imbalance through adoption of the TRQ system. The second asymmetry occurred through the modest impact of the URAA on the policies of industrial countries, which was further diluted by 'skillful manipulation of the interpretation of the implementation criteria'. For instance, the carrying over of unused export subsidy allowances from one year to the next, and use of disaggregated product classifications to limit tariff reductions on sensitive products to the minimum, while still reducing 'average' tariffs by the minimum required amount (Brooks *et al.*, 2004).

Export subsidies, both explicit and implicit, are widely considered the most detrimental of all trade policy instruments. These subsidies blighted the exporting capabilities of those developing economies that could compete in world markets in several agricultural products, as set out earlier in this chapter. The Uruguay Round did lead to reduction commitments on export subsidies, and reduction or removal in export subsidies was expected to produce widespread net benefits to this set of developing economies. Export subsidies often led to an unhealthy competition among subsidy-providing economies, much to the detriment of those exporters that do not receive any such subsidies. The latter group was unsuccessful at exporting, despite having a strong comparative advantage in the products in question. These subsidies were frequently resorted to when world market prices were low, thus tending to exacerbate price volatility in trade in agricultural products. While they were helpful for some importing developing economies by lowering their import bill, they had crippling effects over world markets. The URAA commitments to lower export subsidies were not kept by the industrial economies and they continued to distort world markets to the hilt. During 1995–97, they declined for some commodities because this was a period of steep world market prices, but in general they recorded a rise.

During the Uruguay Round, reduction commitments were also obtained on domestic support, and these commitments were honoured by most industrial countries. They applied to aggregate domestic support, and therefore even after meeting the aggregate decline objective, countries were able to maintain high levels of domestic support for sensitive commodities. A shift towards greater decoupling in OECD economies would surely limit distortions in the world markets.

What came to transpire was not surprising because at the end of the Uruguay Round the CPs were aware of the possibility of a limited pay-off from the URAA. Since the beginning, it was clear to any observer that the tariffs at rates that were being set in the TRQ arrangement were higher than the NTBs they replaced. Another indication of this awareness was that the WTO members who were being asked to reduce or eliminate protectionist measures under the URAA, deliberately overestimated the level of agricultural protection for 1986–88, which was the reference period.[15] The objective of overestimating was that they could continue with virtually the same level of protection between 1995 and 2001, when the transition period for the URAA expired (OECD, 2002; Messerlin, 2003).

This made the tariffication exercise dirty. The TRQs which were accepted as a transitional instrument and were expected to contribute to transparency of the protectionist regime, and thereby arouse public opinion in favour of liberalization, failed to work as intended. Another reason for the loss of transparency was that during the closing days of the Uruguay Round the negotiators developed negotiation fatigue and allowed a significant amount of specific tariffs under the URAA. Specific tariffs are much less transparent than *ad valorem* tariffs, and therefore as already noted, over 40 per cent of the EU and US agricultural tariffs lines are still specific. What was worse was that their protectionist impact worsened with a fall in world prices of agricultural products. They frequently declined in the post-1997 period.

The persistence of high tariff regimes after the Uruguay Round

Although non-tariff barriers were transformed into TRQs during the Uruguay Round, tariffs on agricultural exports managed to remain much higher than those on manufactured goods. This applies to both developing and industrial economies. In 2000, the average tariff rate on manufactured goods imports in the industrial economies was 1.5 per cent if they originated from the other industrial economies, but 11.5 per cent if they originated from the developing economies. Similarly, for agricultural imports the average tariff rate in the industrial economies was 15.6 per cent if they originated in the other industrial economies and 21.1 per cent if they originated in the developing economies (Hertel *et al.*, 2000). As computed by WB (2004), average most-favoured-nation (MFN) tariffs in the Quad economies in 2001 on agricultural products were 10.7 per cent, while on manufactured good they were 4.0 per cent. In the large middle-income countries (like Brazil, China, India and Korea), average tariffs on agricultural products were 26.6 per cent and those on manufactured products 13.1 per cent. In smaller middle-income developing countries (like Bulgaria, Costa Rica, Hungary and Jordan) the former figure was 35.4 per cent, while the latter figure was 12.7 per cent.[16] Tariff rates in the developing economies are much higher than those in the industrial economies. For instance, Morocco (64 per cent) and Korea (42 per cent) had the highest rates, while Indonesia (8.5 per cent) and Malaysia (2.8 per cent) were at the other extreme. These tariff rates, for various technical reasons, are underestimates.

A high dispersion in tariff rates has continued to be another problematic issue; that is, as already noted, tariff peaks were found to be frequent and high. On average, tariffs are lower in the industrial economies than in the developing economies, but tariff peaks abound in the former, and represent sector- and industry-specific protection. The highest tariff peak is as high as 506 per cent in the EU and 306 per cent in the USA. Tariff peaks are infrequent in the developing economies, although Korea is an exception in this regard, having tariff peaks as high as 1,000 per cent. Reforms of agriculture trade policies in the OECD economies are acknowledged to be slow, but as opposed to this, developing economies made significant improvements during the 1990s. Their average agricultural tariffs came down from 30 per cent in 1990 to 18 per cent in 2000. They also followed complementary policies like the elimination of QRs and licensing systems.[17]

Implementation of the URAA and its impact

Although the OECD (2002) statistics showed that the share of total agricultural support measured as a proportion of GDP in the OECD countries impressively declined between the reference period (1986–88) and the late 1990s, this decline in agricultural support did not represent success of the URAA. Instead it reflected the decline in the proportion of agricultural value-added in the GDP during the period under consideration. The real decline in the proportion of agricultural support to gross value-added was very small, from 75.9 per cent to 61.9 per cent during the period under consideration. However, this level of support is still high. According to Messerlin's (2003) calculations, the average support per farmer in the OECD economies increased from 1995, albeit public opinion in the OECD economies paradoxically holds that the URAA has substantially liberalized the agricultural sector. Trade officials, local politicians and the anti-globalization lobby are the principal purveyors and propagators of this fabrication. Empirical analysis by Diakosavvas (2001) also concluded that the contribution of the URAA was inconsequential to agricultural trade practices as well as support in the OECD economies.

However, Australia and New Zealand are two conspicuous exceptions to this general observation regarding a limited decline in agricultural support. Their agricultural support has been reduced dramatically over the reference period (1986–88) and during the late 1990s. In New Zealand, support to agricultural value-added declined by four-fifths and in Australia by one-third. These declines led to a growth in the share of agriculture in GDP in New Zealand. In Australia, declining agricultural support caused a much smaller decline in the share of agriculture in

GDP compared to the decline recorded in the protectionist OECD economies (Messerlin, 2003).

To examine the impact of the URAA, a study was conducted by the Food and Agricultural Organization (FAO, 2002) entailing 23 country case studies which included the various categories of economies; that is, least developed countries (LDCs), net food importers and exporters of agricultural products. To be sure, assessing the impact of the URAA faced methodological problems; simulation modelling using country models and cross-sectional statistical analyses to examine the average relationship between trade liberalization and agricultural production are some of the commonest approaches. Since the FAO (2002) project was based on country case studies, issues could be examined in their specific disaggregated context, allowing detailed analysis not possible with either the simulation modelling or statistical approaches.

The FAO case studies indicated that with advancing globalization and the changing global economic environment, an increasing number of developing economies have been rationally endeavouring to integrate into the global economy and are, *inter alia*, trying to access global markets in agricultural and agro-industrial products in which they have comparative advantage. They are aware of the benefits of integration with the global economy. Gains from trade in agriculture cannot materialize if trade barriers and distortions continue to inhibit trade and restrict the growth of their agricultural sectors. For instance, the Egyptian case study showed that with improved market access Egypt would adopt a strategy of allocating an increasing amount of productive resources to high-value horticultural crops in which it has comparative advantage. However, limits on market access in the EU economies forced Egypt to a less efficient use of its agricultural resources. The EU is the principal market for Egypt, and the highly protected agricultural sector in the EU is a disincentive for Egypt to bring in structural changes in its agricultural sector in the foreseeable future. During the Uruguay Round, tariff escalation was somewhat reduced in the agricultural sector, but thereafter tariff escalation has continued to be a deterrent to making large investments in the high value-added food processing sector in the developing economies. Besides, these case studies also confirmed the presence and detrimental effect of tariff peaks, which continued to abound even after the URAA. The SPS measures adopted by the developing exporting economies were not readily recognized by importing industrial economies. These case studies proved that the URAA did not deliver the liberalization dynamics intended (Messerlin, 2003). Due to their experiences during the Uruguay Round and with the implementation of the URAA, most developing economies remained sceptical about benefits from future negotiations on agriculture (Lindland, 1997; Mathews, 2002). Therefore, at the time of the launch of the Doha Round, the developing economies were largely unconvinced and disenchanted about the value of any future negotiations on agriculture.

Agriculture negotiations in the Doha Round

The Doha Ministerial Communication pragmatically recognized that appropriate trade policies for developing and industrial economies differ substantially, and trade ministers participating in the Doha Ministerial Conference expected that any future trade agreement should take full account of this fact. Agriculture is a make-or-break issue of the Doha Round of MTNs. Paragraphs 13 and 14 of the Doha Ministerial declaration reconfirm the long-term objective already agreed in the present WTO Agreement, that is to establish a fair and market-oriented multilateral trading system through a programme of fundamental reform of agricultural trade (WTO, 2001). This ambitious objective clearly laid down what was expected of the OECD economies. It encompassed strengthened WTO rules and specific commitments on elimination of domestic support to agriculture by governments. It aimed for an end of protection for agriculture. The ultimate purpose was to correct and prevent the myriad restrictions and countless distortions in world agricultural markets. During the Doha Round, 'without prejudging the outcome', the member governments committed themselves to comprehensive negotiations aimed at

1 substantial reductions in barriers to market access;
2 reductions of exports subsidies with a view to phasing them out; and
3 substantial reductions in domestic support that distorts trade.

These three became the principal areas of negotiation, and are also referred to as the three 'pillars' of negotiations in trade in agriculture. Special treatment for the developing economies and LDCs is considered an element of all the three areas, and it needs to be recalled that these three pillars are not a novel invention of the Doha Round. As pointed out earlier the member countries had agreed to deal with these issues in principle during the Uruguay Round as well.

An innovation of the Doha Ministerial was that it made special and differential treatment (SDT) for developing countries integral throughout the negotiations. SDT applies to both new commitments made by the member economies, and to any relevant new or revised rules and disciplines initiated during the Doha Round. The SDT requires that the outcome of negotiations should be effective in practice and should enable developing countries, in particular the LDCs, to meet their needs. Their food security and rural development has to be paid extra attention during the negotiations. Without achieving this, the Doha Round cannot be regarded as a successful 'development round'. Ministers also took note of the non-trade concerns such as environmental protection, food security, rural development and so on. These were reflected in the negotiating proposals submitted by members. The participating ministers confirmed that the negotiations would take these into account, as provided for in the URAA (WTO, 2001).

Under the mandate of Article XX of the URAA, negotiations in agriculture began in early 2000 and culminated at the end of March 2001. This was called the first phase of negotiations on agriculture. The interest of members was high, and 126 members out of a total of 142 submitted 45 proposals and three technical documents. In addition, six negotiating meetings, called 'Special Sessions' were also held during the first phase. During the Doha Ministerial Conference, in November 2001, the agriculture negotiations were treated as a part of the Single Undertaking. The second phase in negotiations began in March 2002. As opposed to the first phase, meetings held during the second phase were informal, and their records of proceedings were treated as a summary report by the chairperson.

Member countries submitted proposals containing the starting positions of their negotiations during the first phase, and these proposals spanned all the principal areas of agriculture negotiations. Proposals submitted by the EU, the USA, Japan, Mauritius[18] and Switzerland were comprehensive and in-depth, submitted after thoroughly researching the issues in question. Some proposals were area-specific; for instance, each member of the Cairn Group submitted a proposal dealing with a different sub-area in Agriculture trade. Each of these proposals was discussed by the participating members.

The second phase – also called the 'modalities' phase – was of critical importance. It was visualized that members would finalize formulae and other modalities or numerical targets for country commitments by March 2003, and their draft commitments by September 2003, before the Fifth Ministerial Conference began in Cancún. The deliberations during this phase were issue-specific and included technical details. These discussions allowed members to develop specific proposals and eventually reach a consensus agreement on changes in the rules and commitments in agriculture. Their objectives included the three pillars of negotiations in trade in agriculture, and during this phase rules were also to be agreed for determining the future shape of negotiations. The modalities were to be used for producing the first offers or the 'comprehensive draft commitments'. All this was to be completed before the Fifth Ministerial Conference. The initial three meetings covered TRQ administration, tariffs, domestic support in keeping with the concept of the three 'boxes',[19] export subsidies, export credits, state trading enterprises, export taxes, food security, food safety, rural development and the special agricultural safeguards.

The complete lack of progress before the Cancún Ministerial

The Chairman of the Special Session on Agriculture circulated a draft text on modalities on 12 February 2003 among the WTO members. His draft was made with a view to create a consensus and therefore took a middle of the road stand on issues. It was hoped that such a draft would make a consensus feasible. In the mini-ministerial meeting in Tokyo during the same month, members commented on that draft. Their reaction was negative and the draft failed to win their support, let alone reach a consensus. Members did not even agree on the status of the draft, finally agreeing to call it a 'catalyst'. Despite rejection, a second draft submitted by the chairman the next month made few significant improvements before recirculation.

During the next mini-ministerial during 28–30 July 2003 in Montreal, the EU displayed some signs of flexibility. In its new offer it proposed to increase cuts in trade-distorting farm support marginally and some willingness to eliminate farm subsidies. This mini-ministerial was also lacklustre and failed to enthuse members to move in any reasonable direction, and consequently the impasse continued.

What was visualized in the second or 'modalities' phase did not come to pass; deliberations on all the three pillars of negotiations continued with no new breakthroughs. Delegations merely repeated their 'maximum positions', and in addition most proposals lacked specificity as well as precision. Members demonstrated no sign of movement towards a common ground and the impasse persisted. Political commitment and direction from member governments was completely absent from the negotiations, and deadlines after deadlines were missed. However, before the Fifth Ministerial, concerned members began to shed their entrenched positions and move towards a common ground.

The first overtures towards a compromise were made possible by a 'joint text' negotiated by the two major trading powers, the EU and the USA, in August 2003. They belatedly showed leadership and chose to work on a 'framework' of key issues instead of 'modalities', and a compromise draft was ready in mid-August as an unofficial document. This approach proposed a blended formula for tariff reduction. However, the 'joint text' had numerous gaps and was imprecise in its proposals. Both leaders had left out numbers, percentages and coefficients for tariff reduction. In addition, there was no mention of special treatment for the developing countries and LDCs because they thought that it would be appropriate for these two country groups to do so. In addition, there was no mention of special treatment for the developing economies and LDCs because it was believed that these two country groups would present their own cases. Their reaction was to present alternative drafts and soon six more drafts were circulated. The sources of these alternative drafts were the Group-of-Twenty-One (G-21)[20] countries, four Central American economies, Japan, a European–East Asian grouping (of Korea and Switzerland), Norway and Kenya. No consensus on these drafts emerged. They were followed by the submission of five more drafts during the Fifth Ministerial Conference.[21] Four African cotton-producing countries launched a Sectoral Initiative on Cotton, and asked for the removal of all cotton subsidies. They also demanded financial compensation while subsidies were being removed.

A revised draft of the framework text on agriculture was prepared by the WTO secretariat and submitted to the members during the Fifth Ministerial Conference on 13 September. It was officially christened the Luis Ernesto Derbez text after the Mexican Foreign Minister who chaired the Cancún Conference (see Chapter 3). This revised draft addressed the concerns of all principal negotiating groups, but next day the negotiations broke down because of, *inter alia*, the industrial countries' emphasis on the Singapore issues. Ironically, at this point some agreement among members had begun to develop regarding the Derbez text (WTO, 2003c).

An emerging 'framework' deal: post-Cancún developments

In countries that heavily protect their agriculture sector as well as in the middle-of-the-roaders, there is a certain public opinion towards protecting the agriculture sector and policy-makers are generally predisposed to that. This will take time to change, but what can be achieved during the Doha Round of MTNs should be realistically attempted and assessed. Given the history of intransigence on this issue, one way to negotiate could be to deal with the lightly protected areas first, where progress can be made relatively faster and some results can be obtained at an earlier stage of negotiations.

This is called the early harvest approach. Messerlin (2001) considered this approach 'a trap', a short-cut, and unworthy because it is sure to magnify existing distortions in agricultural trade. Public opinion in these countries may be drawn to the fact that the manner in which the agricultural sector in these countries is protected is inefficient because of a low transfer efficiency of the transfer instruments. A mere 20–30 per cent of the transfers becomes part of farm income; the balance is dissipated into high prices of land and inputs. One possible manner of taming the high protection in the economies that heavily protect their agriculture and the middle-of-the-roaders is to change the instruments of agricultural protection in such a manner that the appropriate target groups can be directly benefited. This should result in a considerable decline in protection in the short term.

The failure in Cancún to reach agreement on a framework text on negotiating modalities in September 2003 is well-known and much debated among policy mandarins and academics (see Chapter 3). A meeting of the WTO General Council on 15 December 2003 also failed to provide any momentum to the moribund negotiations. However, the broad contours of a potential agreement began to emerge in early 2004, with a general consensus gradually emerging to build on the work done before and during the Fifth Ministerial Conference. The consensus was to tackle the 'framework' first, and then to address the 'modalities'. The framework deal is to set the general terms of detailed negotiations. Major participants had agreed to move in the context of a package that broadly resembled the text on the table when the Cancún ministerial had collapsed, namely, the Derbez text (WTO, 2003).

WTO members agreed to focus negotiations on reduction of the most trade-distorting – amber-box – domestic support measures. In addition, they agreed that the blue box first needed capping with a possible reduction commitment thereafter. Lastly, it was widely felt that reviewing the green-box criteria was necessary. A framework deal based on these basic contours was finalized in July 2004. The Derbez text had made meaningful proposals in this regard, which were available to the members for deliberations. One of them was of specific reductions in the first year of implementation of the total financial support under the amber-box, blue-box and *de minimis* ceilings. There was some discontentment among the G-21 group because they had pressed for stronger discipline under the blue-box support. They wanted it capped at 2.5 per cent of the value of farm production in the initial phase of implementation, and subsequently phased out using a linear phasing-out formula.

Members also agreed to the need of further clarifying the 'blended formula approach' to market-access commitments, which needed to be done with reference to the concerns of the developing economies. This approach was proposed in the joint text prepared by the EU and the USA. It divided tariff cuts into three categories. In the first, known as the Uruguay Round 'formula', weak cuts on a select number of high tariffs were made for sensitive products with an average and minimum reduction. It involved quota increases for these products. The second set of tariff cuts involved a more ambitious approach with reductions based on the 'Swiss formula', which meant deeper cuts on a broader category of less-sensitive products. The third part of the blended formula approach was trimming down some tariff lines to zero.

Members sought commitment to reductions or elimination of all forms of unfair export competition with the view that a 'commitment to the elimination of all forms of export subsidies is a must for these negotiations to be successful'. There was general acceptance of the concepts of 'Special Products' and the special safeguard mechanism for the developing countries. Furthermore, trade in cotton was to be assigned priority in negotiations. To this end, it was considered necessary to identify specific development support measures on cotton that might be implemented in a shorter timeframe than that likely for the multilateral trade negotiations as a whole (AITIC, 2004).

As the foregoing discussion shows, export subsidies have been an extremely problematic aspect of trade in agriculture, and therefore were assigned an important place in the negotiations. Success on this front would represent an enormous achievement for the Doha Round. To be sure, in 2004 export subsidies were less than what they were a decade ago when the Uruguay Round ended, but they still distort many commodity markets and are a source of unpredictability for producers. The Cairns Group, the G-21 and the USA, all made it known that they want export subsidies eliminated by an agreed date. Taking a flexible stance, this group has also made it known that they can live with a decision to eliminate *in principle*, with the precise schedule for elimination agreed later in the negotiations on modalities.

The issue of export subsidies relates to only one country group, the EU. There is no pressing need of these subsidies for the EU because of large-scale agricultural surpluses. According to the most recent WTO notification, the cost of EU export subsidies is currently in the vicinity of $2 billion – less than one-tenth of its total Common Agricultural Policy (CAP) subsidy costs.[22] These subsidies essentially go to dairy products, beef and sugar. Export subsidization of cereals and coarse grains is very low, much less than the Uruguay Round commitments of the EU. Indeed this may grow if the euro continues to remain strong *vis-à-vis* the dollar.[23]

Other products that are being, or have been, traded with export subsidies include wheat and wheat flour, pig meat, poultry, eggs, wine, fruit and vegetables, alcohol and rice. All the products that have been benefiting from export subsidies are of particular interest to the developing economies. It is likely that the EU could commit to eventual elimination of export subsidies – albeit over a long period for some products.

An agreement for establishing modalities

On 1 August 2004, a comprehensive framework for establishing negotiation modalities in agriculture was agreed among members. Its legal status is that of a non-binding agreement, and was made an Annex of the so-called July Package. This framework establishing modalities was essentially based on the URAA and has been reformed to establish a fair and market-oriented trading system. It is highly significant in that it would determine the future course of action in the Doha Round negotiations on agriculture. Its objective is to eventually achieve the Doha mandate. Objectives and partial modalities have been established in this agreement, and the basis for the negotiations of full modalities is to be taken up in the next phase of negotiations. As in the Doha Development Agenda (DDA), it was again agreed in the framework agreement that as agriculture is a critically important sector for the developing economies, the modalities to be developed would need to incorporate operationally effective provisions for SDT. Also, the developing economies must be able to pursue agricultural policies that are supportive of their development goals as well as poverty alleviation. The framework agreement clearly noted that the 'reforms in all three pillars form an interconnected whole and must be approached in a balanced and equitable manner' (WTO, 2004b).

West African concern over trade in cotton was specifically recognized by the General Council because cotton is regarded as a vitally important commodity for several developing countries, particularly LDCs. Within the framework of agricultural negotiations, this issue would be addressed without delay. The Special Session of the Committee on Agriculture would ensure appropriate prioritization of the cotton issue independently from other sectoral initiatives.

The framework agreement highlighted the fact that the Doha Ministerial Declaration called for 'substantial reductions in trade-distorting domestic support'. With a view to achieving these substantial reductions, the negotiations in this pillar would ensure the following:

- SDT for the developing economies and LDCs would remain an integral component of domestic support. For this group of economies, modalities to be developed would include longer implementation periods and lower reduction coefficients for all types of trade-distorting domestic support and continued access to the provisions.

- There will be a strong element of harmonization in the reductions in domestic support made by industrial country members. Also, it would be ensured that higher levels of permitted trade-distorting domestic support would be subject to deeper cuts.
- Each industrial country member is expected to make a substantial reduction in the overall level of its trade-distorting domestic support from bound levels.
- In addition, Final Bound Total 'aggregate measurement of support' (AMS)[24] and permitted *de minimis* levels will be subject to substantial reductions.

A tiered formula was adopted for reduction in the overall base level of all trade-distorting domestic support, as measured by the final bound total AMS plus the permitted *de minimis* level and the level agreed for blue-box payments. Under this formula, members having higher levels of trade-distorting domestic support need to make greater overall reductions in order to achieve a harmonizing result. As the first instalment of the overall cut, in the first year and throughout the implementation period, the sum of all trade-distorting support will not exceed 80 per cent of the sum of final bound total AMS plus permitted *de minimis* plus the blue box.

Reductions in *de minimis* are to be negotiated taking into account the principle of SDT. Accordingly, developing economies that allocate almost all *de minimis* support for subsistence and resource-poor farmers will be exempt. Again, if members choose to do so, they may make greater than formula reductions in order to achieve the required level of cuts in overall trade-distorting domestic support.

Members recognize the role of the blue box in promoting agricultural reforms, and for this reason Article 6.5 of the URAA is to be reviewed so that members may have recourse to the following measures: (1) direct payments under production-limiting programmes, or (2) direct payments that do not require production. Criteria to ensure that blue-box payments are less trade-distorting than AMS measures have been left open for negotiations. The blue box support must not exceed 5 per cent of a member's average total value of agricultural production during a historical period, which is to be established in the negotiations.

Green-box criteria would also be reviewed and clarified with a view to ensuring that such measures have no, or at most minimal, trade-distorting effects on agricultural production. Such a review and clarification would need to ensure that the basic concepts, principles and effectiveness of the green box remain and take due account of non-trade concerns. Obligations for monitoring and surveillance of all new disciplines are to be improved.

As the Doha Ministerial Declaration calls for 'reduction of, with a view to phasing out, all forms of export subsidies', WTO members have agreed to establish detailed modalities ensuring the parallel elimination of all forms of export subsidies and disciplines on all export measures with equivalent effect by a credible end date. It has been decided that the various types of export subsidies will be eliminated by the end date, which has not been agreed as yet.

The Doha Ministerial Declaration also calls for 'substantial improvements in market access'. Members also agreed that special and differential treatment for developing members would be an integral part of all elements in the negotiations. To ensure that a single approach adopted for industrial and developing country members meets all the objectives of the Doha mandate, tariff reductions would be made through a tiered formula that takes into account their different tariff structures.

To ensure that such a formula will lead to substantial trade expansion, the following principles will guide its further negotiation:

- Tariff reductions will be made from bound rates. Substantial overall tariff reductions will be achieved as a final result from negotiations.
- Each member (other than LDCs) will make a contribution. Operationally effective SDT for developing country members would be an integral part of all elements.
- Progressivity in tariff reductions will be achieved through deeper cuts in higher tariffs with flexibilities for sensitive products. Substantial improvements in market access will be achieved for all products.

The number of bands, the thresholds for defining the bands and the type of tariff reduction in each band were under negotiation. The role of a tariff cap in a tiered formula with distinct treatment for sensitive products would be further evaluated.[25]

The potential impact of multilateral liberalization in the Doha Round

It is widely agreed that there is an imperious and immediate need to create a simple, uncomplicated, transparent and, within the limits of feasibility, low-tariff trade regime in agricultural products. Future liberalization can be subsequently based on this regime. The Doha Round of MTNs offers an opportunity to consolidate the achievements of the Uruguay Round and strengthen trade reforms in the crucial areas referred to as the three pillars. The preceding section has presented the elaborate details of framework agreement in this regard.

Welfare gains from liberalization

Fairly long ago, Anderson (1994) had the prescience to posit that as an economy grows, industrializes and transforms into a high-income economy, it begins protecting its farm sector heavily. Korea is the best illustration of this penchant, which has maintained the highest degree of agricultural support among the OECD economies. In addition, the new OECD members (like Hungary, Poland, Mexico and Turkey) have recently recorded significantly rising rates of agricultural support. This buttresses Anderson's view of the existence of dynamic forces that support heavy protection of the agricultural sector with rising per capita GDP. This trend needs to be cautiously watched during the Doha Round of MTNs.

Due to high trade barriers and a distorted trade regime, agricultural and commodity markets are at present thin, and trade volumes are small. Also, there are only, a small number of agents in the market, and consequently there is a high variability in trade flows and volatility in prices. There are two policy-related reasons behind the lack of market depth. First, large trade distortions reduce trade flows, force world market prices downwards and discourage market entry. Second, export subsidies are the other reason having the same impact over the market. They impede trade flows and discourage market entry by encouraging surplus production by non-competitive producers. Export subsidies seriously stifle comparative advantage in trade in agriculture and agro-industrial products. Liberalization in agricultural trade would induce increased prices in world markets, calculated to rise 10–20 per cent for cotton, 15–20 per cent for groundnut, 20–40 per cent for sugar and dairy products and up to 90 per cent in rice markets (Beghin and Aksoy, 2003). Liberalization would also induce a shift in production from the industrial economies to the developing economies in a small way. To benefit from liberalization in trade, developing economies will need to deal with their supply-side bottlenecks. Their exports can be constrained by a weak farm credit support, poor financial and physical infrastructure, inadequate port facilities and a lack of export financing. Developing economies commonly suffer from these limitations.

Welfare gains from liberalization of trade in agriculture have been estimated to be significantly higher than those from the liberalization of trade in manufacture. Recent World Bank (2002) estimates show that the former would produce welfare gains of $248 billion, compared to $111 billion from the liberalization of trade in manufactures. This is despite the fact that multilateral trade in agriculture is only a small part of that in manufacture as noted earlier in this chapter. This is due to the fact that, as seen in the foregoing analysis, an exceedingly high level of protection exists in this sector of multilateral trade in the high-income industrial economies. A GTAP-based empirical study on the potential gains from the Doha Round was conducted by Anderson *et al.* (2001) which quantified welfare gains from the Doha Round. This exercise took as its base period the time when all the recommendations of the Uruguay Round are implemented. It concluded that of all the economic gains to be had in 2005 from removing trade barriers, almost half (48 per cent) would come from reforms in one single area, namely in the agriculture trade regime of the OECD economies. The second area that would produce significant welfare gains was the reforms in the agricultural policies of the developing economies.[26] These results have enormous significance for the public policy-making community (Anderson, 2004).

Another comprehensive empirical exercise by Beghin *et al.* (2003), based on computable general equilibrium (CGE) modelling, broadly inferred that real commitments to reduce agricultural support of all the different kinds in the industrial economies will induce substantial changes in world food prices, domestic agricultural rates of return and output, and dramatic shifts in agricultural trade patterns. Total trade will expand and real output, wages and incomes in developing countries, especially among the rural poor, would increase substantially. In particular, rural incomes in low- and middle-income countries would increase by over $60 billion per annum, a figure that comfortably exceeds even the most ambitious goals for increased development assistance. It may also result in substantial savings to OECD taxpayers, since the OECD economies are the principal donors of official development assistance. At the same time, the EU and Japanese agricultural exports would fall sharply and, *pari passu*, their imports would rise. Other OECD countries would see a more balanced aggregate trade growth, although a number of strategic sectors would be adversely affected.

Van der Mensbrugghe and Beghin (2004) used a global LINKAGE model to assess the impact of agricultural policy reforms. This model is based on a standard neoclassical general equilibrium model with firms maximizing profits in competitive markets and consumers maximizing consumption under budget constraints. The LINKAGE model is a dynamic one, with a scenario spanning 1997 to 2015. It computed global gains of $385 billion from agricultural trade reforms, divided roughly evenly between the developing and industrial economies, albeit the developing countries gained significantly more as a share of initial income. The Cairns Group countries and the USA were found to gain substantially from agricultural trade reforms.

Welfare gains for the low-income developing economies

That the proportion of the global population of the absolute poor first soared over the nineteenth and twentieth centuries and then began a decline from the late 1970s has been discussed in Chapter 4. It has been noted in the preceding section that if all the trade barriers are removed that have persisted since the implementation of the recommendations of the Uruguay Round, 48 per cent of all welfare benefits to the global economy will come from the reforms of policies in the areas of agricultural products and processed-food-related industries in the OECD economies. An additional 17 per cent of welfare gains will originate from the same set of industries in the developing economies. In addition, these reforms would underpin agricultural trade between developing economies. Agricultural trade between developing economies has been rising; its proportion has grown from 28 per cent in 1980 to 37 per cent in 2001 (Anderson *et al.*, 2001 and Anderson, 2004).

Beghin *et al.* (2003) and Anderson (2004) estimated that full liberalization of the OECD farm policies – whenever it takes place – would result in a 50 per cent increase in global agricultural trade. This would accompany a price rise of 5 per cent in agricultural products according to Anderson (2004) and a trifle higher, around 7 per cent, according to Beghin *et al.* (2003). As the developing economies are a heterogeneous group, the impact of liberalization in the Doha Round would vary a great deal from country to country. The low-income developing economies and LDCs that are net food importers would suffer from an adverse terms-of-trade effect. However, this effect would be small because such reforms are generally phased in gradually, and it would only be felt weakly by a few net food-importing developing economies. The sub-Saharan economies benefit twice as much in terms of aggregate welfare gains from participating in agricultural trade liberalization under the aegis of the Doha Round than from not liberalizing their agricultural policies (Anderson and Yao, 2003).

The adverse terms-of-trade effect might be small, but some of the low-income developing economies and the LDCs that are net food importers have been concerned. They consider that liberalization on the lines of the three pillars in the OECD economies, as suggested by the July Package or the framework agreement, may make their food import bill unaffordable. However, withdrawal of farm support in the OECD economies need not mean a necessary loss to this group of developing economies, since many of them are close to self-sufficiency in food. When international prices rise, these economies may try to become self-sufficient sooner. It is also possible that these economies may attempt to switch to an export orientation because it would enhance their national welfare. Secondly, in their attempt to sustain and bolster industrialization, many developing economies follow domestic policies that tend to be biased against their agricultural sector. This turns them into net food importers despite their comparative advantage in food crops. International price rises would impel such economies to turn their policy structures towards an export orientation. Higher food prices would attract more investment, which in turn would be attracted from more distorted sectors of the economy. The ultimate outcome would be an improvement in the efficiency of resource allocation. Due to these two possibilities, the number of developing economies that could face hardship due to agricultural price rises is far smaller than those that are net exporters of agricultural products and stand to benefit.

The potential to ameliorate the plight of the rural poor

For several developing economies, particularly the low-income developing economies and the LDCs, which are at an early stage of development and industrialization, the agricultural sector is large and represents a significant proportion of their GDP. For this group of developing economies, the agricultural sector is the primary engine of growth due to two reasons. First, its relative size *vis-à-vis* the rest of the economy is large, and second because it provides important growth linkages to the rest of the economy. A large proportion of the poor households in these countries are in rural areas, and therefore this country group is known for its chronic incidence of rural poverty. According to estimates made by Alderman (2001), three-fourths of the world's poor reside in rural areas. This situation is likely to persist and the rural poor may outnumber their urban counterparts for at least two more decades. The results of the above GTAP exercise supports the view that the rural poor stand to benefit from liberalization of the agriculture sector under the auspices of the Doha Round.

In a healthy agricultural sector which is well-integrated with the global economy, liberalization of agricultural policies and the resulting growth in the agricultural sector can lead to a myriad of benefits for this group of developing economies. It would particularly benefit the rural poor inhabiting these economies. The channels of benefits to this group would include food security, a reduction in *real* food prices, and underpinning employment and rural incomes. An expansion of the agricultural sector would also create important economic linkages in the production chains in these small economies. Apparently, improvements in incomes of the rural households can lead to amelioration of the plight of the rural poor. In low-income developing economies a small percentage increase in agricultural GDP per capita can lead to a greater gain in the per capita income of the lowest 20 per cent or so of the population. If the Doha Round succeeds in progressing on the lines proposed by the framework agreement, and achieves the important objective of liberalization of multilateral agricultural trade and thereby give an impetus to agricultural trade, it would logically upgrade the plight of the rural poor in the low-income developing economies.

Conclusions and summary

High tariffs and NTBs as well as subsidization have been age-old chestnuts in agricultural trade. Agricultural trade regimes are markedly more complex and distorted than those of trade in manufactured products. Heavy traditional subsidization of agriculture by the industrial economies has led to ineffable distortion of multilateral trade regime. Protection of trade in agriculture *inter alia* compounds the losses associated with inefficient domestic policies in the industrial economies. Notwithstanding the adoption of the URAA, tariff barriers in agriculture remain extremely high even after the Uruguay Round. Recent estimates indicate that average agricultural tariffs are approximately six times as high as industrial tariffs. The agriculture sector is also well known for tariff peaks, which are sometimes as high as 500 per cent against agricultural exports from the developing economies. Furthermore, tariff escalation impedes exports of processed foods and agro-industrial products in the EU and the US markets. Tariff escalation also affects exports of processed tropical products, obstructing exports of high value-added farm products from the tropical countries. Long enduring export subsidies is another instrument of acute distortion of agricultural trade in several agricultural commodities. The EU has had a long tradition of heavily subsidizing its agricultural exports, which frequently results in depression of world market prices.

One recent development in this regard is that in the industrial economies direct subsidies have been delinked in a small way from the level of production, which reduced incentives to over produce. It is acknowledged that France has had a long-term antagonism to multilateral liberalization of agricultural trade. Since the early 1980s, France took the most inflexible and illogical stand on reform of Common Agricultural Policy and multilateral agricultural trade.

To be sure, the URAA represented a turning-point in the way agriculture was treated under the multilateral trade regime. It established the first ever framework for a long-overdue transformation in agricultural trade regime. Bringing trade in agriculture under multilateral discipline is considered a momentous achievement of the Uruguay Round. There is a flip-side of this coin. Although a watershed agreement, the URAA did not succeed in influencing high levels of subsidies, agricultural support and protection in any manner. The Doha Ministerial Communication pragmatically recognized that appropriate trade policies for developing and industrial economies differ substantially. Agriculture is a make-or-break issue of the Doha Round of MTNs.

An innovation of the Doha Ministerial Conference was that it made special and differential treatment (SDT) for developing countries integral throughout the negotiations. SDT applies to both new commitments made by the member economies and to any relevant new or revised rules and disciplines initiated during the Doha Round. After prolonged negotiations, there was little agreement on issues of significance and a complete lack of progress before the Cancún ministerial conference.

The proposals made in the Derbez text, tabled at the Cancún ministerial conference, had made a certain amount of meaningful proposals, which were available to the members for deliberations. One of them was of specific reductions in the first year of implementation of the total financial support under the amber box, blue box and *de minimis* ceilings. There was some discontentment among the G-21 group because they had pressed for stronger discipline under the blue box support.

The framework agreement or the so-called July Package establishing modalities was essentially based on the URAA and has been reformed to establish a fair and market-oriented trading system. It is highly significant in that it would determine the future course of action in the Doha Round negotiations on agriculture. Its objective is eventually to achieve the Doha mandate. Objectives and partial modalities have been established in this agreement. Negotiations on the lines of the framework agreement would indeed help in achieving the Doha mandate.

Welfare gains from liberalization of trade in agriculture have been empirically estimated to be significantly higher than those from the liberalization of trade in manufacture. Several CGE modelling exercises have confirmed this result.

7
Intellectual Property Rights and the Doha Round

Intellectual property rights

Over the preceding half century, ideas and knowledge have become a progressively important part of world trade. A creative mind is a scarce commodity, to be found only infrequently. Inventions, innovations, high-technology products and processes, and medicines have an intellectual origin and high commercial value, as do works of literature and arts. Their inventors and creators deserve to be compensated for the creative value inherent in these products, processes and creations. They are the intellectual property or assets of the inventors and creators. Logically, ethically and morally they deserve to have a right to negotiate the commercial value of their intellectual assets. International law does not allow unauthorized use of intellectual assets that have significant commercial value.

International exploitation of intellectual assets is a central feature of not only trade, but also of foreign direct investment (FDI) and transfer of technology. That all these flows have increased at an exceedingly rapid pace in the last half century is a widely acknowledged fact. Along with that, the commercial exploitation of intellectual property has also increased at an equally brisk pace. The present trend of progressively integrating the global economy has provided further impetus to the cross-border commercial exploitation of intellectual assets. The extent of protection and enforcement of the rights of inventors and creators have varied widely around the world, and as intellectual assets have become more important in trade, FDI and technology transfer, these differences have become a source of tension in international trade and economic relations.

The World Trade Organization (WTO) defines intellectual property rights (IPRs) as the 'rights given to persons over the creations of their minds'. For Keith Maskus (1998), IPRs exist to

> the extent to which their owners may exclude others from activities that infringe or damage the property. Thus, IPRs set out and protect the boundaries of legal means of competition among firms seeking to exploit the value of creative assets. Efforts to extend the rights beyond these boundaries are denied in principle. In this context, it is more fruitful to conceive of IPRs as rules regulating the terms of static and dynamic competition, rather than mechanisms for creating legal monopolies, which is the standard economic concept.

An established IPR regime gives the inventor or creator an exclusive right over the use of his or her creation, albeit for a certain period of time. The IPRs customarily fall in two areas: rights related to copyrights (or artistic property) and those related to industrial property. The first category of IPRs are those possessed by authors and artists for their literary writings, artistic works, musical compositions, paintings, sculpture, computer programs and movies. These IPRs are protected for half a century after the death of the author or artist. The fundamental objective of protecting IPRs is to 'encourage and reward creative work'[1] and its owner, which can be an individual or a corporate entity.

The IPRs that relate to industrial property are further subdivided into two principal areas. One area can be characterized as the protection of distinctive signs, in particular trademarks, or in indications of geographical origin, commonly referred to as geographical indications (GIs). The latter identify a product as originating in a place where a given characteristic of the product is essentially attributable to its geographical origin. The GIs play an important role in signalling a certain level of quality. The best illustration of GIs is Champagne, which originated in the Champagne region of France and is respected for its superior quality by consumers.[2] Its quality imparts its commercial value.

Trademarks are used commercially to distinguish goods and services of one business corporation from another, thus aiding both the consumer and the producer. Trademarks are sign and symbols that enable consumers to make informed choices in the market-place full of myriad competing products. The objective of protecting these distinctive signs is to stimulate and ensure fair competition, and such protection can last indefinitely. The IPRs in other areas of industrial property, like invention, innovation, technological advancement, designs and industrial processes, are protected by patents. Such protection primarily stimulates invention, innovation, design and technological advancement. The objective of providing protection to inventors and designers is to protect their investment in the development of new technology as well as 'giving them incentive and means to finance research and development activities'.[3] Patents for inventions, trademarks for commercial branding and copyrights for artistic and literary works are all a form of monopoly power in a commercial context, and the need to regulate this monopoly power is universally recognized. A functioning IPR regime facilitates the transfer of technology in the form of FDI, joint ventures and licensing of patented technology. Such a regime usually provides protection for a finite term, usually 20 years in the case of patents. The IPR regime espoused by the WTO accepts these international norms.

Trade-related aspects of the intellectual property rights agreement

It bears repeating that in a globalizing world economy, with brisk expansion of trade, FDI and technology transfer, there has been a rapid growth in the commercial exploitation of intellectual assets. International law in the area of IPRs has historically been fairly underdeveloped and unable to serve the rapidly integrating global economy in an efficacious manner. During the decade of the 1980s, a pressing need for systemic improvement was felt by both the developing and industrial country members of the WTO. One consequence of this pressure was the increasing number of bilateral, regional and sometimes multilateral negotiations on IPRs. Important as IPRs and their protection were, they were taken up at all three levels. The industrial economies had fairly well-developed norms in this regard, and over the decade of the 1990s, several developing and transition economies also developed minimum standards in an extensive manner.

The Uruguay Round (1986–94) was a watershed period in this regard. Before the launch of the Uruguay Round, there was no specific agreement on IPRs within the framework of the multilateral trading system. IPRs were regarded as the domain of specialist organizations, treaties and conventions in this area. However, some principles contained in the General Agreement on Tariffs and Trade (GATT) had a bearing on intellectual property measures taken on imports or exports. Article XX(d) of GATT-1947 (now Article XX(d) of GATT-1994) specifically referred to intellectual property rights.[4] Under this provision, measures which would otherwise be inconsistent with the GATT could be taken to secure compliance with laws or regulations relating, among other things, to IPRs.

The multilateral negotiations during the Uruguay Round altered this status by incorporating IPRs into the multilateral trading system. The TRIPS agreement negotiated during the Uruguay Round, and which came into force on 1 January 1995, introduced IPRs into the multilateral trading system for the first time. Conclusion of the TRIPS agreement was a noteworthy and key achievement of the WTO, widely regarded as a significant institutional improvement, and is often described as one of the three 'pillars' of the WTO; the other two pillars being trade in goods and trade in services.

The TRIPS agreement is still considered a work in progress; it is the first step in the consolidation of multilateral regulations in the area of IPRs. As it deals with a complex issue, it will surely take a while before the structure of multilateral regulations in IPRs reaches maturity. Its language and terminology is far from perfectly clear, and it is expected that clarifications on meanings and implications will take some time. Many terms do not have their legal definitions as yet, and there is little case law regarding implementation of the agreement. WTO members face commercial and legal pressure to adopt the TRIPS agreement in their legal systems, but members can still question and contest any of the TRIPS articles that is in conflict with their existing domestic or international law. Also, member countries can define the terminology to suit their national interest. All this is presently tolerated under 'constructive ambiguities' to conceal major disagreements.

Attempts to improve and strengthen the contemporary IPR regime and take it beyond its current minimum-standards status are constantly being debated and even negotiated in bilateral, regional and sometimes multilateral negotiations on IPRs. A propensity to widen the scope and subject matter of IPR protection is clearly discernible among a sub-group of WTO members, namely the industrial economies. The IPR regime would eventually be progressively harmonized for all WTO members and is expected to be strong on enforcement. One likely outcome would be a weakening of special and differential treatment (SDT) for the developing economies in this area, as well as a reduction of some of the flexibilities that they presently benefit from.

It is to be expected that countries with widely varying levels of economic development and capability for innovation and technological development would have dissimilar interests in protecting intellectual assets. They would also have disparate inclinations and abilities to enforce the protection of IPRs in their respective economies. A multilateral agreement could be instrumental in bringing much needed uniformity in this regard. The TRIPS agreement that was negotiated during the Uruguay Round was an attempt to narrow the gap in the manner in which the protection of IPRs are protected around the world. It is formally known as Annex 1C of the Marrakesh Agreement or the GATT-1994.[5] The Marrakesh Agreement is the cornerstone of the contemporary global trading system. A body called the Council for TRIPS was created for administering and monitoring the TRIPS agreement, particularly its operational aspects, and it is open to all members of the WTO. The Council for TRIPS also meets in 'special sessions', that are intended for negotiations on a multilateral system for notifying and registering GIs for wines and spirits under the Doha Development Agenda (DDA).

The World Trade Organization and IPRs

At the top of the international hierarchy of treaties and conventions lies the WTO's agreement on Trade Related Aspects of Intellectual Property Rights, or the TRIPS agreement. Like the General Agreement on Trade and Services (GATS), this is another agreement that extended the reach of the GATT system to issues beyond trade in goods in the WTO system. The five broad issues covered by the TRIPS agreement are:

1 how basic principles of the trading system and other international intellectual property agreements should be applied;
2 how to give adequate protection to intellectual property rights;
3 how countries should enforce those rights adequately in their own territories;
4 how to settle disputes on intellectual property between members of the WTO; and
5 special transitional arrangements during the period when the new system is being introduced.

Different kinds of intellectual property rights and how to protect them also come within the ambit of the TRIPS agreement, with the purpose of ensuring that adequate standards of IPR protection exist and are maintained in all the WTO member countries. The TRIPS agreement starts by ensuring that the main international agreements of the World Intellectual Property Organization (WIPO), which came into force long before the WTO was created, are observed. As the TRIPS agreement is essentially based on the WIPO framework, it is worthwhile to know what that is. The genesis of the WIPO goes back to 1883. The early 1880s are known for several famous innovations, works of art and intellect, including Johannes Brahms' composition of his Third Symphony, the publication of Robert Louis Stevenson's *Treasure Island*, and construction of New York's Brooklyn Bridge by Emily and John Roebling. The two principal conventions on IPRs that come under the WIPO are the Paris Convention for the Protection of Industrial Property (1884), which was the first international treaty which helped people of one country obtain protection in other countries for their intellectual creation, covering patents, trademarks and industrial designs; and the second was the Berne Convention for the Protection of Literary and Artistic Works (1886) covering copyright on novels, poems, plays, songs, operas, drawings, paintings and sculptures. The current membership of WIPO is 180 countries.

In accordance with WTO customs and norms, the TRIPS agreement allows different WTO members different time periods to delay applying its provisions. The industrial economies were granted a transition period of one year, while the developing and transition economies had four years to comply with its provisions. The LDCs were granted a longer transition period, of a total of 11 years, with the possibility of extension.[6] For pharmaceutical patents, the application of patent provision has been extended to 1 January 2016. This was decided by trade ministers at the Fourth Ministerial Conference in Doha, Qatar, in November 2001.

Also, in keeping with the contemporary policy penchant of the WTO, the TRIPS agreement paid particular attention to the needs of the developing economies, particularly the least developed countries (LDCs). This concern is noted in its preamble. That developing economies, in particular the LDCs, need to develop a technological base was identified as an important concern by the WTO member economies. Therefore, this country group has been allowed 'maximum flexibility' in domestic implementation of the TRIPS agreement in that these economies are able to develop and sustain an increasingly sound technological base, which in turn may provide an impetus to their real GDP growth rate. This is one of the noteworthy objectives of the TRIPS agreement. Article VII of the TRIPS is important in this regard, as it focuses on 'transfer and dissemination of technology, to the mutual advantage of producers and users of technological knowledge' (explored further later in this chapter).

Some stylized facts about the TRIPS regime

IPRs form a complex subject matter with interrelationships with regulatory systems and economic structures. The primary characteristic of the

TRIPS agreement is that it makes protection of IPRs an integral part of the multilateral trading system, as embodied in the WTO. As alluded to above, the TRIPS regime imposes the norm of minimum standards of IPRs on WTO members. Under the principle of a 'single undertaking' devised during the Uruguay Round, all the WTO agreements apply to all members without exceptions. Accordingly, the TRIPS agreement applies to all members of the WTO, which also means that the provisions of the TRIPS agreement are subject to the integrated WTO dispute-settlement mechanism, contained in the so-called Dispute Settlement Procedures (DSP). Another set of provisions that this agreement deals with relate to the domestic procedures and remedies for the enforcement of the IPRs. The TRIPS agreement lays down certain general principles applicable to all IPR enforcement procedures.

All the WTO members, including those availing themselves of the longer transition periods for the implementation of the TRIPS agreement, were required to comply with the two fundamental principles of the multilateral trading system, namely national treatment and the most-favoured-nation (MFN) clause. Article III and Article IV of the TRIPS agreement enshrine these basic principles; Article III deals with national treatment, that is equal treatment has to be given to foreign and domestic firms and individuals, while Article IV stands for the MFN treatment, that is the non-discrimination clause which requires that no discrimination can be made between foreign firms or individuals when dealing with IPRs issues. Although special transition rules have been devised under the TRIPS agreement for a developing economy that does not provide product patent protection, certain basic regulations have to be applied. That is, for pharmaceutical and agricultural chemicals such a developing country must accept the filing of patent applications from the beginning of the transitional period. If the government allows the relevant pharmaceutical or agricultural chemical product to be marketed during the transition period, it must – subject to certain conditions – provide the patent applicant an exclusive marketing right for the product for five years, or until a decision on granting a product patent is taken, whichever is shorter.

The TRIPS agreement follows an additional important principle, additional to the two fundamental principles of the multilateral trading system. This principle requires that protection of IPRs should contribute to covering technical innovation as well as transfer of technology. The agreement underpins it because, first, both producers and users benefit from transfer of technology, and second it is a vitally important instrument of significantly enhancing global economic and social welfare.

The TRIPS agreement was built upon the framework of two WIPO-administered agreements, as discussed earlier in the chapter. Although it requires members to comply with certain minimum standards for the protection of IPRs, members may indeed choose to implement laws which give more extensive protection than is required under the agreement. This is permissible, even encouraged, so long as the additional protection does not contravene the provisions of the TRIPS agreement. Members also have the freedom to determine appropriate methods of enforcing the provisions of the agreement in their domestic legal system.

After the TRIPS agreement came into force, multilateral protection of IPRs increased discernibly, particularly in the developing economies. The newly industrialized economies (NIEs) and the emerging-market economies (EMEs) and the high-income developing economies did better in this respect than the other developing economies. The NIEs and the EMEs were in the forefront of adhering to the TRIPS agreement and ushering-in related domestic institutional and policy reforms. A significant number of developing countries have ratified the two IPR-related treaties, namely the Paris Convention and the Berne Convention, and this number is gradually growing.

The TRIPS agreement gave the WTO limited authority to enforce IPRs and obligated member nations to enforce their private IPRs. Several regional integration agreements (RIAs) and countries that were bound in bilateral trade agreements (BTAs) also determined their own IPR standards, in turn contributing to the same objective of improvement in the IPR regime. Separate chapters on IPRs have become a common feature of the RIA and BTA agreements. IPR protection under RIAs and BTAs is generally more stringent and goes beyond the TRIPS agreement. They tend to take a TRIPS-plus approach. One recent illustration of this is the Free Trade Area of the Americas (FTAA),[7] that established a Negotiating Group on Intellectual Property Rights (NGIPRs), with the objective to 'promote and ensure adequate and effective protection to intellectual property rights' (Das, 2004). When IPR regimes are determined within the context of RIAs, they tend to first grow TRIPS-plus, and second lead to internal harmonization of IPR protection norms in the RIAs. Favourable initial results of strengthened IPR regimes are to be seen in significant gains in FDI and technology licensing in the developing economies, albeit it that trade has been influenced only moderately. However, this outcome of a potential TRIPS-plus regime has been challenged.[8]

Development dimension of the IPR regimes

Like the strong development emphasis in the DDA, integration of the development dimension into the IPR regime is presently being debated in international fora. For instance, in the WIPO Convention on 26 August 2004, several member countries proposed integration of the development dimension into the WIPO activities.[9] The objective of this proposal is to integrate intellectual property norm-setting, transfer of technology to developing economies and technological cooperation into the activities of the WIPO (Gabrieloni, 2004). The new perspective of the IPRs that is currently being debated holds that an IPR protection regime should take a two-pronged approach. It should be an instrument to promote technological innovation, as well as dissemination of technology. Bridging the significant technology gap between the industrial and developing economies, particularly the LDCs, needs to be made into a conscious policy objective and tangible steps are needed to be taken to meet it. The IPR regime needs to respond to the zeitgeist, and to ensure that the cost of protecting the IPRs is not so high that it outweighs the benefits of protection. In its 2002 report, the Commission on Intellectual Property Rights of the Government of the United Kingdom (GUK, 2002), had proposed this objective to be adopted by the multilateral and national IPR regimes.

In the present and future treaties on IPRs, there must a preservation of policy space for all member states, including the unique constraints of the developing economies, particularly the LDCs. Pragmatic strategies should be devised to fulfil these growth-related necessities. Adoption of high-level declarations on the lines of the Millennium Development Goals on IPRs addressing growth concerns would indeed be helpful. Articles VII and VIII of the TRIPS agreement do make such a declaration in an unambiguous manner.

TRIPS in the Doha Round

The TRIPS agreement appears on the agenda for the Doha Ministerial Conference in numerous ways. It appears in the context of (i) negotiations on geographical indications, (ii) a separate declaration on TRIPS and public health emergencies, (iii) work on clarifying the relationship between the TRIPS agreement and the UN Convention on Biological Diversity and (iv) implementation issues, including current obligations on technology transfer under the TRIPS agreement. Given the significance and magnitude of the issue, the TRIPS agreement is directly covered by three paragraphs (17 through 19) of the Doha Ministerial communiqué (WTO, 2001). In the Doha Declaration, participating trade ministers stressed that it is important to implement and interpret the TRIPS agreement in a way that supports public health emergencies – by promoting both access to existing medicines as well as the invention and development of new medicines. They agreed to authorize the Council for TRIPS to complete work on the implementation of Article XXIII, Paragraph 4, 'to negotiate the establishment of a multilateral system of notification and registration of geographical indicators for wines and spirits' by the time the next Ministerial Conference started in Cancún. They also gave clear mandate to the Council for TRIPS for establishing a work programme on Article XXVII.

The participating ministers in the Doha Round also referred to their separate declaration in the DDA on TRIPS and public-health emergencies, which was designed to respond to concerns about the possible implications of the TRIPS agreement for access to generic drugs and medicines in low-income developing economies (see later in the chapter). In the separate declaration, the ministers emphasized that the TRIPS agreement does not and should not prevent member governments from acting in times of epidemics and emergencies from protecting public health. This declaration affirmed governments' right to use the TRIPS agreement's flexibilities in order to avoid any reticence the governments may feel. The separate declaration also clarified some of the modes of flexibility available, in particular compulsory licensing and parallel importing.[10]

Technology transfer and the Doha Round

The developing economies at varying rungs of economic growth pin high hopes on the capability of technology for raising their total factor productivity (TFP) and eventually their real GDP growth rates. Development of new knowledge and higher-level technologies has virtually been reduced to a monopoly of the industrial economies. Transfer of technology from the industrialized economies and its dissemination in the developing economies, that have succeeded in developing a technology infrastructure and have a strong base of human capital, is the *sine qua non* of economic development. It is not a surprise that the DDA also calls on industrial economies to find ways to facilitate technology transfer to the developing economies, in particular to the LDCs. This is in keeping with Article MXVI, Paragraph 2, of the TRIPS agreement (see below).

In Paragraph 37 of the DDA, the Doha Ministerial Declaration included a binding mandate for WTO members to study the intricate relationship between trade and transfer of technology, and to this end the Working Group on Trade and Transfer of Technology (WGTTT) was established. The developing economies were the *demandeurs* for establishing this working group, while the industrial economies treated WGTTT as a mere academic exercise of little future consequence. The initial focus of the WGTTT was limited to the definitional and analytical issues. The developing country group showed a good deal of interest in the operations of the WGTTT and submitted several proposals. The EU emphasized definitional issues, while the USA showed little enthusiasm about the prescriptive message of the WGTTT. The Fifth Ministerial Conference in Cancún reviewed the mandate of the WGTTT and its work continued, although deliberations progressed at an exceedingly slow pace. In the latter half of 2004, members reported that while the working group has done some useful work on the analytical issues, 'further work was needed to elaborate and develop a common and a shared understanding of the issues'. Also, proactive recommendations for the transfer of technology should follow the analytical work of the Working Group (WTO, 2004). Deliberations on these recommendations were still ongoing at the time of writing (November 2004).

Before the TRIPS agreement came into force, some developing economies had posed a threat of duplication or imitation of high-technology imported products by way of reverse engineering. In the areas of medium- and high-technology manufactured products, IPRs have faced a serious threat of reverse engineering from the developing economies that have a relatively stronger human capital base and poor enforcement of IPRs. Two groups of countries do not pose a threat of imitation, duplication and reverse engineering – those not having a strong base of human capital, and those having a strong system of IPR protection and enforcement. The LDCs come in the former category, while the Organization for Economic Cooperation and Development (OECD) economies fall in the latter group.

Technology transfer and protection of IPRs

International technology transfers and the protection of IPRs are closely related. The principal channels of technology transfer are trade, FDI and licences, which are affected by the strength of the IPR protection regime in the recipient country. Under certain circumstances, an orderly and stringent patent regime can retard technology transfer. Firms may refuse to transfer technology to some countries or firms for competitive reasons, and the patent regime can certainly be developed in such a manner as to discourage technology transfer to local firms. This can impede them from learning new technology by imitation or reverse engineering. It is the mission of a forward-looking IPR regime to strike a balance between protection of new technology on the one hand, and meeting the needs of economic development in the host developing economies on the other.

Within the parameters of an IPR regime, technology transfer *per se* is a complex, difficult and costly process, entailing transferring and relocating codified knowledge in return for contractual obligations. The costs of such transfers depend upon the channels used. The theoretical literature does not give an unambiguous indication regarding the impact of general improvements in the protection of IPRs and technology transfer,[11] and debate on the aggregate impact of protection of IPRs on trade, FDI and licensing has still not come to categorical conclusions, although some proclivities are evident. It was, however, palpable that robust protection of IPRs in the recipient economy has a positive and significant correlation with trade volume in manufactured goods within the OECD economies, as well as in trade between the OECD economies and large developing economies (Maskus, 2000; Smith, 1999). The strength of the IPRs was measured by an index in these studies.

Creating a TRIPS-consistent IPR regime has apparent consequences. As the IPR regime is strengthened in an economy or adherence to the TRIPS agreement is seen as improving, technology exporting firms in the OECD economies respond. Smith (1999) found that in response to strengthening IPR regimes, technology-intensive large international corporations expand their exports to large- and middle-income developing economies having a strong technology base. Furthermore, Maskus (2000) concluded that harmonization brought about by TRIPS could increase manufactured imports in large developing economies by as much as 9 per cent, which could, *inter alia*, produce gains in terms of TFP for the importing economy.

As opposed to a strong link between trade in high-technology manufactured products and improvements in an IPR regime, a strong correlation between improvements in the IPR regime and FDI and technology licensing was not so obvious. However, recent empirical research does point to a positive association between licensing fees and IPR enforcement, measured by the Ginarte–Park patent index. A regression analysis of real volume of licence fees for industrial processes paid by unaffiliated firms in 26 countries to US firms revealed that such fees were positively and significantly correlated to the enforcement of patent laws in the technology importing countries. On average, every 1 per cent rise in the IPR index led to a 2.3 per cent increase in licensing volume. This shows that technology transfers are elastic and sensitive to how well the IPRs are protected in an economy (Yang and Maskus, 2001). However, Yang and Maskus (2001) believed that their study was flawed and needed further refinement, to the extent that it did not have a true measure of licensing contracts or contents.[12]

A more comprehensive study by Smith (2001) found that better enforcement of patent laws would increase technology sales to affiliates and licensing payments from them would rise. It buttressed the weak results of Yang and Maskus (2001). Using statistics related to a large number of trade, FDI and licensing contracts, Puttitanun (2003) concluded that increases in the patent index significantly raised the flows of FDI and licensing. These results are similar to those arrived at by Smith (2001). A general observation in this regard is that in high- and middle-income developing economies, having reasonable levels of technological capabilities, the quality of technology transfer rises with the strength of IPR protection. As the IPR regime improves in terms of enforcement and as domestic firms display higher capacity to absorb advanced technology, technology-intensive firms from the industrial economies grow better disposed to transact more advanced products and processes (Maskus, 2004).

The TRIPS agreement and the lead-up to the Doha Round

During the Uruguay Round the EU and the USA were most interested in making the TRIPS agreement a part of the multilateral trading system. They based their arguments on the premise that a uniform and harmonious IPR regime would increase technology transfer to the developing economies and favourably affect TFP in a large part of the world economy. This perspective did not go unchallenged. Antagonists were certain that the TRIPS agreement would enhance the market power of information and knowledge-developers, who would use it in a monopolistic and abusive manner, ultimately resulting in a slowing-down of technology transfer (Correa, 2003). Not only did these two extremes of views exist in this regard, but the developing economies also considered the TRIPS agreement unbalanced and skewed in favour of the industrial economies. In their view the TRIPS mechanism and its provisions are not sufficient for ensuring enhanced technology transfers to the developing economies. This concern was raised by them before the commencement of the Doha Round.

Neither of the above extreme views can stand close logical scrutiny, since technology transfer is a complex and multifaceted process in which IPRs and their enforcement form only one important dimension. That said, IPRs are necessary but not sufficient for a robust transfer of technology. There are a host of other micro, meso and macro variables involved in deciding whether technological transfer is likely to be swift, slow or be stalled. The domestic investment climate in the host economy, the macroeconomic policy structure, competition in the domestic market, corporate governance policies, proximity to major markets and labour mobility will all have an impact over the pace of technology transfer. For instance, a country may have improved its IPR regime and still have restrictive entry and distribution laws, which may not be conducive to new technology transfers. These so-called 'other' factors also need to be worked upon along with the IPR regime for an improved technology transfer.

Article VII of the TRIPS agreement is related to transfer and global dissemination of technology. It has been noted above that in emphasizing technology transfer this article emphasized the need for 'maximum flexibility' so that the TRIPS agreement makes a tangible contribution to buttressing the technological base in the developing economies, particularly in the LDCs. Making Article VII of the TRIPS agreement into the guiding star of the Doha Round negotiations would indeed have far-reaching ramifications. Some aspects of it have been further clarified in Article MXVI, Paragraph 2, which states that

> Developed country members shall provide incentives to enterprises and institutions in their territories for the purpose of promoting and encouraging technological transfer to LDC members in order to enable them to create a sound and viable technological base.

Article VII is precise in its demand of the industrial countries, which have a specific obligation towards the LDCs at the exclusion of the developing and transition economies. The Doha Ministerial Declaration further defined that this is a positive obligation and that the industrial economies must proactively find ways to achieve these objectives (Becker Consulting, 2003). However, these requirements of Article MXVI, Paragraph 2, have not been translated into a clear course of action, for two reasons. First, the objective of technology transfer is exceedingly broad and somewhat difficult to quantify. Second, there are neither specific obligations in terms of reporting for member countries nor are there any consequences of not adhering to this requirement. For these reasons the obligations of Article MXVI, Paragraph 2, have been reduced to mere wishful thinking of the multilateral trading community.

Proposed measures for the Doha Round

To ensure that the industrial economies take their Article MXVI, Paragraph 2, obligations seriously, it is essential for the Council for TRIPS to develop a clear implementation mechanism. Along with that there should be a process of periodically monitoring the implementation task under Article MXVI, Paragraph 2, and a half-yearly progress report may be published for WTO members. This is not a novel concept. A parallel notion was deliberated during the Doha Ministerial Conference, according to which the industrial countries were to submit a progress report at the end of 2002, which was required to be updated annually. However, this proposal did not go far and various forms of reporting mechanism were further discussed in the Council for TRIPS. Eventually no consensus emerged. An important step to be taken during the ongoing negotiations is to finalize the reporting/monitoring system, with close surveillance on how the obligations under Article MXVI, Paragraph 2, are being adhered to by the industrial economies. This would indeed indicate significant progress towards the basic mandate of the DDA.

The Doha Round and public health concerns

Many developing economies, particularly the low-income ones and the LDCs, face serious and frequent outbreaks of epidemics and public health disasters. For example, according to WHO estimates, in the early years of the twenty-first century, 3 million people died of human immunovirus/ acquired immune deficiency syndrome (HIV/AIDS) annually, with 2.3 million in only one region, sub-Saharan Africa. Mortality from malaria was estimated at 1 million per year and tuberculosis 2 million. These three diseases alone removed 168 million disability-adjusted life years. The economic cost of these and other diseases in terms of reduced productivity and non-participation in the labour force is large. In addition, there is the bloated fiscal cost of healthcare budgets in the low-income countries.[13]

Therefore, at the time of the launch of the Doha Round, the issue of access to generic drugs and essential medicines in developing countries was assigned a great deal of significance by the participating trade ministers. As noted earlier, given the importance of this issue, participating ministers had made a separate 'Declaration on TRIPS Agreement and Public Health', reflecting their concerns regarding the TRIPS agreement becoming a roadblock in matters related to public health. This separate declaration was adopted at the end of the Doha Ministerial Conference, in addition to the general Ministerial Declaration.

The long-simmering controversy between the industrial and developing countries regarding this issue was a consequence of two conflicting needs: the need to ensure accessibility to essential medicines in developing countries on the one hand, and the interest of the pharmaceutical companies in the industrial countries to profit from manufacturing and selling such medicines after years of investment in research and expensive licensing procedures, on the other hand. The two contending sides took logical and self-righteous stands, and neither could be easily flawed in its position. The pharmaceutical companies that invest in research and development (R&D) and invent and manufacture medicines expect to be rewarded for promoting R&D in new medicines. To be sure, there is public interest in encouraging them in making this investment, which is also one of the fundamental rationales of the IPRs and patent law. On their part, the developing economies need the life-saving generic drugs, especially during periods of epidemics and medical disasters when these drugs are required at short notice. This was a complex issue which entailed not only protection of IPRs, but also strands of basic human rights, politics and economics. The complex issue of health markets in low-income developing countries is characterized by both market and government failures. Therefore, there is a strong need for consistent and aggressive intervention by public authorities to increase the supply of available drugs.

The Doha Round and patented essential medicines

The debate on generic drug production to meet public health emergencies on the one hand, and normal trade in generic drugs on the other became so intense that for a while protection of IPRs became synonymous with it. The 'Declaration on the TRIPS Agreement and Public Health' by WTO members, in Paragraph 4, encouraged 'flexibility' in interpreting the TRIPS agreement in such a way that it reflects the interests of member states and allows them to protect public health in general, and promote the access of populations in developing countries to essential generic drugs specifically. It is further pointed out in Paragraph 5 that the flexibility should be specifically adopted in the area of compulsory licensing of life-saving generic drugs and exhaustion of the intellectual property rights. Paragraph 6 recognized and drew attention to the difficulties of WTO members that did not have sufficient manufacturing capability in their pharmaceutical sector, or did not have a pharmaceutical industry at all. These countries cannot make effective use of the system of compulsory licences under the TRIPS agreement. Therefore, Paragraph 6 instructed the Council for TRIPS 'to find an expeditious solution to this problem and to report to the General Council before the end of 2002'.

In the Fourth Session of the Doha Ministerial Conference the negotiators were charged by the DDA with resolving the issue of TRIPS *vis-à-vis* public health emergencies. As noted earlier, many developing countries, including LDCs, face potential public health crises in the areas of HIV/AIDS, tuberculosis, malaria or similar epidemics that call for urgent medical treatment. Against the backdrop of these distressful situations faced by several WTO members, an expeditious resolution of this issue was needed.

Before the launch of the Doha Round, there was a great deal of rancorous disagreement on this tangled subject. Discussions over patent exemptions reached a total impasse at the end of 2002, although members were eager to reach some sort of agreement before the start of the Fifth Ministerial Conference in Cancún. After long deliberations and negotiations, this vitally important issue was eventually resolved on 30 August 2003. Members agreed to adopt the 'Decision of the TRIPS Agreement and Public Health', which allowed developing economies greater access to needed categories of vital medicines when their governments are faced with outbreak of diseases that threaten public health (WTO, 2003). This decision allows developing countries to import generic drugs for the treatment of diseases that are public-health threats, and has far-reaching ramifications for those developing countries and LDCs that do not have a pharmaceutical industry, or where it is in its infancy.

Agreement on an implementation procedure

An implementation procedure in which countries that have manufacturing capacities can acquire permission to export medicines that are manufactured in accordance with a compulsory licence, while providing proper guarantees that the export destination will be limited to member states that lack such manufacturing capacity and face a public-health crisis, and guaranteeing that the exported medicines will not be transferred to third countries, was created to meet the expectations of all countries. Developing countries were satisfied that the agreement did not limit them to emergency situations or designate only a short list of diseases for which generic drugs could be produced. Instead, it permitted them to produce or import drugs to address the particular diseases that affected their countries.

Although in general this agreement was heralded as a success because it addressed a major concern of small developing countries, some analysts criticized it for adding red-tape for developing countries that want to file for a patent exemption. Some prominent non-governmental organizations (NGOs) were critical of the agreement for adding more bureaucratic burdens to the process of issuing compulsory licences.[14] They believed that the burden of proof fell on the developing economies, which may be problematic because they usually do not have time and liquid and professional resources to present their case to the WTO. In addition, it was not clear in the agreement how developing countries that want to import generic drugs could prove that their domestic pharmaceutical industry is unable to satisfy domestic demand. It was realized that the WTO could end up approving import requests from countries that lack domestic industries altogether and reject requests based on the inefficiency of a domestic industry. Also, the specific prerequisite that generic drugs may only be produced for 'public, non-commercial purposes' is vague and open to contention.

The agreement permitted eligible WTO members to obtain from an eligible exporting WTO member, which had the manufacturing capabilities in the vital drugs, pharmaceutical supplies to meet a public health emergency. LDC members could automatically avail themselves of this pharmaceutical import system, although other developing countries were required to notify the Council for TRIPS regarding the public-health emergency, or 'circumstances of extreme urgency that required a patented medicine for public, noncommercial use'. The importing developing country is also required to notify the Council for TRIPS the name and quantity of the patented medicine required. Under the 'Decision of 30 August 2003' it is also expected to notify of its inadequate manufacturing capability and ask for a compulsory license under TRIPS Article XXXI for a patented pharmaceutical product (WTO, 2003). Several well-conceived measures have been devised to monitor the exporting firm and country. The exporting WTO member is issued a compulsory licence, and the amount of pharmaceuticals manufactured under the licence should be what is required to meet the emergency needs of the importing member. The IPRs is a complex subject matter with interrelationships with regulatory systems and economic structures. At the top of the international hierarchy of treaties and conventions to protect the IPRs lies the WTO's Agreement on Trade Related Aspects of Intellectual Property Rights, or the TRIPS Agreement. It extended the reach of the GATT system to issues beyond trade in goods in the new WTO system. Different kinds of intellectual property rights and how to protect them come within the ambit of the TRIPS agreement. Its purpose is to ensure that adequate standards of IPRs protection exist and are maintained in all the WTO member countries.

The international law in the area of IPRs has been fairly underdeveloped. The Uruguay Round (1986–94) is a watershed period in this regard. Like the strong development emphasis in the DDA, integration of the development dimension into the IPR regime has been debated in the international fora. The TRIPS appear on the agenda for the Doha Ministerial

Conference in numerous ways. Given the significance and magnitude of the issue, the TRIPS agreement is directly covered by three paragraphs of the Doha Ministerial communiqué. In the Doha Declaration, participating trade ministers stressed that it is important to implement and interpret the TRIPS agreement in such a way that supports public health – by promoting both access to existing medicines and the creation of new medicines. They stated that the TRIPS should be supportive of public health by promoting both access to existing medicines and research and development into new medicines.

It is not a surprise that the DDA also calls on industrial economies to find ways to facilitate technology transfer to the developing economies, in particular to the LDCs. This is in keeping with the Article MXVI, Paragraph 2, of the TRIPS agreement. Debate on the aggregate impact of protection of IPRs on trade, FDI and licensing has still not come to categorical conclusions, but some proclivities are evident. It was, however, palpable that robust protection of IPRs in the recipient economy has a positive and significant correlation with trade volume in manufactured goods within the OECD economies as well as in trade between the OECD economies and large developing economies.

During the Uruguay Round the EU and the US were most interested in making the TRIPS agreement a part of the multilateral trading system. They based their arguments on the premise that a uniform and harmonious IPR regime would increase technology transfer to the developing economies and thereby favourably affect TFP in a large part of the world economy. This perspective did not go unchallenged. Antagonists were certain that TRIPS would enhance the market power of information and knowledge developers who will use it in a monopolistic and abusive manner. It would ultimately result in slowing down the transfer of technology. Not only two extremes of views existed, but the developing economies also considered the TRIPS agreement unbalanced.

Article VII of the TRIPS is related to transfer and global dissemination of technology. In emphasizing technology transfer this article emphasized the need for 'maximum flexibility' so that the TRIPS agreement makes concrete contributions to buttressing the technological base in the developing economies, particularly in the LDCs. Article VII of the TRIPS agreement can be made into the guiding star of the Doha Round negotiations. Article MXVI, Paragraph 2, deals with the implementation mechanism of Article VII.

Many developing economies, particularly the low-income ones and LDCs, face serious health problems. Therefore, at the time of the launch of the Doha Round, the issue of access to essential medicines in developing countries was assigned a great deal of significance by the participating trade ministers. Given the importance of this issue, they had made a separate 'Declaration on TRIPS Agreement and Public Health', which obviously reflected their concern regarding the TRIPS agreement becoming a roadblock in the matters related to public health. Debate on generic drug production and trade became so intense that for a while protection of IPRs became synonymous with it. The 'Declaration on the TRIPS Agreement and Public Health' by the WTO members, in Paragraph 4, encouraged 'flexibility' in interpreting the TRIPS agreement in a way that it reflects the interest of member states to protect public health generally, and promote the access of populations in developing countries to essential generic drugs specifically.

Deliberations, debates and academic symposiums on the best mechanisms for ensuring an adequate and sustainable supply of essential generic drugs to patients in poor countries preceded the 'Decision of 30 August 2003', as it was christened by the WTO. It is also referred to as the 'implementation decision'. Nothing short of a landmark, this decision was taken carefully, bearing in mind the needs of the member countries facing public-health emergencies on the one hand and the interests of pharmaceutical exporting firms and countries on the other. This decision invented a system for meeting the expectations of both the country groups, the *demandeur* developing economies and the industrial economies that are the principal inventor and producers of drugs and essential medicines.

Notes

1 The Doha Round of Multilateral Trade Negotiations

1 For more details refer to Das (2001), chapter 1. See also Hoekman and Kostecki (2001).

2 Its genesis owes to the failure of an attempt to form an international trade organization during a meeting of the United Nations Conference on Trade and Employment in Havana, Cuba, in 1947.

3 In October 2004, the WTO had 148 members. Cambodia was the last country to accede to the WTO on 13 October 2004; it belongs to the category of least-developed countries (LDCs). In addition, 30 countries had observer status. With the exception of the Holy See, observers must start accession negotiations within five years of becoming observers.

4 Its formal title is *The Results of the Uruguay Round of Multilateral Trade Negotiations: The Legal Text*, and it was published by the General Agreement on Tariffs and Trade (GATT) in 1994.

5 Most of the WTO agreements are the result of the multilateral trade negotiations during the Uruguay Round (1986–94). They were signed at the Marrakesh Ministerial meeting on 15 April, in Marrakesh, Morocco, 1994. The so-called 'Final Act' signed in Marrakesh was like a cover note. Everything else was attached to it. Foremost was the Agreement Establishing the WTO, which serves as an umbrella agreement. Annexed were the agreements on goods, services and intellectual property, dispute settlement, the trade policy review mechanism and the plurilateral agreements. The schedules of commitments also form part of the Uruguay Round agreements. The Marrakesh Agreement was developed out of the General Agreement on Tariffs and Trade (GATT), which it included. However, it supplemented the GATT with several other agreements on such issues as trade in services, sanitary and plant health measures, trade-related aspects of intellectual property rights, and technical barriers to trade. The Marrakesh Agreement also established a new, more efficient and legally binding means of dispute resolution.

6 See Romer (1994a, 1994b) for an empirical and theoretical treatment of the welfare costs of trade distortions.

7 Das (2000 and 2001) provide a succinct analysis of this ignominious failure.

8 See speech by Commissioner Pascal Lamy 'Can the Doha Development Agenda Live up to its Name?' delivered in Cancún on 10 September 2003.

9 In 2004, the United Nations classification of least-developed countries (LDCs) included 50 countries, of which 30 are members of the WTO and five are observers.

10 We divide the various groups of developing economies according to the World Bank (2004) definition, which is available in *Classification of Economies* on the Internet at http://www.worldbank.org/data/countryclass/countryclass.html, where economies are divided according to 2003 per capita

gross national income. The groups are: low-income developing countries with per capita gross national income of $765 or less; lower-middle income, $766–$3,035; upper-middle income, $3,036–$9,385; and high income, $9,386 or more.

11   This sub-group of developing economies comprised Argentina, Bangladesh, Brazil, China, Colombia, Costa Rica, Cote d'Ivoire, the Dominion Republic, Haiti, Hungary, India, Jamaica, Jordon, Malaysia, Mali, Mexico, Nepal, Nicaragua, Paraguay, the Philippines, Rwanda, Thailand, Uruguay and Zimbabwe.

12   See, for instance, Dollar (1992), Ben-David (1993), Sachs and Warner (1995), Coe and Hoffmaister (1997), Frankel and Romer (1999) and Edwards (1998). World Bank (2002a) provides a good survey of this literature.

13   See McCulloch, Winters and Cirera (2001), particularly chapter 2. Berg and Kruger (2002) survey the links between trade liberalization and growth. Winters (2002) provides a theoretical survey.

14   At the Third Plenary Session of the 11th Central Committee of the Chinese Communist Party (CCP) in December 1978, the People's Republic of China adopted its 'open door policy'. This became famous as the Deng doctrine, because Deng Xiaoping was the intellectual father of this liberal economic strategy. This marked a turning point in Chinese economic performance as well as economic history. It grew at a healthy rate through the 1980s and 1990s, and gross domestic product (GDP) increased by 10 per cent per annum in real terms over the 1980–2000 period. In a short span of two decades China economically transformed itself. Between 1978 and 2000, the GDP grew almost fivefold, per capita income quadrupled, and 270 million Chinese were lifted out of absolute poverty (*The Economist*, 2001). In 1990, China's GDP was $378.8 billion and per capita GDP was $341.60. A decade later, in 2000, GDP reached $1,080 billion, while per capita GDP rose to $853.40. Between 1981 and 2001, China succeeded in bringing down the population living below the World Bank poverty line of $1.08-a-day from 634 million to 211 million, a reduction of 66.7 per cent. If the poverty line is moved up to $2.15-a-day, the population below the poverty line declined from 875.8 million to 593.6 million, a decline of 32.2 per cent (Chen and Ravallion, 2004).

15   On the first page, in the first paragraph, of the Doha communiqué one finds a reaffirmation of these objectives. It reads as follows: 'The multilateral trading system embodied in the World Trade Organization has contributed significantly to economic growth, development and employment throughout the past fifty years. We are determined, particularly in the light of the global economic slowdown, to maintain the process of reform and liberalization of trade policies, thus ensuring that the system plays its full part in promoting recovery, growth and development' (WTO, 2001).

16   Recent empirical studies that have come to these conclusions include Ben-David (2001) and Greenaway, Morgan and Wright (2002).

17   The classical theory of comparative advantage (1817) was a simple, albeit robust concept, and based on inherent difference in countries' capacity and costs of producing different products. Although the theory is still robust, we no longer live in the simple and pristine world of Portuguese wine and British textiles. To be sure, factor endowments are an important source of

comparative advantage, but so are increasing returns to scale, product differentiation and technological differences.

18   For a detailed discussion refer to Mendoza (2002) and Mendoza and Bahadur (2002).

19   See Mendoza and Bahadur (2002) for an analysis of balance and imbalance in the Uruguay Round and in various WTO agreements.

20   The Rorschach test is a test for revealing the underlying personality structure of an individual by the use of a standard series of ten ink-blot designs to which the subject responds by telling what image or emotion each design evokes.

21   Refer to Das (2001), chapter 3, for a detailed treatment of the achievements of the Uruguay Round. It cites results from the empirical studies that have computed the welfare gains for the global economy and different sub-groups. For a discussion and survey of various projections, see Safadi and Laird (1996) and Rodrik (1994). See also the discussions in the edited volume by Martin and Winters (1996).

22   See UNDP (1997), pp. 80–6.

23   According to mercantilist philosophy, exports are good and imports are bad. Adam Smith was the first economist to discredit mercantilism in the most vigorous manner.

24   Similar views were also expressed by Stoeckel (2004).

25   Sir Leon Brittan, Vice-President of the European Commission, was the first to use this nomenclature. After that it caught on with academics as well as the economic and financial press.

26   The four Singapore issues are (i) trade and foreign investment, (ii) trade and competition, (iii) transparency in government procurement, and (iv) trade facilitation. They are referred to as the Singapore issues because they were broached for the first time during the Singapore Ministerial Conference by the industrial economies.

27   The birth date of the WTO is 1 January 1995.

28   The ASEAN was established on 8 August 1967 in Bangkok by the five original member countries, namely, Indonesia, Malaysia, Philippines, Singapore and Thailand. The ten present ASEAN members are Brunei Darussalam, Cambodia, Indonesia, Lao PDR, Malaysia, Myanmar, the Philippines, Singapore, Thailand and Vietnam.

29   The GATT had 23 signatories when it came into effect in January 1948, and 84 signatories at the time of the beginning of the Tokyo Round in 1973. More than 110 countries signed the Uruguay Round accord in Marrakesh, Morocco, in April 1994.

30   Pascal Lamy, the EU trade Commissioner, called the negotiation process 'medieval', as reported in *Financial Times*, 6 December 1999.

31   It is also known as the Seven Wise Men's report. Its formal title is *Trade Policies for a Better Future: Proposals for Action*, and it was published by the GATT Secretariat in 1985.

32   The various agreements which make up the Marrakesh Agreement combine as an indivisible whole, or a 'Single Undertaking'. No entity can be party to any one agreement without being party to them all.

33   Technically a vote could be taken and it was done only at the time of new accessions. Technically there could be a vote for other purposes as well, but it was never done. The new WTO system operates expressly by consensus.

34 Although most-favoured nation (MFN) sounds like a contradiction, implying some kind of special treatment to a particular trade partner, in the WTO jargon it means non-discrimination. That is, treating all trade partners under the WTO regime equally. Each WTO member treats all the WTO members as 'most-favoured' trading partner. If any country improves the market benefits to one trading partner, it is obliged to give the same best treatment to all the other WTO members so that they all remain 'most-favoured'. However, historically MFN did not mean equal treatment.

35 World Trade Organization (WTO, 2001), 'Doha Declaration Explained'. Available on the Internet at http://www.wto.org/english/tratop_eldda_e/work_organi_e.htm. 15 December.

36 As Archbishop of Cracow in Poland, Pope John Paul II was a passionate supporter of globalization. However, as the 1990s wore on, the Pope became increasingly uneasy about 'unbridled capitalism'. He expressed his disapproval in his Apostolic Exhortation to the Catholic Church in the Americas in January 1999 by enumerating the following ill effects of globalization: 'the absolutizing of the economy, unemployment, the reduction and deterioration of public services, the destruction of the environment and natural resources, the growing distance between the rich and the poor, unfair competition which puts poor nations in a situation of ever increasing inferiority ...'.

37 More manifestations of the same backlash against globalization were seen soon after Seattle in Davos (against the World Economic Forum), Bangkok (against the UNCTAD X conference), and Washington DC (against the spring meeting of the International Monetary Fund and the World Bank).

2 Equilibrating the Global Trading System

1 The 23 founding members were: Australia, Belgium, Brazil, Burma, Canada, Ceylon, Chile, China, Cuba, Czechoslovakia, France, India, Lebanon, Luxembourg, the Netherlands, New Zealand, Norway, Pakistan, Southern Rhodesia, Syria, South Africa, the United Kingdom and the United States.

2 Enshrined in Article I of the GATT, and subsequently the WTO, the most-favoured-nation (MFN) principle is the cornerstone of the multilateral trading system. It is Article II of the General Agreement on Trade in Services (GATS) and Article IV of the Agreement on Trade-Related Aspects of Intellectual Property Rights (TRIPS). According to this principle, countries cannot normally discriminate between their trading partners. The expression most-favoured-nation (MFN) sounds like an oxymoron. It suggests some kind of special treatment for one particular country, but it means non-discrimination, that is treating everybody equally. Each member of the WTO treats all other members equally as 'most favoured' trading partners. If a member country improves the benefits that it gives to one trading partner, it is obliged to give the same 'best' treatment to all the other WTO members so that they all remain 'most favoured'. The expression MFN originated in the nineteenth century, when its meaning was just the opposite of what it is at present. A number of MFN treaties were signed during this period. Being a 'most favoured' trading partner was like being in an exclusive club, because only a few countries enjoyed the privilege.

3   The NIEs group comprises Chile, Hong Kong SAR, Korea, Singapore and Taiwan.
4   In a trade agreement, the negotiating parties make reciprocal concessions to put their trade relationships on a basis deemed equitable by each. The principle of reciprocity is extremely old, and in one form or another it is to be found in all trade agreements. The concessions exchanged by the negotiating parties are, however, in different areas.
5   See, for instance, Winters (2000a), Rodrik (2001b) and Hoekman *et al.* (2003).
6   Refer to WTO (2004), Appendix table 1.
7   The Group-of-Seven (G-7) was founded in 1978 by French President Giscard d'Estaing and German Chancellor Helmut Schmidt. Paul Martin, the erstwhile Canadian Finance Minister, is credited with founding the Group-of-Twenty (G-20) in 1999 which comprised 10 industrial economies and 10 EMEs. The first group was composed of the G-7 economies, plus Australia, Russia and the President of the EU. The second group included Argentina, Brazil, China, India, Indonesia, Korea, Mexico, Saudi Arabia, South Africa and Turkey. With the passage of time, G-7 has become inadequate to address the economic challenges of the global economy. The G-20 is a more representative group of finance ministers that has attracted worldwide attention as a useful forum for discussing and negotiating policies on global economic issues (Bradford and Linn, 2004).
8   See, for instance, Parsley and Wei (2001), Rogers (2001), Hufbauer, Wada and Warren (2002) and IMF (2002).
9   In economics of international trade, the two expressions, namely, the GATT-1947 and the GATT-1994, are frequently used. The difference between the two is that the latter is the revised version of the original GATT Agreement of 1947. The text of the Agreement was significantly revised and amended during the Uruguay Round and the new version was agreed upon in Marrakesh, Morocco. Apparently, the GATT-1994 reflected the outcome of the negotiations on issues relating to the interpretations of specific articles. In its renewed version, the GATT-1994 includes specific understandings with respect to GATT Articles, its obligations and provisions, plus the Marrakesh Protocol of GATT-1994.
10   Refer to GATT-1994, Article XXVIII *bis*, in GATT (1994).
11   The concept of national treatment is as basic to the WTO system as the most-favoured-nation (MFN) principle. A tariff reduction at the border would provide absolutely no benefit if the imported goods are later discriminated against in the marketplace (beyond the border) by the host government by way of a differential sales tax, or other requirements of inspection on packaging. It is the principle of giving others the same treatment as one's own nationals. The requirement of national treatment prohibits against negative discriminatory treatment of imports. Imports cannot be accorded less-favourable treatment than products of national origin. GATT and WTO Article III requires that imports be treated 'no less favourably than the same or similar domestically produced goods' once they have passed customs. The General Agreement on Trade in Services (GATS) Article XVII and Agreement on Trade-Related Intellectual Property Rights (TRIPS) Article III also deal with national treatment for services and intellectual property protection, respectively.

12 For the logic behind it, see Das (2004b), chapter 2.

13 See, for instance, Deardorff and Stern (2002) and Miller (2003).

14 Relatively high tariffs, usually on 'sensitive' products, amidst generally low tariff levels, are known as tariff peaks. For industrial countries, tariffs of 15 per cent or above are generally considered as high tariffs or spikes.

15 David Ricardo's theory of comparative advantage was propounded in 1817.

16 Seekers of more information should refer to Deardorff and Stern (2003) and Brown *et al.* (2003).

17 In 2004, the United Nations classification of least-developed countries (LDCs) included 50 countries, of which 30 are members of the WTO and five are observers.

18 Tariff-binding is defined as commitment not to increase a rate of duty beyond any agreed level. Once a rate of duty is bound, it may not be raised without compensating the affected trading partners. Tariff binding is enshrined in Article II of GATT-1994.

19 Bound tariff rates of 15 per cent and above are known as international peaks or tariff spikes. As opposed to this, when tariffs are three times or greater than the domestic mean tariffs they are called national peaks.

20 Its full name is Mercado Comun del Sur, or the common market of the south. Its membership includes Argentina, Brazil, Paraguay and Uruguay.

21 Hoda and Verma (2004) provide details regarding each proposal culled from the WTO documents.

22 Such as catalytic converters, air filters, etc.

23 These statistics were cited in the *OECD Policy Brief, October 2003*.

24 See Das (2001), chapter 5, for a detailed treatment of the GTAP model.

25 The details of their modelling framework are documented in Hertel (1997).

26 Conclusions presented are only an abridged version. For complete results of the CGE exercise refer to Lippoldt and Kowalski (2004).

3 Setback in Cancún

1 As noted earlier, thus far five Ministerial Conferences of the World Trade Organization have taken place. They were: Singapore (9–13 December 1996), Geneva (18–20 May 1998), Seattle (30 November to 3 December 1999), Doha (9–13 November 2001) and Cancún (10–14 September 2003). The sixth Ministerial Conference is scheduled for December 2005 in Hong Kong SAR.

2 Refer to, for instance, Evenett (2003) and Srinivasan (2003).

3 Arthur Dunkel, a former member of the Swiss trade delegation, was the Director General of the GATT between 1980 and 1992.

4 The United States Trade Administration (USTA) signed eight bilateral trade agreements between September 2003 and May 2004.

5 See Bacchetta and Bora (2003) for these statistics. Also refer to Lall (2000) for a detailed exposition on the changing structure of developing country exports over the last two decades.

6 At the time of writing, the G-21 has the following 22 members: Argentina, Bolivia, Brazil, Chile, China, Colombia, Costa Rica, Cuba, Ecuador, Egypt, Guatemala, India, Indonesia, Mexico, Nigeria, Pakistan, Paraguay, Peru, Philippines, South Africa, Thailand and Venezuela. The role of collegial leaders of G-21 was played by Brazil, China, India and South Africa.

7 Fifty countries are presently designated by the United Nations as 'least-developed countries' (LDCs). The list is reviewed every three years by the Economic and Social Council (ECOSOC) of the United Nations. In its latest triennial review in 2003, the ECOSOC used the following three criteria for the identification of the LDCs, which were proposed by the Committee for Development Policy (CDP): (i) a low-income criterion, based on a three-year average estimate of the gross domestic product per capita (under $750 for inclusion, above $900 for graduation); (ii) a human-resource weakness criterion, involving a composite Augmented Physical Quality of Life Index (APQLI) based on indicators of: (a) nutrition; (b) health; (c) education; and (d) adult literacy; and (iii) an economic vulnerability criterion, involving a composite Economic Vulnerability Index (EVI) based on indicators of: (a) the instability of agricultural production; (b) the instability of exports of goods and services; (c) the economic importance of non-traditional activities (share of manufacturing and modern services in GDP); (d) merchandise export concentration; and (e) the handicap of economic smallness (as measured through the population in logarithm); and the percentage of population displaced by natural disasters.

8 See the following section for a definition of the Singapore issues.

9 Refer to the inaugural address of Mike Moore given in Doha, Qatar, on 9 November 2001, as well as his speech before the Third Ministerial Conference in Seattle.

10 See paragraph 45 of the Doha Ministerial Declaration, 14 November 2001.

11 They are referred to as the Singapore issues because they were raised for the first time by the industrial economies during the Singapore Ministerial Conference in 1996.

12 Bound tariff rates of 15 per cent and above are known as international peaks or tariff spikes. As opposed to this, when tariffs are three times or greater than the domestic mean tariffs, they are called national peaks.

13 See WTO (2001a), paragraph 2.

14 See note 10, Chapter 1.

15 For instance, the US Farm Bill of 2002 (or the Farm Security and Rural Investment Act of 2002) promised greater domestic support to farmers. Likewise, the European Commission's Luxembourg reform of the Common Agricultural Policy (CAP) declared in June 2003 failed to reduce the total level of European agricultural support. Japan also announced a programme of increased self-sufficiency in agriculture, implying higher production subsidies and trade barriers.

16 When the Cancún Ministerial Conference began, Chairperson of the Ministerial Conference, Luis Ernesto Derbez, Foreign Minister of Mexico, had warned of dangers of failure. He described the Cancún Conference as a 'once-in-a-generation opportunity', and that a failure would mean loss of momentum and that negotiations would take 'a long time to recover'. Pascal Lamy, who was confirmed the Trade Commissioner of the EU in 1999 by the European Parliament, was the EU's chief negotiator in Cancún. He had admonished the congregation at the outset to eschew 'the confrontational north–south ambiance of the 1970s and 1980s'.

17 This category of exportables includes textiles and apparel, toys, sporting goods, iron and steel products, and engineering products like engines, pumps and other instruments.

18 Borrowing an expression from Paul Krugman.
19 See, for instance, Deardorff (2001) and Hummels, Ishii and Yi (2001) for interesting analyses of production networks and the newest trends.
20 See WB (2003), in particular chapters 2 and 6.
21 $1.08 a day is one of the two reference lines of poverty defined by the World Bank. The other reference line is $2.25 a day.
22 See Hoekman (2003), who also provides a list of instances of creating such splits among the developing economies in the past.
23 These countries were Benin, Burkina Faso, Chad and Mali.
24 See Paragraph 16 of the Doha Ministerial Declaration, which states the aim of reducing 'or as appropriate eliminate' these three forms of persistent protection. 'Product coverage shall be comprehensive and without *a priori* exclusions.'
25 See studies like Cernat, Laird and Turrini (2002), Supper (2001) and WTO (2001).
26 The exceptions are Peoples' Republic of China, Hong Kong SAR, Macao and Singapore, which have low simple average bound tariffs.
27 Tariff binding implies commitment not to increase a rate of duty beyond an agreed level. Once a rate of duty is bound it may not be raised without compensating the affected parties.
28 The sample comprised 18 countries, the Quad economies (namely, Canada, the EU [of 15], Japan, and the USA), Australia, Brazil, China, Hong Kong SAR, Mexico, India, Korea (Republic of), Malaysia, Poland, Singapore, Switzerland, Taiwan, Thailand and Turkey.
29 See the previous footnote for a list of sample countries.
30 See Bacchetta and Bora (2001 and 2003) who provide a detailed analysis identifying each product with its four digit HS classification.
31 Between the biannual meetings of Ministerial Conferences, the main governing body of the WTO is the General Council. The Council meets in two other forms, namely the Dispute Settlement Body (DSB) to oversee the dispute settlement procedures and as the Trade Policy Review Board (TPRB) to conduct regular reviews of WTO members' trade policies. The main bodies that report to the General Council are the Council for Trade in Goods, the Council for Trade in Services, and the Council for Trade Related Aspects of Intellectual Property Rights. All the WTO councils and committees are open to all members (Das, 2001).
32 It must be acknowledged that all the implementation-related information and statistics regarding progress in the Doha Round of multilateral trade negotiations comes from WTO (2003d).
33 Movement of natural persons implies entry and temporary stay of people supplying a service. They could be either self-employed or employees of a services company.
34 Under this system, governments can issue compulsory licences to allow a competitor to produce the product or use the process under licence, but only under certain conditions aimed at safeguarding the legitimate interest of the patent holder.
35 They are also known as anti-trust or anti-monopoly laws.
36 Vertical agreement refers to agreements between suppliers and distributors.
37 Cartels are known to operate in the following industries: graphite electrodes, vitamins, citric acid, seamless steel tubes, lysine and bromine.

38   Cited in WTO (2003), p. 32.
39   See Paragraph 16 of the Doha Declaration, November 2001.
40   This number includes notifications made under GATT Article XXIV, GATS Article V, and the Enabling Clause.
41   These four issues are: (1) interpreting what is meant by 'substantially all trade', (2) trade-restricting regulations such as rules of origin (ROO), (3) the impact of RIAs on economic growth and (4) the primacy of the multilateral trading system and the possible negative effect of RTAs on non-member countries.
42   The European development cooperation policy is run in conjunction with the 77 ACP countries and, following the Lomé Convention, is governed by the Cotonou Agreement.
43   Pascal Lamy did not inform the negotiating group until the last morning in Cancún. Even at that late hour hints were dropped that the EU could drop three Singapore issues, leaving only negotiations on trade facilitation on the table.
44   See, for instance, Hoekman (2003) and Evenett (2003).
45   'Implementation-related issues' are one of the 20 agenda items of the Doha Round.
46   This was reversal of the US commitment embodied in its 1996 Farm Bill, which aimed at increasing the reliance of farmers on market-determined prices rather than government price support.
47   In WTO terminology, subsidies in general are identified by 'boxes' which are given the colours of traffic lights: green implies permitted; amber means slow down or reduce; while red stands for forbidden. In agriculture, things are in general more complicated. The Agriculture Agreement has no red box, although domestic support exceeding the reduction commitment levels in the amber box is prohibited; and there is a blue box for subsidies that are tied to programmes that limit production. All domestic support measures considered to distort production and trade (with some exceptions) fall into the amber box, which is defined in Article 6 of the URAA as all domestic supports except those in the blue and green boxes. These include measures to support prices, or subsidies directly related to production quantities. These supports are subject to limits: '*de minimis*' minimal supports are allowed (5 per cent of agricultural production for developed countries, 10 per cent for developing countries); the 30 WTO members that had larger subsidies than the *de minimis* levels at the beginning of the post-Uruguay Round reform period had committed to reduce these subsidies.
48   See Das (2001) for this debate.
49   This section draws on the following two sources: Hoekman (2003) and Hoekman, Michalopoulos and Winters (2003).
50   Jacques Chirac, the French President, declared that the draft framework was 'profoundly unbalanced'.
51   A petition was filed by Brazil in the WTO Dispute Settlement Panel challenging the annual payments of approximately $3 billion to its cotton farmers by the USA. It constituted a violation of WTO rules. The WTO Dispute Settlement Panel gave a preliminary ruling on 27 April 2004, against US cotton subsidies, which is both a political victory and a financial gain for the cotton farmers from western and central Africa, including Benin and Burkina

Faso and Mali. Africa's cotton production is concentrated on small farms. Approximately ten million cotton farmers earn on average of $400 per year, and lose an estimated $250 million annually to heavily-subsidized cotton producers from the world's wealthier nations, in large part because subsidies enable American producers to offer their cotton at much lower prices and still record profits. In June 2003, led by Benin, Chad, Burkina Faso and Mali, West Africa presented a proposal for phasing out cotton subsidies to the World Trade Organization. Three months later, this issue was placed on the agenda at the Cancún Ministerial, which proved both a setback and a victory for West Africa's cotton farmers. Although the US Trade Representative Robert Zoellick had initially signalled a willingness to negotiate meaningful agricultural reforms, the USA ultimately joined the EU in opposing the demands. However, because of the pressure from the G-20 group, the EU and the USA were unable to force a compromise on this issue at Cancún (Rice and Smith, 2004).

4 The Doha Round and the Developing Economies

1 See Das (2001), in particular chapter 1.
2 This chapter draws on chapter 6 of *Global Economic Prospects* (2004) published by the World Bank; see pp. 205–31.
3 As discussed in the preceding chapter, the G-21 achieved in Geneva what they could not in Cancún.
4 Canada, the EU, Japan and the USA are the four Quadrilateral (or Quad) countries.
5 For a detailed discussion on this issue refer to Stiglitz and Charlton (2004).
6 See note 9, Chapter 2.
7 See note 34, Chapter 1.
8 For instance, the Generalized System of Preferences (GSP), the Caribbean Basin Initiative (CBI), the Lomé Convention, the Cotonou Agreement, the NAFTA Parity Act, the Central American Common Market (CACM) and the CARICOM Common Market, are some of the PTAs that were created under the Enabling Clause.
9 The definition of absolute poor is based on subsistence, the minimum standard needed to live. Robert McNamara defined it as 'a condition of life beneath any reasonable standard of human dignity'. There has been a long drawn debate in the discipline regarding whether income or consumption poverty lines should be defined in absolute or relative terms. Most international organizations define the poverty line in an absolute way as the 'level of income necessary for people to buy the goods necessary to their survival'. In keeping with this concept, the dollar-a-day line, at 1985 purchasing power parity, is extensively used (Bouguignon, 1999).
10 See, note 7, Chapter 3.
11 See note 10, Chapter 1.
12 See, for instance, Brenton (2003) and Brenton and Manchin (2002).
13 Some of the recent studies include Oyejide (2002), Hart and Dymond (2003), Hoekman *et al.* (2003) and Hoekman *et al.* (2004).
14 *Ibid.*

15 See Das (2004) for these details, in particular chapter 3, as well as Schiff and Winters (2003).
16 Several researchers have addressed these issues. See for instance Hoekman *et al.* (2003), and Messerlin (2003) and Wolf (2003).
17 See also Hoekman *et al.* (2002).
18 As noted earlier, bound tariff rates of 15 per cent and above are known as international peaks (also tariff spikes). As opposed to this, when tariffs are three times or greater than the domestic mean tariffs they are called national peaks.
19 Francois and Martin (2003) deal with this issue at great length.
20 The WB (2003) forecast the real GDP growth rate for the developing economies for 2003–15 at 4.7 per cent per annum, and that for the industrial economies at 2.5 per cent. Similarly, the medium-term forecast of the IMF (2003) for the 2003–07 period was 5.7 per cent for the developing economies and 3.1 per cent for the industrial economies.
21 The source of all the statistical data used here is WTO (2003).
22 *The Economist*, 13 November 2004, provides a detailed account of the possibility of such transformations in trade in textiles and apparel. See 'The Looming Revolution' on pages 75–7.
23 See paragraph 16 of the Doha Ministerial Declaration.
24 See two recent works of Winters (2000b) and McCulloch *et al.* (2001).
25 See Chen and Ravallion (2004), tables 2 and 3.
26 See World Bank (2002), chapter 6.

5 Trade in Services and the Doha Round

1 The sources of these statistics are the WTO, *International Trade Statistics*, various issues, and WTO (2004).
2 Das (2004a) discusses the onward march of globalization, global economic integration and its economic consequences in enormous detail.
3 This is a large well-researched document (190 pages) which took years to finalize. It was published in 2002.
4 The source of these statistics is WTO (2004), Appendix table 3.
5 *Ibid.*
6 Some analysts believe that the technological advances of the preceding quarter century have led to the creation of the so-called New Economy. They contend that the rules governing economic performance have been transformed due to a permanent improvement in the economy's efficiency and productivity. The technological advances they refer to include increased use of faster computers with new software and the widespread availability of information that the Internet provides. Economists are trying to determine whether these factors are behind the sharp upward revision in worker productivity in the USA. Chairman of the Federal Reserve Board, Alan Greenspan, recently stated that he did not know whether the current 'good performance of the economy' is a part of 'a once- or twice-in-a-century phenomenon that will carry productivity trends nationally and globally to a new higher track, or whether we are merely observing some unusual variations within the context of an otherwise generally conventional business cycle expansion.' However,

Paul Krugman disagrees and argues that we are still operating under the same rules that applied to the earliest, most basic market economies.

7 In the audiovisual industry, international markets provide an important source of earnings for the Indian movie industry. Although Indian movies are exported to 95 countries, Canada, the UK and the USA are the largest markets. In 1998, a total of 198 titles were exported. This number exceeded 500 in 2001. Export earnings of the Indian movie industry rose from Rs2 billion to Rs5.25 billion between 1998 and 2001. Hong Kong SAR is one of the largest producers and exporters of movies in the world, franking third after the USA and India. Thailand has also emerged as an active player in the audiovisual industry, producing movies, TV programmes, music and animation. Firms from Thailand provide production and post-production services for large clients like 20th Century Fox and Warner Brothers at competitive prices. Many developing economies have emerged as successful providers of port services, and several of them figure in the list of top 20 container terminals, in terms of throughput. Together they provided 54.3 per cent of the total container shipping services in 2002. Four of the five largest containers shipping terminals are in developing countries, namely Singapore, Taiwan, Korea and Hong Kong SAR. Likewise, in the construction industry, 51 of the largest 150 construction firms in the world were from developing countries. Firms from China, Turkey, Korea (Republic of), Brazil and Taiwan, in that order, were among the most active in this service area. Expertise in health services became an import source of foreign exchange earnings in Chile, Costa Rica, Cuba, South Africa and Thailand (OECD, 2003a).

8 The source of these statistics is NASSCOM (2004).

9 There are about 60 agreements and decisions in the text of the Uruguay Round agreement, or the WTO-1994, published in 550 pages.

10 This is the complete and formal name of the GATS.

11 Its date of coming into force is the same as that of the WTO, 1 January 1995.

12 Refer to WTO (2001a) for a simple and lucid exposition on the functions and operations of the General Agreement on Trade in Services (GATS).

13 This section is based on the WTO publications in this area. See in particular WTO (2003) 'Negotiators Agree on Modalities for Treatment of Autonomous Liberalization'. Press Release. no. 335. 10 March.

14 *Ibid.*

15 Cattaneo and Nielson (2003) have discussed the methodological imperfections in such empirical exercises and ways to resolve them.

16 See *Towards a Fair Deal for Migrant Workers in the Global Economy*, International Labour Conference, 92nd Session, October 2004. Report VI. Geneva. See Chapter 4 in particular for current regulations in this area.

17 For more details refer to the *Background Paper* prepared for the Trade and Migration Seminar by the IOM/WB/WTO (2004).

6   Trade in Agriculture and the Doha Round

1 See table IV.6, on page 106 of *International Trade Statistics 2003*, published by the WTO in August 2003.

2 See table IV.4, on page 105 of *International Trade Statistics 2003*.

3   A Corn Law was first introduced in Britain in 1804, when the landowners, who dominated Parliament, sought to protect their profits by imposing a duty on imported corn. During the Napoleonic Wars it had not been possible to import corn from Europe, which led to an expansion of British wheat farming and to high bread prices. However, farmers feared that when the war came to an end in 1815, the import of foreign corn would lower prices. This fear was justified and the price of corn fell by 50 per cent during 1812 and 1815. In 1846, the Corn Law had to be finally repealed.

4   These five rounds of MTNs were Geneva (1947), Annecy (1949), Torquay (1951), Geneva (1956) and the Dillon Round (1960–61).

5   The Cairns Group of 17 agricultural exporting countries, formed in 1986, has effectively put agriculture on the multilateral trade agenda and kept it there. The Cairns Group is an excellent example of successful coalition-building in the trade area. The 17 members of this Group are Argentina, Australia, Bolivia, Brazil, Canada, Chile, Colombia, Costa Rica, Guatemala, Indonesia, Malaysia, New Zealand, Paraguay, the Philippines, South Africa, Thailand and Uruguay. The members of the Cairns Group come from four continents and include a wide range of economies, from industrial to the least developed.

6   See WB (2004), chapter 3, as well as Beghin and Aksoy (2003), OECD (2003a) and Ingco and Nash (2004).

7   New Zealand's Ambassador, Tim Groser, is the current Chairman of the Committee on Agriculture of the WTO.

8   Early in 2004 Pascal Lamy and Supachai Panitchpakdi exchanged accusations of using 'contestable' statistics.

9   See Tangermann (2004) for more details.

10 The legal basis of an agricultural policy for the entire European Community is defined in Articles 32 through 38 in Title II of the EC Treaty. Agriculture sat high on the agenda of European policy-makers, especially at the time when the Treaty of Rome was being negotiated during the 1950s. The memory of postwar food shortages was still vivid and thus agriculture constituted a key element from the outset of the European Community. The Treaty of Rome (1957) defined the general objectives of a common agricultural policy. The principles of the Common Agricultural Policy (CAP) were set out at the Stresa Conference in July 1958. In 1960, the CAP mechanisms were adopted by the six founding member states and two years later, in 1962, the CAP came into force. The CAP is comprised of a set of rules and mechanisms which regulate the production, trade and processing of agricultural products in the European Union (EU), with attention being focused increasingly on rural development. Among the European Union's policies, the CAP is regarded as one of the most important policy areas. Not only because of its share of the EU budget (almost 50 per cent, and decreasing over the years), the vast number of people and the extent of the territory directly affected, but also because of its symbolic significance, and the extent of sovereignty transferred from the national to the European level. The significance of the CAP, nowadays, is also portrayed by the fact that it is directly related to the Single Market and EMU, two key areas in achieving European integration. The objectives of the CAP, as set out in Article 33 of the EC Treaty, are: (i) 'to increase agricultural productivity by promoting technical progress and by

ensuring the rational development of agricultural production and the optimum utilization of the factors of production, in particular labor; (ii) to ensure a fair standard of living for the agricultural community, in particular by increasing the individual earnings of persons engaged in agriculture; (iii) to stabilize markets; (iv) to assure the availability of supplies; (v) to ensure that supplies reach consumers at reasonable prices.'

11   These CAP reforms were announced in Luxemburg on 26 June 2003.

12   GTAP stands for Global Trade Analysis Project and is based on Hertel (1997). The GTAP model is a standard, multi-sector model that has become highly popular with researchers.

13   In *Financial Times*, 2 August 2004, Herve Gaymard the Agriculture Minister of France was quoted as saying that he would seek a 'proper' timetable for the cuts looking 'towards a horizon of 2015 or 2017'.

14   These non-tariff barriers (NTBs) included variable import levies, discretionary import licensing and voluntary export restraints.

15   This was taken up as the reference period because during these years the OECD economies maximized their support to the agricultural sector.

16   See World Bank (2004), chapter 3, table 3.8.

17   The source of statistics in this section is WB (2004), chapter 3.

18   Mauritius had submitted a proposal on behalf of the African countries.

19   According to WTO terminology, subsidies in general are identified by 'boxes' which are given the colours of traffic lights: green implies permitted, amber means slow down or reduce, while red stands for forbidden. In agriculture, things are in general more complicated. The Agriculture Agreement has no red box, although domestic support exceeding the reduction commitment levels in the amber box is prohibited; and there is a blue box for subsidies that are tied to programmes that limit production. All domestic support measures considered to distort production and trade (with some exceptions) fall into the amber box, which is defined in Article 6 of the URAA as all domestic supports except those in the blue and green boxes. These include measures to support prices, or subsidies directly related to production quantities. These supports are subject to limits: *'de minimis'* minimal supports are allowed (5 per cent of agricultural production for developed countries, 10 per cent for developing countries); the 30 WTO members that had larger subsidies than the *de minimis* levels at the beginning of the post-Uruguay Round reform period had committed to reduce these subsidies.

20   At the time of writing, the G-21 has the following 22 members: Argentina, Bolivia, Brazil, Chile, China, Colombia, Costa Rica, Cuba, Ecuador, Egypt, Guatemala, India, Indonesia, Mexico, Nigeria, Pakistan, Paraguay, Peru, Philippines, South Africa, Thailand and Venezuela. The role of collegial leaders of the G-21 was played by Brazil, China, India and South Africa.

21   See WTO (2003a, 2003b, 2004a) for more details.

22   Cited in AITIC (2004).

23   Of the three most important international currencies, the euro acquired a position of strength during the fourth quarter of 2004. High budget and current-account deficits caused concern regarding the future health of the US economy. Coupled with weakness of the US economy, Europe's interest yield advantage, and geo-political tensions sent the euro soaring. It peaked on 10 November 2004 at $1.30. Although it soon came down from its high

perch by a small margin ($1.20), it continued to remain strong. In addition, fears surrounding the new respiratory virus hitting Asia left the yen at its lowest level in four years *vis-à-vis* the euro. Japanese investors were aggressively purchasing euro-denominated assets during the fourth quarter.

24 Under the Uruguay Round Agreement on Agriculture (URAA), the United States and other countries agreed to keep the total value of trade-distorting domestic support to farmers from exceeding predetermined ceiling levels for the years 1995–2000. Ceilings were established for each country based on their level of trade-distorting domestic support in the base period 1986–88. Under the URAA, ceilings decline from 97 per cent of 1986–88 base levels in 1995 to 80 per cent in 2000 for the industrial economies. Countries also agree to notify the WTO about the current level of domestic support for each year in the implementation period, 1995 to 2000. The annual level of such support, called the 'aggregate measurement of support' (AMS), is measured as the sum of certain trade-distorting commodity-specific and non-commodity-specific farm programme benefits, as defined in the URAA. These AMS benefits include those from direct government payments as well as market price supports that are provided to farmers based on the level of current production, price, resource use or input benefits.

25 These details on agreement on modalities have been gleaned from WTO (2004b). Seekers of more detail should refer to this source.

26 See Hertell and Martin (2000).

7 Intellectual Property Rights and the Doha Round

1 Refer to the website of the World Trade Organization (WTO) 'What are intellectual property rights?' available at http://www.wto.org/english/tratop_e/trips_e/intel1_e.htm. September 2004.

2 Trademarks and indications of geographical origin are markedly different from each other. For instance, trademarks belong to a commercial enterprise, and are not limited by any territorial link, whereas geography is at the heart of the geographical indications (GIs). Besides, the GIs are not limited to any particular commercial enterprise, but enjoyed by all enterprises within the demarcated geographical area that meet the stipulated requirement for use of the geographical indication.

3 *Ibid.*

4 See note 9, Chapter 2.

5 The Marrakesh Agreement was signed on 15 April 1994 in Marrakesh, Morocco. Trade ministers who participated in the Uruguay Round signed the results of the seven-and-a-half years of trade negotiations – about 60 agreements and a decision totalling around 550 pages – as the Uruguay Round was formally concluded.

6 In 2004, the UN classification of least-developed countries (LDCs) included 50 countries, of which 30 were members of the WTO and five were observers.

7 The Free-Trade Area of the Americas (FTAA) has 34 members. Countries participating in the negotiations of the FTAA held their Seventh Ministerial Meeting in Quito, Ecuador, on 1 November 2002 with the intent to review progress in the FTAA negotiations to establish guidelines for the next phase of

these negotiations. The negotiations are scheduled to conclude on January 2005 in accordance with the terms agreed by the heads of state and government at the Third Summit of the Americas, held in Quebec City in April 2001. The negotiations are to seek FTAA's entry into force as soon as possible after January 2005, but in any case no later than December 2005. The 34 members of the FTAA are Antigua and Barbuda, Argentina, Bahamas, Barbados, Belize, Bolivia, Brazil, Canada, Chile, Colombia, Costa Rica, Dominica, Dominican Republic, Ecuador, El Salvador, Grenada, Guatemala, Guyana, Haiti, Honduras, Jamaica, Mexico, Nicaragua, Panama, Paraguay, Peru, St Lucia, St Kitts and Nevis, St Vincent and Grenadines, Suriname, Trinidad and Tobago, Uruguay, the United States of America and Venezuela.

8 See, for instance, Vivas-Eugui (2004).

9 See *A Proposal for Establishing a Development Agenda for the World Intellectual Property Organization*, published by the WIPO.

10 These explanations are provided on the TRIPS pages of the WTO website, where a good deal of relevant information on the TRIPS agreement is available.

11 See the literature survey conducted by Maskus, Saggi and Puttitanun (2004).

12 See also Gould and Gruben (1996) and Carr, Markusen, and Maskus (2004).

13 Related statistics are available on the website of the WTO and UNAIDS as well as in the *World Health Report* published annually by the WHO.

14 NGOs such as Médecins Sans Frontiéres, Oxfam and the Third World Network were among the most critical of the agreement.

References

Agency for International Trade Information and Cooperation (AITIC) (2004) 'Post-Cancún Agenda: The Doha Work Programme Negotiations on Agriculture'. Geneva: Switzerland. April.

Alderman, H. (2001) 'What has Changed Regarding Rural Poverty since Vision to Action?', Washington, DC: The World Bank. Rural Strategy Background Paper No. 5.

Anderson, K. (1994) 'Multilateral Trade Negotiations, European Integration and Farm Policy', *Economic Policy*, vol. 18, no. 2, pp. 28–44.

Anderson, K. (1995) 'Lobbying Incentives and the Pattern of Protection in Rich and Poor Countries', *Economic Development and Cultural Change*, vol. 43, no. 2, pp. 401–23.

Anderson, K. (2003) 'How Can Agricultural Trade Reforms Reduce Poverty?' Adelaide: University of Adelaide. Center for International Economic Studies. Discussion Paper No. 0321. July 2003.

Anderson, K. (2004) 'Agricultural Trade Reforms and Trade Reforms and Poverty Reduction in Developing Countries', in S. Jayasurya and P.J. Lloyd, *International Trade and Development*. London: Edward Elgar Publishers. pp. 130–59.

Anderson, K. and Yao, S. (2003) 'How Can South Asia and Sub-Saharan Africa Gain from the Next WTO Round?', *Journal of Economic Integration*, vol. 18, no. 3, pp. 466–81.

Anderson, K., Francois, J., Hertel, T.W., Hoikman, B. and Martin, W. (2000) 'Potential Gains from Trade Reforms in the New Millennium', Adelaide: University of Adelaide. Centre for International Economic Studies.

Anderson, K., Dimaranan, B., Francois, J., Hertek, T., Hoekmam, B. and Martin, W. (2001) 'The Cost of Rich (and Poor) Country Protection to Developing Countries', *Journal of African Studies*, vol. 10, no. 3, pp. 227–57.

Bacchetta, M. and Bora, B. (2001) 'Post Uruguay Round Market Access Barriers for Industrial Products', *Policy Issues in International Trade and Commodities*, Study Series No. 1. Geneva: United Nations Conference on Trade and Development.

Bacchetta, M. and Bora, B. (2003) 'Industrial Tariff Liberalization and the Doha Development Agenda', Geneva: World Trade Organization.

Baker, D. (2003) 'Agriculture in the EU's Eastern Enlargement: The Current Status of CEECs', *Intereconomics*, vol. 38, no. 1, pp. 19–28. January/February.

Basu, S., Fernald, J.G., Oulton, N. and Srinivasan, S. (2003) 'The Case of Missing Productivity Growth: Or Does Information Technology Explain Why Productivity Accelerated in the US but not in the UK?'. Cambridge, MA: National Bureau of Economic Research. NBER Working Paper No. 10010.

Becker Consulting (2003) 'Incentives for Technology Transfer to Least Developed Countries'. Stockholm (mimeo).

Beghin, J.C. and Aksoy, A. (2003) 'Agricultural Trade and the Doha Round: Lessons from Commodities Studies'. Ames. Iowa, Iowa State University. Center for Agricultural and Rural Development. Briefing Paper 03–42. July.

Beghin, J.C., Ronald-Holst, D. and van der Mensbrugghe, D. (2003) 'How Will Agricultural Trade Reforms in High-Income Countries Affect the Trading Relationship of Developing Economies?', in OECD, Paris: Organization for Economic Cooperation and Development. pp. 39–58.

Ben-David, D. (1993) 'Equalizing Exchange: Trade Liberalization and Economic Convergence', *Quarterly Journal of Economics*, vol. 108, no. 3, pp. 611–31.

Ben-David, D. (2001) 'Trade Liberalization and Income Convergence: A Comment', *Journal of International Economics*, vol. 55, no. 2, pp. 229–34.

Berg, A. and Kruger, A.O. (2002) 'Trade, Growth and Poverty', Paper presented at the Annual Bank Conference on Development Economics, Washington, DC.

Borjas, G.J. (2004) 'Do Foreign Students Crowd out Native Students from Graduate Programs'. Cambridge, MA: National Bureau of Economic Research. NBER Working Paper No. 10349.

Bouguignon, F. (1999) 'Absolute poverty, relative deprivation and social exclusion'. Paper presented at the workshop on the *World Development Report*, organized by the Deutsche Stiftung fur Internationale Entwicklung, Berlin, Germany, during 2–3 Februray.

Bouguignon, F. and Morrisson, C. (2002) 'Inequality Among World's Citizens: 1820–1992', *The American Economic Review*, vol. 92, no. 4, pp. 727–44.

Bradford, C.I. and Linn, J.F. (2004) 'Global Economic Governance at Crossroads: Replacing G-7 with G-20', Washington, DC: The Brookings Institution. Policy Brief No. 131. April 2004.

Brenton, P. (2003) 'Integrating the Least Developed Countries into the World Trading System'. Washington, DC: The World Bank. Policy Research Working Paper No. 3018.

Brenton, P. and Manchin, M. (2002) 'Making the EU Trade Agreements Work', *The World Economy*, vol. 25, no. 1, pp. 22–40.

Brooks, J., Matthews, A. and Wilson, N. (2004) 'Do Developing Countries Need a Development Box?' Paris. Organization for Economic Cooperation and Development (OECD) (mimeo).

Brown, D.K., Deardorff, A.V. and Stern, R.M. (2003) 'Multilateral, Regional and Bilateral Trade Policy Options for the United States and Japan', *The World Economy*, June, vol. 26, no. 6, pp. 803–28.

Carr, D.L., Markusen, J.R. and Maskus, K.E. (2004) 'Competition for Multinational Investment in Developing Countries: Human Capital, Infrastructure, and Market Size', in Robert E. Baldwin and L. Alan Winters (eds), *Challenges to Globalization*. Chicago: University of Chicago Press, pp. 383–409.

Cattaneo, O. and Nielson, J. (2003) 'Services Providers on the Move: The Economic Impact of Mode 4'. Paris: Organization for Economic Cooperation and Development. Trade Directorate. March.

Cernat, L., Laird, S. and Turrini, A. (2002) 'Back to Basics'. Geneva: United Nations Conference on Trade and Development.

Chellaraj, G., Maskus, K.E. and Mattoo, A. (2004) Available on the Internet at http://siteresources.worldbank.org/INTRANETTRADE/Resources/Topics/Services/chellaraj-maskus-mattoo_skilledworkerimpactonusa.pdf.14 September.

Chen, S. and Ravallion, M. (2004) 'How Have the World's Poorest Fared Since the Early 1980s?' Washington, DC. The World Bank. Available on the Internet at http://www.worldbank.org/research/povmonitor/MartinPapers/How_have_the_poorest_fared_since_the_early_1980s. pdf. 20 April.

Coe, D.T. and Hoffmaister, A.W. (1997) 'North – South R&D Spillovers', *The Economic Journal*, vol. 107, no. 1, pp. 134–49.

Collier, P. and Dollar, D. (2002) *Globalization, Growth and Poverty*. New York. Oxford University Press for the World Bank.

Collier, P. and Dollar, D. (2003) *Globalization: Facts, Fears, and an Agenda for Action*, Washington, DC: The World Bank. Policy Research Report.

Collier, P. and Gunning, J.W. (1999) 'Why Has Africa Grown Slowly?', *Journal of Economic Perspectives*, vol. 13, no. 3, pp. 3–18.

Correa, C.M. (2003) 'Can the Trips Agreement Foster Technology Transfer to Developing Countries'. Duke University. Unpublished Manuscript.

Das, D.K. (2000) 'Debacle at Seattle: The Way the Cookie Crumbled', *Journal of World Trade*, September, vol. 12, no. 3, pp. 206–30.

Das, D.K. (2001) *Global Trading System at the Crossroads: A Post-Seattle Perspective*. London and New York: Routledge.

Das, D.K. (2004a) *Regionalism in Global Trade*. Cheltenham, UK and Northampton, MA, USA: Edward Elgar Publishing, Inc.

Das, D.K. (2004b) *Financial Globalization and the Emerging Market Economies*. London and New York: Routledge.

Das, D.K. (2004c) *The Economic Dimensions of Globalization*. Houndmills, Hampshire, UK. Palgrave Macmillan Ltd.

Das, D.K. (2004d) 'Sequences in Financial Liberalization in the Emerging-Market Economies: Growth, Volatility or Both?' *Journal of Economic Integration*, vol. 19, no. 4, December.

Das, D.K. (2005) *Asian Economy and Finance: A Post-Crisis Perspective*. Boston, MA, USA: Kluwer Academic Publishers.

de Jauquières, G. (2004) 'The New Dynamic in World Trade'. 4 August. Available on the Internet at http://www.viewswire.com/login.

Deardorff, A. (2001) 'International Provision of Trade Services, Trade and Fragmentation', *Review of International Economics*, vol. 9, no. 2, pp. 233–48.

Deardorff, A.V. and Stern, R.M. (2002) 'What You Should Know About Globalization and the World Trade Organization', *Review of International Economics*, vol. 10, no. 3, pp. 404–23.

Deardorff, A.V. and Stern, R.M. (2003) 'Enhancing the Benefits for Developing Countries in the Doha Development Agenda Negotiations'. Ann Arbor, MI: University of Michigan. Ford School of Public Policy. Discussion Paper No. 498. 13 August.

Dee, P. and Hanslow, K. (2000) 'Multilateral Liberalization of Services Trade'. Canberra. Government of Australia. Productivity Commission. Staff Research Paper. AUSinfo.

Diakosavvas, D. (2001) 'The Uruguay Round Agreement in Practice: How Open are the OECD Markets?' Paris: Organization for Economic Cooperation and Development. Directorate for Food, Agriculture and Fisheries.

Dollar, D. (1992) 'Outward-Oriented Developing Economies Really Do Grow More Rapidly: Evidence from 95 LDCs', *Economic Development and Cultural Change*, vol. 34, no. 1, pp. 62–96.

Doudeijns, M. and Dumont, J.C. (2003) 'Immigration and Labor Shortages: Evaluation of Needs and Limits of Selection Policies in Recruitment'. Paper presented at a conference on *The Economic and Social Aspects of Migration* organized by the Economic Commission and the OECD Secretariat in Brussels during 21-2 January.

Economist, The (2003a) 'On a Roll'. Available on the Internet at http://www. economist.com/agenda/displaystory.cfm?story_id=1872018. 27 June.

Economist, The (2003b) 'The WTO Under Fire', 18 September. Available on the Internet at http://www.economist.com./PrinterFriendly.cfm?Story_ID = 2071855.

Economist, The (2004a) 'Trade: From Cancún to Can-Do', May 15, pp. 72–3.

Economist, The (2004b) 'Progress at Last, but Still a Long Way to Go', 2 August. Available on the Internet at http://www.economist.com/agenda/Printer Friendly.cfm?Story_ID=2983066.

Edwards, S. (1998) 'Openness, Trade Liberalization and Growth in Developing Countries', Journal of Economic Literature, vol. 31, no. 3, pp. 844–80.

Elbehri, A. and Leetma, S. (2002) 'How Significant are Export Subsidies to Agricultural Trade?', Paper presented at the Fifth Annual Conference on Global Economic Analysis, in Taipei, Taiwan, on 5 June.

Evenett, S.J. (2003) 'The Failure of the WTO Ministerial Meeting in Cancún', CESifo Forum, vol. 4, no. 3, Autumn, pp. 11–27.

Finger, J.M. (2000) 'Implementation of Uruguay Round Commitments: The Development Challenge'. Presented at the WTO/World Bank Conference on Developing Countries in a Millennium Round, 20–21 September held in Geneva, Switzerland.

Finger, J.M. and Nogues, J.J. (2001) 'The Unbalanced Uruguay Round Outcome: The New Areas in Future WTO Negotiations'. Washington, DC: The World Bank. Working Paper no. 2732. December.

Finger, J.M. and Schuknecht, L. (1999) 'Market Advances and Retreats since the Uruguay Round Agreement'. Washington, DC. The World Bank. Policy Research Working paper No. 2232. December.

Florax, R.J.G.M., de Groot, H.L.F. and Heijungs, R. (2002) 'The Empirical Economic Growth Literature: Robustness, Significance and Size'. Discussion Paper TI 2002-040/3. Tinbergen: Tinbergen Institute.

Food and Agricultural Organization (FAO) (2002) Agriculture, Trade and Food Security. Vol. II: Country Case Studies. Rome.

Francois, J. and Martin, W. (2003) 'Formula Approaches for Market Access Negotiations', The World Economy, vol. 26, no. 1, pp. 1–26.

Francois, van Meijl and van Tongeren, P. (2003) 'French Agriculture and Processed Foods in the Doha Round'. Paris: Groupe d'Economie Mondiale de Sciences PO. July.

Frankel, J. and Romer, D. (1999) 'Does Trade Create Growth?', American Economic Review, vol. 89, no. 2, pp. 379–99.

Fugazza, M. and Vanzetti, D. (2004) 'A South-South Survival Strategy: The Potential for Trade among Developing Countries'. Paper presented at the European Trade Study Group, Sixth Annual Conference, at Nottingham, UK, during 9–11 September.

Gabrieloni, M. (2004) 'Establishing a Development Agenda for the World Intellectual Property Organization', Bridges Weekly, vol. 8, no. 8, pp. 1–2. September.

General Agreement on Tariffs and Trade (GATT) (1985) Trade Policies for a Better Future: Prospects for Action. Geneva: GATT.

General Agreement on Tariffs and Trade (GATT) (1994) *The Results of the Uruguay Round of Multilateral Trade Negotiations: The Legal Text*. Geneva: GATT.

Gereffi, J. and Memedovic, O. (2003) *The Global Apparel Value Chain: What Prospects for Upgrading the Developing Economies?*. Vienna: United Nations Industrial Development Organization.

Gibson, P., Wainio, J., Whitley, D. and Bohman, M. (2001) *Profiles of Tariffs in Global Agricultural Markets,* Washington, DC: The United States Department of Agriculture. Agricultural Economic Report No. 796.

Gould, D.M. and Gruben, W.C. (1996) 'The Role of Intellectual Property Rights in Economic Growth', *Journal of Development Economics*, vol. 48, no. 2, pp. 323–50.

Government of the United Kingdom (GUK) (2002) 'Integrating Intellectual Property Rights and Development Policy'. London: The Commission on Intellectual Property Rights.

Greenaway, D., Morgan, W. and Wright, P. (2002) 'Trade Liberalization and Growth in Developing Countries', *Journal of Development Economics*, vol. 67, no. 1, pp. 229–44.

Hall, B.H. (2004) 'Exploring the Patent Explosion'. Cambridge, MA: National Bureau of Economic Research. NBER Working Paper No. 10605.

Hart, M. and Dymond, W. (2003) 'Special and Differential Treatment and the Doha "Development" Round', *Journal of World Trade*, vol. 37, no. 2, pp. 395–415.

Haveman, J.D. and Shatz, H.J. (2003) 'Developed Country Trade Barriers and the Least Developed Countries: The Economic Result of Freeing Trade'. Helsinki. Finland. Discussion Paper No. 2003/46. United Nations University. World Institute of Development Economic Research. June.

Hertel, T. and Martin, W. (2000) 'Liberalizing Agriculture and Manufactures in a Millennium Round: Implications for the Developing Economies', *The World Economy*, vol. 23, no. 3, pp. 455–70.

Hertel, T.W. (1997) *Global Trade Analysis: Modeling and Analysis*. Cambridge and New York: Cambridge University Press.

Hertel, T.W. and Martin, W. (2000) 'Liberalizing Agriculture and Manufactures in a Millennium Round: Implications for the Developing Economies', *The World Economy*, vol. 23, no. 3, pp. 455–70.

Hertel, T.W., Anderson, K., Francois, J. and Martin, W. (2000) 'Agricultural and Non-Agricultural Liberalization in the Millennium Round'. The Centre for International Economic Studies. Adelaide. University of Adelaide. Discussion Paper No. 0016.

Hertel, T.W., Ivanic, M., Preckel, P.V. and Cranfield, J.A.L. (2004) 'The Earning Effects of Multilateral Trade Liberalization: Implications for Poverty', *The World Bank Economic Review*, vol. 18, no. 2, pp. 205–36.

Hoda, A. and Verma, M. (2004) 'Market Access Negotiations on Non-Agricultural Products'. New Delhi. Indian Council for Research on International Economic Relations. Working Paper No. 132. May.

Hoekman, B.M. (2003) 'Cancún: Crisis or Catharsis'. Paper presented at the joint roundtable of the Brookings Institution and George Washington University held on 20 September, in Washington, DC.

Hoekman, B.M. and Kostecki, M.M. (2001) *The Political Economy of World Trading System*, New York: Oxford University Press.

Hoekman, B.M., Ng, F. and Olarreaga, M. (2002) 'Eliminating Excessive Tariffs on Exports of Least Developed Countries', *World Bank Economic Review*, vol. 16, no. 1, pp. 1–21.

Hoekman, B.M., Michalopoulos, C. and Olarreaga, M. (2003) 'Differential and More Favorable Treatment, Reciprocity and Fuller Participation of Developing Economies'. Washington, DC: The World Bank (mimeo).

Hoekman, B.M., Michalopoulos, C., Winters, L.A., Pangetsu, M., Saggi, K. and Tybout, J. (2003) 'Special and Differential Treatment for Developing Countries: Objectives, Instruments, and Options for the WTO'. Geneva. World Trade Organization (mimeo).

Hoekman, B.M., Michalopoulos, C. and Winters, L.A. (2003) 'More Favorable and Differential Treatment of Developing Countries: A New Approach in the WTO'. Washington, DC: World Bank. Policy Research Working Paper No. 3107.

Hoekman, B.M., Michalopoulos, C. and Winters, L.A. (2004) 'Special and Differential Treatment of Developing Countries in the WTO: Moving Forward After Cancún', *The World Economy*, vol. 27, no. 4, pp. 481–506.

Hufbauer, G.C., Wada, E. and Warren, T. (2002) *The Benefits of Price Convergence: Speculative Calculations*. Washington, DC: Institute for International Economics. Policy Analysis in International Economics. No. 65.

Hummels, D., Ishii, J. and Yi, K.M. (2001) 'The Nature and Growth of Vertical Specialization in World Trade', *Journal of International Economics*, vol. 54, no. 1, pp. 75–96.

Inama, S. (2003) 'Trade Preferences and the WTO Negotiations on Market Accedss'. Geneva: United Nations Conference on Trade and Development (mimeo).

Ingco, M.D. and Nash, J.D. (2004) 'What's at Stake? Developing Country Interest in the Doha Development Round', in M.D. Ingco and J.D. Nash (eds), *Agriculture and the WTO*. Washington, DC: The World Bank, pp. 1–23.

International Center for Trade and Sustainable Development (ICTSD) (1999) *Bridges: Daily Update on Third Ministerial Conference*. Geneva. Issue 1. 30 November.

International Labor Organization (ILO) (2004) *Towards a Fair Deal for Migrant Workers in the Global Economy*. Geneva. The International Labor Conference, 92nd Session. Report VI. October 2004.

International Monetary Fund (IMF) (2002) *World Economic Outlook: Trade and Finance*. Washington, DC. September.

International Monetary Fund (IMF) (2003) *Worlds Economic Outlook*. Washington, DC. April.

International Monetary Fund/World Bank (IMF/WB) (2002) 'Market Access for Developing Country Exports: Selected Issues'. Washington, DC. Available on the Internet at http://www.imf.org/external/np/pdr/ma/2002/eng/092602/htm. 26 September.

International Organization for Migration/ World Bank/World Trade Organization (IOM/WB/WTO) (2004) *Background Paper*. Prepared for the *Trade and Migration Seminar* held in Geneva, during 4–5 September.

Irwin, D.A. (2000) *Does Trade Raise Income?*. Cambridge, MA: National Bureau of Economic Research.

Irwin, D.A. (2001) *Free Trade Under Fire*, Princeton, NJ: Princeton University Press.

Karsenty, G. (2000) 'Assessing Trade in Services by Mode of Supply', in P. Sauve and R. Stern (eds), *GATS 2000: New Directions in Services Liberalization*. Washington, DC: The Brookings Institution, pp. 130–62.

Konan, D.E. and Maskus, K.E. (2004) 'Quantifying the Impact of Services Liberalization in a Developing Country'. Washington, DC: The World Bank. Policy Research Working Paper No. 3193. January.

Krugman, P. (1997) 'What Should Trade Negotiators Negotiate About', *Journal of Economic Literature*, XXXV, no. 1, pp. 113–20.

Krugman, P. (1999) *The Return of Depression Economics*. New York: W.W. Norton.

Lall, S. (2000) 'The Technological Structure of Developing Country Manufactured Exports', Queen Elizabeth House Working Paper Series No. QEHWPS No. 44. Oxford: Oxford University Press.

Lamy, P. (2003) 'Can the Doha Development Agenda Live up to its Name?' Available on the Internet at http://europa.eu.int/comm/commissioners/lamy/speeches_articles/spla188_en.htm. 10 September 2003.

Lindland, J. (1997) *The Impact of the Uruguay Round on Tariff Escalation in Agricultural Products*. Rome: Food and Agricultural Organization.

Lindsey, B. (2000) 'Globalization in the Streets Again'. Available on the Internet at http://www.freetrade.org/pubs/articles/bl-4-15-00.html.

Lippoldt, D. and Kowalski, P. (2004) 'The Doha Development Agenda: Welfare Gains from Further Multilateral Trade Liberalization'. Paris: Organization for Economic Cooperation and Development. Trade Directorate. 26 June.

Martin, W. and Winters, L.A. (eds) (1996) *The Uruguay Round and the Developing Countries*. Cambridge: Cambridge University Press.

Maskus, K.E. (1998) 'The International Regulation of Intellectual Property'. *Weltwirtschaftliches Archiv*, Band 123, Heft 2, pp. 186–208.

Maskus, K.E. (2000) 'Intellectual Property Rights in the Global Economy'. Washington, DC: Institute for International Economy.

Maskus, K.E. (2004) 'Encouraging International Technology Transfer'. Geneva. UNCTAD-ICTSD. Issues Paper No. 7.

Maskus, K.E., Saggi, K. and Puttitanun, T. (2004) 'Patent Rights and International Technology Transfer through Direct Investment and Licensing'. Paper prepared for the conference, on *International Public Goods and the Transfer of Technology after TRIPS*, Durham. Duke University Law School, 28 June (revised version).

Mathews, A. (2002) 'Developing Country Experiences with the Implementation of the Uruguay Round Agreement on Agriculture'. Paper presented at the Food and Agricultural Organization symposium on *Implementing the WTO's Agreement on Agriculture* in Geneva on 2 October.

Mathews, A. (2004) 'Agriculture after Cancún'. Dublin. Scotland. Trinity College. Trinity Economic Paper No. 17. 11 March.

Mattoo, A. and Subramanian, A. (2003) 'What Would a Development-Friendly WTO Architecture Really Look Like?' Washington, DC: IMF Working Paper. WP/03/153. August.

Mattoo, A. and Subramanian, A. (2004) 'The WTO and the Poorest Countries: The Stark Reality'. Washington, DC: The International Monetary Fund. IMF Working Paper No. IMF/WP/81. May.

McCulloch, N., Winters, L.A. and Cirera, X. (2001) *Trade Liberalization and Poverty: A Handbook*. London: Centre for Economic Policy Research.

McGuire, G. (2002) 'How Important are Restrictions on Trade in Services?' Background paper for the OECD-World Bank Services Expert Meeting, held in Paris, during 4–5 March.

McLaughan, G. and Salt, J. (2002) 'Migration Policies Towards Highly Skilled Foreign Workers'. London. Report to the Home Office. Migration Research Unit. University College. March.

Mendoza, R.U. (2002) 'The Multilateral Trade Regime: A Global Public for All', in I. Kaul, P. Conceicao, K.L. Goulven and R.U. Mendoza (eds), *Providing Global Public Goods: Managing Globalization*, New York: Oxford University Press, pp. 455–83.

Mendoza, R.U. and Bahadur, C. (2002) 'Towards Free and Fair Trade: A Global Public Good Perspective', *Challenge: The Magazine of Economic Affairs*, September/October, vol. 45, no. 5, pp. 21–62.

Messerlin, P.A. (2001) *Measuring the Cost of Protection in Europe: European Commercial Policy in the 2000s*. Washington, DC: Institute for International Economics.

Messerlin, P.A. (2003a) 'Making the Doha Development Round Work for the Poorest Countries', in P. Griffith (ed.), *Rethinking Fair Trade*. London: The Foreign Policy Center, pp. 22–38.

Messerlin, P.A. (2003b) Agriculture in the Doha Round'. Washington, DC: The World Bank. Working Paper No. 2003.

Micklethwait, J. and Wooldridge, A. (2000) *A Future Perfect*. New York: Random House.

Miller, S. (2003) 'WTO Seeks to Jumpstart Talks, but Finding that Consensus is Difficult', *The Wall Street Journal*, 25 July, p. 16.

Moore, M. (1999) 'Message from the Director General', *WTO Focus* no. 43, November, p. 1.

National Association of Software and Services Companies (NASSCOM) (2004) 'Indian Services and Software Exports: Facts and Figures'. New Delhi, India.

Neilson, J. and Taglioni, D. (2004) 'Services Trade Liberalization: Identifying Opportunities and Gains'. Paris: Organization for Economic Cooperation and Development. February.

Organization for Economic Cooperation and Development (OECD) (2000) *Agricultural Policies in the OECD Countries*. Paris.

Organization for Economic Cooperation and Development (OECD) (2002a) *Agricultural Policies in the OECD Countries: Monitoring and Evaluation*. Paris.

Organization for Economic Cooperation and Development (OECD) (2002b) *Agricultural Policies in the OECD Countries*. Paris.

Organization for Economic Cooperation and Development (OECD) (2003a) 'Agricultural Trade and Poverty: Making Policy Analysis Count'. Paris. September.

Organization for Economic Cooperation and Development (OECD) (2003b) 'Opening up Trade in Services', *OECD Policy Brief*. Paris. August.

Organization for Economic Cooperation and Development (OECD) (2003c) 'Farm Household Incomes: Issues and Policy Responses'. Paris. January.

Organization for Economic Cooperation and Development (OECD) (2003d) 'Services Providers on the Move', *OECD Policy Brief*. Paris. August.

Organization for Economic Cooperation and Development (OECD) (2003e) 'The Doha Development Agenda: Tariffs and Trade', *OECD Policy Brief*, October.

Organization for Economic Cooperation and Development (OECD) (2004) *OECD Agricultural Outlook 2004–13*. Paris.

218   *References*

Ostry, S. (2001) 'WTO; Institutional Design for Better Governance'. R. Porter, P. Sauve, A. Subramanian and A.B. Zampetti (eds), *Efficiency, Equality and Legitimacy: The Multilateral Trading System at the Millennium*. Washington, DC: The Brookings Institution, pp. 76–92.

Ostry, S. (2002) 'The Uruguay Round North-South Grand Bargain: Implications for Future Negotiations', in D.L.M. Kennedy and J.D. Southwick (eds), *The Political Economy of International Trade Law*, Cambridge: Cambridge University Press, pp. 166–84.

Oyejide, T.A. (2002) 'Special and Differential Treatment', in B. Hoekman (ed.) *Development, Trade and the WTO*. Washington, DC: The World Bank.

Panitchpakdi, S. (2003) 'Cancún: The Real Losers are the Poor'. Available on the Internet at http://www.wto.org/english/news_e/news03_e/news_sp_18sep03_e.htm. 18 September 2003.

Parsley, D.C. and Wei, S.J. (2001) 'Limiting Currency Volatility to Stimulate Goods Market Integration: A Price-Based Approach'. Cambridge, MA: National Bureau of Economic Research. NBER Working Paper No. 8468.

Puttitanun, T. (2003) *Essays on Intellectual Property Right, Innovation and Technology Transfer*. Boulder, Colorado. Unpublished Doctoral Dissertation.

Reimer, J.J. (2002) 'Estimating the Poverty Impact of Trade Liberalization'. Policy Research Working Paper No. 2790. Washington, DC. The World Bank.

Rice, S.E. and Smith, G.E. (2004) 'The WTO Hands a Critical Victory to African Farmers', Washington, DC: The Brookings Institution. Available on the Internet at http://www.brookings.edu/views/articles/rice/20040521.htm. 21 May.

Robinson, S., Wang, Z. and Martin, W. (1999) 'Computing the Implications of Services Trade Liberalization'. Paper presented at the Second Annual Conference on Global Economic Analysis, in Ebberuk, Denmark, during 20–2 June.

Rodriguez, F. and Rodrik, D. (1999) 'Trade Policy and Economic Growth: A Skeptic's Guide to Dross-National Evidence'. London: Centre for Economic Policy Research. Discussion Paper 2143. May.

Rodrik, D. (1994) 'Developing Countries after the Uruguay Round'. Paper presented for the Group of 24 Meeting, 14–15 August.

Rodrik, D. (2001a) *The Global Governance of Trade as if Development Really Mattered*, New York: United Nations Development Programme. October.

Rodrik, D. (2001b) 'Trading in Illusions', *Foreign Affairs*, March/April. vol. 123, pp. 55–62.

Rodrik, D. (2002) 'Feasible Globalization'. Cambridge, MA: National Bureau of Economic Research. NBER Working Paper No. W9129. August.

Rogers, J.H. (2001) 'Price Level Convergence, Relative Prices, and Inflation in Europe'. Washington, DC: Board of Governors of the Federal Reserve System. International Finance Discussion Paper No. 699.

Romer, P.M. (1994a) 'New Goods, Old Theory, and Welfare Costs of Trade Distortion', *Journal of Development Economics*, vol. 43, no. 1, pp. 5–38.

Romer, P.M. (1994b) 'The Origins of Endogenous Growth', *Journal of Economic Perspective*, vol. 8, no. 1, pp. 3–22.

Sachs, J. and Warner, A. (1995) 'Economic Reforms and the Process of Global Interaction', *The Brookings Papers on Economic Activity*, no. 1, pp. 1–68.

Safadi, R. and Laird, S. (1996) 'The Uruguay Round Agreement: Impact on Developing Countries', *World Development*, vol. 24, no. 7, pp. 1223–42.

Sala-i-Martin, X. (2002) 'The World Distribution of Income (Estimated from Individual Country Distribution)'. Cambridge, MA: National Bureau of Economic research. NBER Working Paper 8933. May.

Sally, R. (2003) 'Whither the WTO? A Progress Report on the Doha Round', Washington DC: CATO Institute. Center for Trade Policy Studies. 3 March.

Santayana, G. (1905) *Life of Reason*. London: Constable & Company Ltd.

Schiff, M. and Winters, L.A. (2003) 'Regional Integration and Development'. Oxford, UK: Oxford University Press.

Schott, J.J. and Watal, J. (2000) 'Decision Making in the WTO'. Washington, DC. Institute for International Economics. Policy Brief No. 00–2. March.

Scoffield, H. (2004) 'Outsourcing a Major Boon to Canada'. *Globe and Mail, Report on Business*. 2 April, p. B4.

Smith, P.J. (1999) 'Are Weak Patent Rights a Barrier to US Exports?', *Journal of International Economics*, vol. 48, no. 1, pp. 151–77.

Smith, P.J. (2001) 'How Do Foreign Patent Rights Affect US Exports?', *Journal of International Economics*, vol. 50, no. 3, pp. 411–40.

Spinanger, D. (2003) 'Beyond Eternity: What Will Happen When Textiles and Clothing Quotas are Eliminated'. Geneva. UNCTAD Research Paper No. 30. United Nations Conference on Trade and Development.

Srinivasan, T.N. (2003) 'Future of Global Trading System: Doha Round, Cancún Ministerialand Beyond', Paper presented at the conference on *The Future of Globalization: Explorations in the Light of Recent Turbulence*, organized by the Yale Center for the Study of Globalization, Yale University, New Haven, CT, during 10–11 October.

Stern, N. (2003) 'Trade, Aid and Results: Can We Make a Difference'. Paper presented at the *Annual Bank Conference on Development Economics – Europe*, held in Paris, during 15–16 May.

Stiglitz, J.E. (1999a) 'Two Principles for the Next Round: Or How to Bring Developing Countries in from the Cold'. Washington, DC. 21 September (mimeo).

Stiglitz, J.E. (1999b) 'Addressing Developing Countries Priorities and Needs in the Millennium Round'. Speech delivered at the Harvard University, Center for Business and Government, Cambridge, MA, 29 November.

Stiglitz, J.E. (2000) *Economics of Public Sector*. New York: W.W. Norton. 3rd edition.

Stiglitz, J.E. and Charlton, A. (2004) *The Development Round of Trade Negotiations: In the Aftermath of Cancún*. London: The Commonwealth Secretariat.

Stoeckel, A. (2004) 'Termites in the Basement: To Free Up Trade, Free the WTO Foundation'. Canberra. Australia: Center for International Economics. March.

Summers, L. (1999) 'Reflections on Managing Global Integration', *Journal of Economic Perspectives*, vol. 13, no. 3, pp. 19–34.

Supper, E. (2001) 'Is There Effectively A Level Playing Field in Developing Country Exports?' *Policy Issues in International Trade and Commodities*. Studies Series No. 1. Geneva. United Nations Conference on Trade and Development.

Tangermann, S. (2004) 'Farming Support: The Truth Behind the Numbers'. *OECD Observer*. 31 March.

Technical Center for Agricultural and Rural Cooperation (TCARC) (2003) 'The Cancún WTO Ministerial Meeting: What Happened? What Does it Mean for Development?' UK. TCARC Policy Paper. Available on the Internet at http://agritrade.cta.int/wto/analysis.htm

United Nations Conference on Trade and Development (UNCTAD) (2004) 'Assuring Development Gains from the International Trading System and Trade Negotiations: Implications of ACT Termination'. Geneva. 30 September.

United Nations Development Program (UNDP) (1997) *Human Development Report*. New York.

van der Mensbrugghe, D. and Beghin, J.C. (2004) 'Global Agricultural Liberalization: An In-Depth Assessment of What is at Stake'. Ames: Iowa, Iowa State University. Center for Agricultural and Rural Development. Working Paper 04–370. September.

Verikios, G. and Zhang, X. (2001) 'Global Gains from Liberalizing Trade in Telecommunications and Financial Services'. Government of Australia. Productivity Commission. Staff Research Paper. AUSinfo.

Vivas-Eugui, D. (2004) 'Regional and Bilateral Agreements and a TRIPS-Plus World'. Geneva. Trip Issues Paper 1. International Center for Trade and Sustainable Development.

Walkenhorst, P. and Dihel, N. (2002) 'Bound Tariffs, Unused Protection and Agricultural Trade Liberalization'. Presented at the *Fifth Conference on Global Economic Analysis*, Taipei, Taiwan, held during 12–13 September.

Watkins, K. (2003) *Northern Agricultural Policies and World Poverty: Will the Doha Round Make a Difference?* Paper presented at the *Annual Bank Conference on Development Economics*, held in Washington, DC, during 15–16 May.

Whally, J. (1985) *Trade Liberalization Among Major World Trading Areas*. Cambridge, MA: The MIT Press.

Winters, L.A. (2000a) 'Should Concern About the Poor Stop Trade Liberalization?' Paper presented at the Annual Bank Conference on Development Economics (ABCDE) in *Europe 2000, Development Thinking at the Millennium*, 26–8 June.

Winters, L.A. (2000b) 'Trade, Trade Policy and Poverty: What are the Links?' Discussion Paper 2382. London: Center for Economic Policy Research.

Winters, L.A. (2002a) 'Doha and the World Poverty Targets'. Paper presented at the *Annual Bank Conference on Development Economics*, held in Washington, DC, during 24–6 June.

Winters, L.A. (2002b) 'The Economic Implications of Liberalizing Mode-4 Trade'. Paper presented at the joint WTO-World Bank Symposium on *The Movement of Natural Persons (Mode-4) under the GATS*, Geneva, during 11–12 April.

Winters, L.A. (2002c) 'Trade Liberalization and Poverty: What Are the Links?', *The World Economy*, vol. 25, no. 9, pp. 1339–68.

Winters, L.A. and Walmsley, T.L. (2002) 'Relaxing the Restrictions on the Temporary Movement of Natural Persons: A Simulation Analysis' (unpublished manuscript).

Winters, L.A., Walmsley, T.L., Wang, Z.K. and Grynberg, R. (2002) 'Negotiating the Liberalization of the Temporary Movement of the Natural Persons', *Economics Discussion Paper*, vol. 87, no. 4, University of Sussex, pp. 22–42.

WITS/TRAINS (2004) *Database on International Trade and Tariffs*. Geneva/Washington, DC. UNCTAD/World Bank.

Wolf, M. (2003) 'The Abominable No-Men'. *The Financial Times*. 23 September.

World Bank (WB) (2002a) 'Reshaping Global Trade Architecture for Development'. in *Global Economic Prospects*. Washington, DC: The World Bank, pp. 45–82.

World Bank (WB) (2002b) *Global Economic Prospects and the Developing Economies: Investing to Unlock Opportunity*. Washington, DC: The World Bank.

World Bank (WB) (2002c) 'Reshaping Global Trade Architecture for Development', in *Global Economic Prospects*. Washington, DC: The World Bank.

World Bank (WB) (2002d) *Global Economic Prospects and the Developing Countries*. Washington, DC.

World Bank (WB) (2003a) *Global Economic Prospects and the Developing Economies*. Washington, DC.

World Bank (WB) (2003b) *Global Economic Prospects 2004*. Washington, DC.

World Bank (WB) (2003c) *Globalization, Growth, and Poverty*, New York: Published by the Oxford University Press for the World Bank.

World Bank (WB) (2004) *Global Economic Prospects and the Developing Economies*. Washington, DC.

World Trade Organization (WTO) (1998a) 'Economic Effects of Services Liberalization'. Geneva. Council for Trade in Services. 29 May.

World Trade Organization (WTO) (1998b) 'Presence of Natural Persons (Mode 4): A Background Note by the secretariat'. Council for Trade in Services. 15 December.

World Trade Organization (WTO) (2000) 'The Developmental Impact of Trade Liberalization under the GATS'. Geneva. A Note by Secretariat. 26 June.

World Trade Organization (WTO) (2001a) 'Doha WTO Ministerial 2001: Ministerial Declaration'. Geneva. 14 November.

World Trade Organization (WTO) (2001b) *GATS: Facts and Fiction*. Geneva. February.

World Trade Organization (WTO) (2001c) *Market Access: Unfinished Business. Post Uruguay Round Inventory and Issues*. Geneva.

World Trade Organization (WTO) (2003a) 'Negotiators Agree on Modalities for Treatment of Autonomous Liberalization'. Press Release. No. 335. 10 March.

World Trade Organization (WTO) (2003b) 'TRIPS Agreement and Public Health – Decision of 30 August 2003'. Geneva.

World Trade Organization (WTO) (2003c) *World Trade Report 2003*. Geneva. September.

World Trade Organization (WTO) (2003d) 'Draft Cancún Ministerial Text Submitted by General Council Chairperson Carlos Perez del Castillo and Director General Supachai Panitchpakdi'. Geneva, 31 August.

World Trade Organization (WTO) (2003e) 'Fifth Ministerial Conference; Briefing Notes'. Geneva. 9 September.

World Trade Organization (WTO) (2003f) 'Consolidated African Union Position on Agriculture: Communication from Mauritius'. Geneva. 31 August.

World Trade Organization (WTO) (2003g) 'Draft Cancún Ministerial Text submitted by Ministerial Council Chairman Luis Derbez'. Geneva. 13 September.

World Trade Organization (WTO) (2004a) 'Text of the "July package"—the General Council's Post-Cancún Decision'. 1 August.

World Trade Organization (WTO) (2004b) 'Working Group on Trade and Transfer of Technology: Eight Session'. 15 July.

World Trade Organization (WTO) (2004c) *WTO Agriculture Negotiations: The Issues and Where We are Now*. Geneva. 20 April.

World Trade Organization (WTO) (2004d) *World Trade 2003, Prospects For 2004.* Press Release. No. Press/373. 5 April.

World Trade Organization (WTO) (2004e) 'Text of the "July package"—the General Council's Post-Cancún Decision'. 1 August.

World Trade Organization (WTO) (2004f) *Annual Report 2004.* Geneva.

Yang, G. and Maskus, K.E. (2001) 'Intellectual Property Rights and Licensing: An Econometric Investigation'. *Weltwirtschaftliches Archiv*, Band 137, Heft 1, pp. 58–79.

Index

ACP group, 74, 80, 100, 152
African Growth Opportunity Act, 62–3
Agreement on Textiles and Clothing, 14, 109
anti-dumping duty, 72
anti-globalization lobby, 10–11, 27–8,
applied general equilibrium model, 91, 112
ASEAN, 19, 108

balancing modalities, 36–8
balancing WTO architecture, 38–41
bargaining and negotiations, 3
blended formula approach, 163–5
business process outsourcing, 43, 126–8

Cairns Group, 145
Cancún
  failure, 74–9
  impasse, 54–9
Committee of the Whole, 18–19
Common Agricultural Policy, 22, 76, 164
cost of trade barriers, 3–4
Council for Trade in Services, 130, 132
Council for TRIPS, 191–2

Derbez, Luis Ernesto, 77
Derbez Text, 81, 83, 163
developing economies, 59–63
Doha Communiqué, 43–4, 130
Doha Development Agenda, 4, 46–8, 63, 80, 90–2, 189–90
  modalities, 132–4
  special and differential treatment, 96–8, 103–4, 165
  welfare gains, 50–2, 54–9
Doha Round
  agriculture, 137–9
  development round, 90–2
  fourth mode, 137–8
  impact, 167–72
  issues, 5, 32

participation, 63–6
progress, 66–74
services negotiations, 129–31
tariff-slashing, 46–8, 69
TRIPS, 182–8
Doha Work Programme, 25–6

economic needs test, 139–40
environmental goods, 49
European Union, 40–1, 48, 57–8, 65, 165
'Everything But Arms' initiative, 62

Fifth Ministerial Conference, 54–6
fourth mode, 133–7
framework agreement, 47–8, 81–4, 98–9, 162–5

GATT (old system), 24–5
generalized system of preferences, 94, 99–101
  eligibility, 96
genetically modified crops, 27
geographical indicators, 157
global economic governance, 1
global public good, 6, 9–13
Global Trade Analysis Project, 51–2, 83, 91, 107, 109, 112, 123, 152–3
'grand bargain', 12
Green Room consultations, 18–21
  process, 24–5, 41–2
Group-of-Seven, 35, 126
Group-of-Eight, 21, 64
Group-of-Twenty, 35
Group-of-Twenty-One, 21, 74, 77, 78, 81, 82, 89
Group-of-Seventy-Seven, 22
Group-of-Ninety, 35, 58, 63, 79, 84, 101

Hamilton, Alexander, 6

information and communications technology, 122–3, 126–8

integration of goods markets, 35–6
intellectual property rights, 174–6
International Labour Organization, 23

'join text', 161–2
July Package, 47–8, 81–4, 98–9

Kennedy Round, 93

launching the round, 4–6
least developed countries, 99–104,
    107, 108, 110, 133, 179, 187
liberalization of trade in services,
    119–23
LINKAGE model, 169–70
List, Friedrich, 6

market access, 64–6
Marrakesh Agreement, 13–14, 178
mercantilist logic, 15
mergers and acquisitions, 119
Millennium Development Goals, 58,
    104–5, 110, 111
Millennium Round, 16–18
mini-Ministerial meetings, 41–2, 161
most-favoured-nation (MFN), 24,
    109, 131
-based liberalization, 104–5
multilateral trade negotiations, 3–4,
    31–4, 54–5, 66–74, 145
liberalization, 124–6
trade expansion, 8–9
trade and growth, 6–9
Multi-Fibre Agreement, 13, 49–50

Negotiation Group on Market Access,
    46–8
negotiating modalities, 36–8
non-rival good, 10

Palais des Nations, 2
poverty line, 111–12
protectionism in agriculture, 144–7

quadrilateral group, 19, 35, 90
quantitative restrictions, 62, 153

rebalancing the country groups, 34–5
regional integration agreements, 65,
    181
Regional Trade Agreement
    Committee, 72–3

Ricardo, David, 6, 43

Seattle debacle, 54–5
Seattle Ministerial Conference, 17–18,
    78–9
Singapore issues, 69–70
Singapore Ministerial
    Conference, 71
Single Undertaking, 2, 5–6, 25
'slicing the value chain', 60
Smith, Adam, 6
Special and Differential
    treatment, 22, 96–8, 104,
    159–60, 177
structural limitation, 21–2

tariff rate quotas, 147, 153–4
tariff-slashing modalities, 44–8
escalation, 64–5
peaks, 64–5
technical barriers to trade, 32
technology transfer, 184–8
Third Ministerial Conference,
    16–18, 67
Tokyo Round, 19, 68, 94
total factor productivity, 183, 185,
    186, 192
total support estimates, 151
Trade and Development Committee,
    67, 72
Trade and Environment
    Committee, 73
trade and growth, 6–9
trade in services, 115–19
transnational corporations, 27–8,
    118, 128
TRIPS regime, 179–81
TRIPS-plus regime, 181

Uruguay Round, 13–16, 48–9, 54–5,
    88–9, 103, 123–4
agenda, 14–15
agreement on agriculture, 146,
    153–5, 160, 165–6, 157–9
high-tariff regime, 156–8
unbalanced outcome, 15–16,
    28–30, 33

World Intellectual Property
    Organization, 178–9